S0-BXG-855

12⁹⁵

Publications on Russia and Eastern Europe
of the School of International Studies
University of Washington

Volume 11

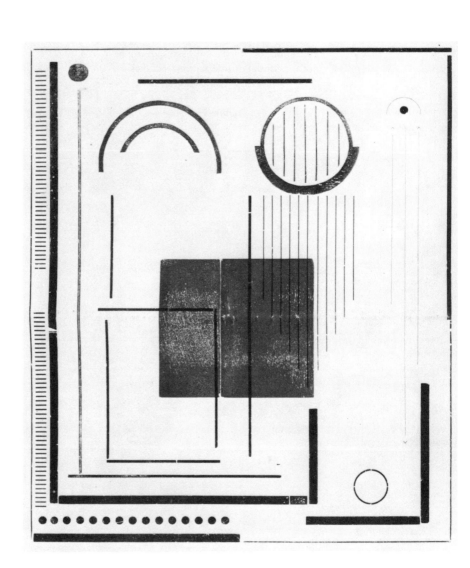

THE POETIC
AVANT-GARDE IN POLAND,
1918–1939

by

Bogdana Carpenter

University of Washington Press
Seattle and London

*Sponsored by the Russian and
East European Program of
the School of International Studies
of the University of Washington*

Frontispiece: Teresa Żarnerówna's "Typography" printed in *Blok,* 1924

Library of Congress Cataloging in Publication Data

Carpenter, Bogdana.
    The poetic avant-garde in Poland, 1918-1939.

    (Publications on Russia and Eastern Europe of the
School of International Studies, University of Washing-
ton ; no. 11)
    Bibliography: p.
    Includes index.
    1. Polish poetry—20th century—History and
criticism. I. Title. II. Series.
PG7070.C37 1983   891.8'517'09   83-1126
ISBN 0-295-95996-7

To John

ACKNOWLEDGMENTS

Much of the research for this book was done with the support of Fulbright and IREX grants (1976-77) as well as a summer research grant from the University of Washington. Part of the second chapter was published previously as the article "Julian Przyboś: the Double Image" that appeared in *The Polish Review,* vol. 26, no. 2 (1981).

I wish to express my gratitude to Professors Czesław Miłosz and Bogdan Czajkowski for their attentive reading of the manuscript and helpful suggestions. I would like to thank Mrs. Alicja Stern for her generosity in offering access to the archives of Anatol Stern and for her support and interest in my project. My deepest gratitude is to my husband John R. Carpenter whose participation in the project includes—beyond moral support—criticism, editorship, typing, and most important the co-translation of all the poems quoted in the book.

CONTENTS

CONTENTS

INTRODUCTION

The term *avant-garde* has an interesting history and requires some comment. It originally derived from French military terminology and designated the most advanced position of an army. The application of the term to literature, like the terms romanticism, realism, naturalism, *fin de siècle,* and modernism before it, has provoked much scholarly discussion. In a seminal book on the theory of the avant-garde Renato Poggioli has traced the use of the term in literary criticism as far back as the middle of the nineteenth century. At that time it carried definite political implications and was used to describe literature that was politically radical. Not until the last quarter of the nineteenth century did it lose its political implications and begin to be applied to artistic phenomena. Poggioli considered the concept from a broad historical and sociological perspective, and he saw the first stage of the modern avant-garde movement in nineteenth-century naturalism, decadence, and symbolism. However, in most contemporary literary and art criticism—this is especially true of continental Europe, but to a lesser degree of Great Britain or the United States—the term *avant-garde* has been used in a narrower sense and designates specific historical, literary, and artistic movements of the first third of our century. It is the more specific use of the term that is followed in this study. Considering the avant-garde as primarily artistic and aesthetic, we limit its period to thirty years with 1909 and 1939 serving as approximate boundaries.[1]

Our choice of the year 1909 as the beginning of the avant-garde is motivated by the appearance of the first futurist manifesto in *Le Figaro* in Paris on February 20 of that year. The publication of the manifesto was a momentous event in the history of the avant-garde. It was the first *public* and *collective* declaration of avant-garde aesthetics.[2] While certain elements in Marinetti's manifesto were characteristic only of futurism, for example his enthusiasm for modern civilization and technology, others—such as the absolute break with the past and tradition, the desire to start from an entirely new position, and the tone of provocation—all of these would be repeated although each time in a different pattern by all avant-garde movements. The use of the form of the manifesto, belonging to revolutionary tactics and an a priori declaration of one's position, became the characteristic outward sign of other avant-garde groups. The most important of these common traits was the break with tradition.[3] If we adopt a dialectical point of view all literature is to some extent a reaction against the style, manner of thinking, and approach to reality of a preceding period, but never in the history of literature and art did writers and artists reject the past in such a thorough manner—not only the immediate past but the entire centuries-long literary and artistic tradition. It is this total negativism toward tradition that explains the passionate, provocative tone of their declarations and is the basis for the desire not only to renew but to reinvent poetic and artistic language. In poetry the futurists' *parole in libertà*—"words in freedom"—the nonsense of dada, and surrealist automatic writing were not simply new devices, but attempts to create an entirely new poetic language.

The avant-garde endeavors in the domain of poetic language are best described by the word "experiment," and its scientific connotations very well capture the philosophical attitudes of the avant-garde poets. No longer believing in a theological universe in which creation is identified with an inspired gesture, they based their concept of creation on the analogy with science, which in the twentieth century had superseded theology, and with the experiment. This new attitude toward poetic creation entailed a new system of evaluation in which the measure of value was not the success or failure of the experiment, but its ultimate goal. The experiment was necessary and valuable because without it the future "discovery" was impossible; it was valuable as a step and therefore could not be judged in absolute terms. Avant-garde aesthetics are a priori and futuristic in orientation: by pushing the ultimate aesthetic moment into the future they limited themselves to the experiment and the manifesto that, using the language of computers, might be described as "programming" the experiment.[4] The pitfalls of avant-garde aesthetics are obvious: they created the danger of the experiment becoming a value in itself and the possibility of never stepping outside its enchanted but limited circle. The short life of so many avant-garde movements, and their rapid burning-out from within, are proofs that the danger was real. Yet the poetic and artistic ferment they caused, their opening up of perspectives and above all the manner in which they revolutionized poetic language make the period in which they took place—from 1909 to 1939—one of the most lively, fascinating, and creative periods in the history of literature and art.

THE AVANT-GARDE IN POLAND

In Poland the avant-garde movements echoed though at the same time substantially differed from those of Western Europe. The artistic ferment in Poland had a considerably later start than in either Russia or Western Europe. From 1918 to 1939 there were two main movements to which the label avant-garde applies: futurism and the Cracow Avantgarde. The name of the latter group—in Polish *Awangarda*—poses certain problems of terminology. For the sake of clarity the word *Avantgarde* spelled with a capital *A* will designate the specific group known in the history of Polish literature as the Cracow Avantgarde, while the same word written with a small *a* and a hyphen, *avant-garde,* will refer to all the avant-garde movements and their characteristic traits, Polish or foreign, that have been defined above.

While Polish futurism and the Cracow Avantgarde shared many common characteristics with the avant-garde movements of Western Europe, their poetic programs significantly differed from those of their European or Russian counterparts. Many of the special traits of the Polish avant-garde movements were due to Poland's particular historical and cultural situation. In Polish history the period between 1918 and 1939 was unique. After one hundred and twenty-three years of non-existence, in 1918 as a result of the collapse of the central powers in World War I Poland gained independence. The Treaty of Versailles, signed on June 28, 1919, ratified the independent Polish republic. The impact was enormous not only on the social and political life of the country, but also on its literature. For over a century political and moral concerns had dominated Polish literature and above all poetry, which was always the most representative and in quality the strongest of all genres in Poland. Stefan Żeromski's concept of literature as "the conscience of the nation" had been prevalent ever since romanticism and echoed Mickiewicz's image of the poet as a "ruler of souls." The messianism of the great romantics had continued to the movement of Młoda Polska or "Young Poland"; because of the lack of autonomous political organizations, Polish literature assumed the task of political and moral leadership. Independence and the establishment of the Polish state liberated literature from the sense of moral obligation imposed upon it by the romantic tradition, which Stanisław Wyspiański already had felt to be a burden. With the realization of an independent state a new sense of commitment emerged, but it was social rather than political, critical rather than idealistic; it expressed the desire to participate in the life of the young state. In the early twenties it found expression in the positivism and optimism of the Cracow Avantgarde and gave rise to a number of civic poems. In the thirties, increasing political instability and economic crisis made writers adopt a much more critical stance and led on the one hand to politically committed literature—most frequently of a leftist and Marxist orientation—and on the other to the emergence of a "catastrophist" literature that was profoundly pessimistic and philosophical. But in 1918 the feeling of euphoria caused by independence was accompanied by a sense of liberation. Jan Lechoń spoke for an entire generation when he wrote the well-known line in 1920, "And in spring let me see the spring, not Poland." ("A wiosną niechaj wiosnę, nie Polskę, zobaczę.") With independence, writers were freed from narrow commitment and from the obsessive concern for unrealized independence.

In 1918 Polish literature was no longer restrained by either external or internal bonds and it acquired a new vitality. The period between the two world wars was a true literary renaissance, a time of animated poetic and artistic discussion, new poetic movements and programs, and outlandish experiments in the novel and theater. Poetry was no longer a mainstay of national identity and it turned to problems of poetic craft. In 1918 Polish poetry was behind Western or Russian poetry—there had been no symbolist school in Poland nor poets like Mallarmé, Yeats, Bely, or Blok. The period of Young Poland—the Polish equivalent of symbolism—was important in the philosophical rather than artistic domain. Some critics have seen Young Poland as a turning point in Polish literature and pointed out that an aggravated crisis in the nineteenth-century Weltanschauung, above all religious, began with that very generation; questions posed by writers for the first time in

1890 continued to be asked in similar forms for the next ninety years. It is important to remember, however, that each successive generation drew from them
different philosophical and artistic conclusions. The generation of Young Poland
reacted against materialism and the empiricism of positivism by turning to idealism,
individualism, and metaphysics. Influenced by the two philosophers Arthur Schopenhauer and Friedrich Nietzsche, the poets of Young Poland proclaimed art to
be a reflection of the absolute and the highest religion, while the artist was a priest
communicating with metaphysical forces and interpreting them for ordinary men.
Since the absolute expressed itself through the individual soul of the poet and was
even synonomous with it, the revelation of the absolute implied the need to understand one's own inner self, to penetrate the hidden motives of actions and feelings.
In the writings of Young Poland, metaphysical and psychological categories were
considered to be identical. The excessive emphasis on psychology accounts for the
prevalence of the poetry of mood and subjective confession, often sentimental in
tone. The style of Young Poland tended toward ornamentation, verbosity, and
pounding rhythmicality. The movement produced no great poet, with the exception of Bolesław Leśmian; but Leśmian's first volume of poetry appeared only in
1912, and he published the bulk of his work during the period between the two
wars. A superb and deeply philosophical poet, Leśmian came twenty years too late.
Possibly the most important and influential Polish symbolist poet was—paradoxically—Juliusz Słowacki, one of the great romantics. A spiritual ancestor of Young
Poland, Słowacki's grandiose mystical poem *The King-Spirit* was a major source for
the revival of romantic mysticism and messianism of the period, and its striking
imagery made it a symbolist work *avant la lettre*.

The reaction against Young Poland of the generation of poets beginning to
write in 1918 was both pervasive and multifaceted. While the futurists derided and
parodied the more superficial traits of the style of Young Poland—its sentimentalism
and ornamentation—the Avantgarde's dispute with it was much more fundamental.
The Avantgarde's reaction led it to define its own positions, and this was the
indirect cause pushing it in the particular direction it took. The Avantgarde opposed
the spiritualism of Young Poland with materialism, it opposed the idealism and
mysticism of that movement with its call for the union of art and life, and with its
concept of "the present moment." In place of an emphasis on intuition and the
subconscious it proposed the use of the intellect, in place of the concept of the poet-
priest it proposed that of the poet-craftsman, and in place of the idea of the poem
as expression of the soul it advocated that of the poem as an object made of
language. The Avantgarde attacked the laxity of style of the Yound Poland movement—melodiousness and rhythmicality at the expense of strict composition, and
the unrestrained outpouring of feelings *(bebechowatość)*—recommending indirectness of expression and rigorous construction. Instead of the symbol used as a means
of self-expression they argued for the symbol as an artistic device. The Polish
Avantgarde reacted against Young Poland but it also went beyond that, reacting
against the romanticism that had preceded it; it took a stand similar to positivism
on the one hand and, on the other, close to such Western poets as Mallarmé and
their own contemporaries T. S. Eliot and Ezra Pound. In the Polish literary tradition
only a single poet can be seen as a precursor of Avantgarde aesthetics: Cyprian

Kamil Norvid (1821-83), the last of the romantics. There are several points of contact between the Avantgarde poets and Norwid. Common to both are interest in formal literary techniques and the concept of the artist as craftsman rather than inspired being. Like the Avantgarde poets but unlike the romantics, Norwid was a poet of culture and civilization, not nature—of the city, not the countryside—and he was a cosmopolitan rather than national poet. At the same time, however, Norwid's emphasis on the processes of history, in keeping with the romantic tradition, brings him close to the post-Avantgarde generation of poets, the catastrophists, and especially to the post-World War II poets. A poet of ruins, Norwid is antithetical to the futurist orientation of the Avantgarde.

As a result of the peculiarities in the development of Polish poetry in the second half of the nineteenth century and the beginning of the twentieth, Polish avant-garde poets found themselves in a situation different from that of the majority of their Western contemporaries. Young poets beginning to write during the years from 1918 to 1925 had no models to follow either spiritually or formally. Their rebellion was total and their need to invent a new poetic language overwhelming. They had to absorb simultaneously both the lessons of European symbolism and the experiments of the most recent poetic movements such as futurism, dada, and surrealism—Mallarmé together with Apollinaire, Marinetti with Mayakovski. But this also explains what is the most strikingly original feature of the Polish avant-garde and what sets it distinctly apart from the other European movements of the time. While nearly all the Western avant-garde movements were anti-intellectual and called for the loosening of formal structure (dada, surrealism, futurism), the Polish avant-garde was intellectual and constructivist. Syntax, the main target of the Italian futurists, was never questioned even by the Polish poets of the most extreme dada and futurist leanings. Quite on the contrary, it was rigidly preserved. The poets of the Polish avant-garde did not adopt the principles of associationism advocated by French surrealism, nor did they follow the dadaists in their use of chance as a determining element of composition. The *zaum* poetry of the Russian futurists found only a few sporadic and modest imitations in Poland. In its theoretical premises and to a great extent in its poetic practice, the Polish avant-garde was intellectual, formalistic, and constructivist. For these reasons it constitutes a distinct and fascinating chapter in the history of the European avant-garde. Curiously, what might have appeared to be a disadvantage to the Polish avant-garde turned out to be its biggest strength. This was its ability to avoid such poetically unproductive experiments as automatic writing, nonsense verse, or *zaum,* all of which proved to be sans issue and led other avant-garde movements to dead ends.

Between 1918 and 1922 was a period of extreme poetic ferment. It was the moment of experimentation and hence the time of the avant-garde par excellence. The historical situation gave the antitraditionalism of the Polish avant-garde additional weight and meaning. Three avant-garde poetic movements followed closely one after the other—formism, futurism and the Cracow Avantgarde. Polish avant-garde poetry had a special intensity—it was highly compressed, its development taking place in a period of merely ten years. This accounts for its liveliness, openness, and renaissance-like atmosphere. Within a period of twenty years Polish poetry made an enormous leap—not only did it elaborate its own avant-garde poetics, but as early as 1933 it was able to assimilate them and then to overcome them with new, highly original poetic proposals that both included the avant-garde experiment and went far beyond it. This new poetry, represented above all by Józef Czech- owicz and the young poets of *Żagary,* was philosophically oriented and stressed the commitment of the poet, not in the narrow sense of party allegiance but in its broadest humanistic meaning. By giving poetry a new philosophical scope these writers helped to shape Polish poetry after World War II.

The avant-garde experiment did not encompass all Polish poetry written between 1918 and 1939. Two groups, the expressionists and Skamander poets, remained outside the avant-garde; the latter were in open opposition to it. Polish expressionism and its magazine *The Source (Zdrój),* published in Poznań between 1917 and 1922, continued the traditions of romantic messianism and Young Poland—these three movements shared the same concept of poetry as the expression of the soul, the belief in intuition, and a somewhat mystical apprehension of the creative act as a moment of contact with the absolute. The pathos and rhetorical style of expressionist poetry accentuated its link with the poetry of Young Poland; its mysticism and lack of outstanding personalities put it at the margin of the poetry of the period.[5]

The poetic group most popular and influential with the reading public was Skamander. Its main strength was the talent of the individual poets belonging to the group. Jarosław Iwaszkiewicz, Julian Tuwim, Jan Lechoń, Antoni Słonimski, and Jerzy Wierzyński constituted its core; several other poets were associated with Skamander, among them Kazimiera Iłłakowiczówna, Maria Jasnorzewska-Pawlikowska, and Józef Wittlin. Compared to other contemporary artistic groups, Skamander proved to be exceptionally tenacious—in fact, its life span covered the entire interwar period and its popularity with readers continued well after World War II. The unusual success of its poets was due to their artistry and accessibility: by combining the familiar everyday world with traditional forms their poetry corresponded best to the needs of the public. The desire to reach a wide audience was a major goal of Skamander; they wanted their poetry to be "democratic" and "populist." Their poetic program was loose and retained traditional versification, while their innovations were primarily the introduction of new subjects (in particular the city), a new hero (the everyday man), colloquial language, a certain sensualism and predilection for the concrete. Reacting like the avant-garde against Young Poland, Skamander created what could be called a poetics of everyday life. Their desire to participate in contemporary life also found expression in numerous satirical poems and the founding of a literary café.

The points of contingency between Skamander and the avant-garde were their reactions against Young Poland's aestheticism and against the romantic tradition of moral and didactic poetry subordinate to the national cause. This similarity of negative reactions accounts for the brief collaboration between Skamander poets and the futurists in the sporadic publication of early avant-garde poetry in the magazine *Skamander;* it also accounts for the confusion among contemporary critics in drawing a line between the two movements. With time the differences became sharper, even irreconcilable, and by 1921 Aleksander Wat considered the collaboration with Skamander to be "one of the biggest tactical mistakes of Polish futurism." The split between Skamander and the avant-garde concerned their attitude toward poetic expression and their definition of poetry. While Skamander's innovations were generally limited to thematics, the avant-garde's break with tradition was far more radical and went beyond thematics, questioning concepts of poetic language and of the poetic act. Polish critics often speak of two poetic models, "creationist" and "veristic," represented by the avant-garde and Skamander. While the avant-garde wanted their poems to be above all creations of language, Skamander's poetry was traditionally descriptive. Avant-garde critics reproached Skamander for its conservative attitude toward language, the absence of a poetic program, passéism, and poetic minimalism. The Skamandrites for their part did not ever debate the avant-garde program, reasserting talent and individuality as the only poetic criteria. The dispute between Skamander and the Cracow Avantgarde became one of the major events in the literary life of the period between the wars— it lasted, unresolved, until the outbreak of the Second World War. It was a profound argument between tradition and antitradition, a quarrel "des Anciens et des Modernes."

This book is a study of the Polish avant-garde poetry and poetic programs. Although the avant-garde did not represent the entire poetic output of Poland between the two world wars, the role it played in the development of Polish poetry was crucial. In their own time the avant-garde poets lost to those of Skamander in their attempt to win public approval, their poetry being too difficult and too new for the average reader, but this was fully compensated by the prestige and influence they exerted among other poets. Without Skamander Polish poetry would have been incomparably poorer, but without the avant-garde experiment Polish poetry would never have evolved from its nineteenth-century models, it would never have moved to the forefront of European poetry where it is now one of the most original and vital contributors. Acting as an evolutionary catalyst, the avant-garde was responsible for the changes in Polish poetry that took place at several different points in the period between 1918 and 1939. The present study seeks to pinpoint these evolutionary stages, analyzing their causes and the direction in which they developed.

Chapter one, devoted to futurism, traces the two different paths followed by its participants after the movement evolved from its initial dadaist negativism. These two tendencies—one of social commitment, the other of constructivist art—reflect the dichotomy typical of all Polish avant-garde poetry. The representatives of the first tendency made poetry subordinate to social and political causes, thus continuing nineteenth-century traditions and swerving away from the avant-garde. The second tendency was to become central to the Polish avant-garde, finding its fullest expression in the theory and poetry of the Cracow Avantgarde, the discussion of which constitutes chapter two of the book. Chapter three considers two poets, Adam Ważyk and Józef Czechowicz, who did not belong to any group and whose work is situated outside, although not in opposition to, the main constructivist stream. While Ważyk's surrealism broadened the spectrum of avant-garde poetry, Czechowicz's introduction of the metaphysical element into avant-garde aesthetics marked a new stage in the development of its poetic consciousness. It provided a bridge between the avant-garde and the next generation of poets. Chapter four traces the fate of avant-garde ideas in the nineteen thirties. A brief discussion of the catastrophists points to the new stage in Polish poetry when the avant-garde experiment had become a well-assimilated tradition. Aside from presenting the theoretical programs and poetry of the movements, this study also includes a large number of translations appearing for the first time in English. Polish avant-garde poetry constitutes a very important part of the poetic thought of the twentieth century, and yet it remains virtually unknown outside of Poland. This book is intended to fill that gap.

THE POETIC
AVANT-GARDE IN POLAND,
1918–1939

1

FUTURISM

THE MANIFESTOES

Futurist Publications, Provocations, and Events

Polish futurism might be said to have started as early as 1914 when a little-known poet, Jerzy Jankowski—"the tragic forerunner and John the Baptist of Polish futurism"[1] published his first poems, which used phonetic orthography and were very much in the spirit of Italian futurism. However, Jankowski's early poems were isolated and passed almost without response. The true futurist movement began four years later, when the three poets Tytus Czyżewski, Bruno Jasieński, and Stanisław Młodożeniec organized The Street Organ (Katarynka), a futurist club in Cracow. They were joined by a group of artists who were exhibiting their works under the name of formism, and who published between 1919 and 1921 a magazine entitled *Formists (Formiści)*. In addition to theoretical articles on formist painting, the magazine printed the first futurist poems. In 1919 two poets from Warsaw, Aleksander Wat and Anatol Stern, created the first futurist literary evening or poetry reading in Warsaw, called "A subtropical evening organized by White Negroes." In 1920 Wat and Stern published a joint collection of futurist poems, *These Are the Blue Feet Which Have to Be Painted (To są niebieskie pięty które trzeba pomalować)*, as well as the first futurist manifesto in the brochure *Gga. The First Polish Almanac of Futurist Poetry (Gga. Pierwszy polski almanach poezji futurystycznej)*. The groups from Cracow and Warsaw met and began to collaborate. In 1921 they jointly published several futurist manifestoes and in 1922 the leaflet *(jednodniówka)* called *Knife in the Stomach (Nuż w bżuhu)*, a poster-size publication, caused an outcry from the critics and from the public. It was the last collective publication of the futurist group.

Most of the individual volumes of the futurist poets were published between 1919 and 1922. In 1919 Anatol Stern's *Futurisias (Futuryzje)* appeared, as well as *Naked Man Downtown (Nagi człowiek w sródmieściu)*. Jerzy Jankowski's *Tram across the Street (Tram wpopszek ulicy)*, Aleksander Wat's *I at One Side and I at the Other Side of My Pug Iron Stove (Ja z jednej strony i Ja z drugiej strony mego mopsożelaznego piecyka)*, Tytus Czyżewski's *The Green Eye. Formist Poetry, Electric Visions (Zielone oko. Poezje formistyczne, wizje elektryczne)* were all published in 1920. These were followed in 1921 by Bruno Jasieński's *Shoe in the Buttonhole (But w butonierce)*, Stern and Wat's collaboration *The Immortal Volume of Futurisias (Nieśmiertelny tom futuryz)*, and Stanisław Młodożeniec's *Lines and Futurines (Kreski i futureski)*. In 1922 Czyżewski published *Night-Day. Electric Mechanical Instinct (Noc-dzień. Mechaniczny instynkt elektryczny)*.

After 1922 the poems published by the futurists changed in tone, became more politically oriented, and could not be properly classified as futurist. The movement ended in 1923 when Jasieński, one of the leading futurists, wrote in an essay with the significant title "Polish Futurism, an Appraisal": "Futurism is a form of consciousness that should be overcome. I am no longer a futurist while all of you are futurists."[2]

The history of Polish futurism—like that of many other twentieth-century avant-garde movements—would be incomplete without mention of the "futurist evenings" and scandals that accompanied them. In 1920 and 1921 the futurists toured the country and organized readings of poetry and manifestoes in many Polish cities that were enlivened by eccentric performances in the dada style. Provocation, eccentricity, and flamboyance were indispensable and even essential to Polish futurism. Aleksander Wat described the "Subtropical evening organized by White Negroes" that took place in 1919 as "the most grotesque literary reading in Poland." The futurist part of the evening included

> the performance of a Negro, the authentic Yusuf ben Mchim, who danced half-naked shivering with cold and singing Negro songs: . . . poems by myself and Stern with outrageous syntax and pornographic Rabelaisian content. The climax of the program was a naked man with a light gauze strip on his hips. He read Stern's poem with the title, "The Burning of the Fig Leaf." He was supposed to burn a fig leaf but he didn't do it.[3]

And Jasieński described a futurist happening in Warsaw:

> I remember one of our first big readings in the Warsaw Philharmonic Hall on February ninth, 1921, which gathered 2,000 persons. People were crowding the aisles and surrounded the stage. Somebody in the audience brought a snake, a woman came with a monkey. Warsaw was manifesting in its way that it was futurizing itself. We read some poems. People stood on their chairs and tried to interrupt us. The poems were bad, but the audience was the least concerned about that.[4]

Occasionally futurist readings ended in a more violent fashion. In the Polish resort town of Zakopane in 1921 the audience was ready to beat Aleksander Wat who read the nonsense poems he called "namopaniki," and after the evening was over they threw stones in the street at Jasieński who had also read his poetry. Negative reactions were not confined to the public. Drastic administrative measures were taken, such as the confiscation of poems and manifestoes, police intervention during readings, expulsion of the poets from certain counties, refusal to lease large

comp. to L. — Zamość

halls for readings, and even the temporary arrest of Anatol Stern in Wilno, after he
had read a poem that was accused of being a blasphemy against Saint Mary. In the
press the futurists were frequently accused of bolshevism and communist sympathies. Although the public manifestations and publications of the Polish futurists
did not surpass the daring and provocativeness of similar manifestations of dadaists
in Zurich and Paris, the provincialism and political insecurity in Poland during these
years resulted in harsher administrative repression of the futurists than in Western
Europe.

The Early Period: Dada and Anarchy

Adam Ważyk, a poet of the same generation as Stern, Wat, and Jasieński, considers the absurd manifestoes and scandals provoked by the Polish futurists as
modest and inconsequential in comparison with the similar provocations of the
Russian futurists and French surrealists—he sees them as an expression of the
adolescent rebellion of young men who have just finished high school: "The rebellion of youth that before was a family affair finds an outlet in public literary
activity, in the strategy of scandal, in giving oneself a bad name. Childish humor,
as in the title of the manifesto *Gga*, took turns with black humor, as in the title
Knife in the Stomach."[5] Ważyk's observations are especially pertinent to the Warsaw futurists, who at least in the beginning were more interested in the rebellious
gesture for its own sake than in a poetic or social revolution. The major characteristic of adolescent rebellion is negativism, and hence the resort of the Polish futurists to techniques of shock, destruction, anarchy, and the absurd. All these emotions—and it is more appropriate to speak of emotions than of beliefs or convictions—found expression in the first futurist manifesto *Gga* written by Aleksander
Wat and Anatol Stern in 1920. In a single outburst in the opening lines it throws
overboard the whole of Western civilization and literature:

> *the big rainbow monkey called dionysus died long ago.* we throw away
> its rotten heritage we declare
> I. CIVILIZATION, CULTURE, WITH THEIR MORBIDITY—ONTO
> THE TRASH HEAP.[6]

Making references appropriate to Poland's history and cultural tradition, the manifesto repeats similar destructive calls of both Italian and Russian futurist manifestoes:

> WE CROSS OUT HISTORY AND PROGENITY . . .
> poland should repudiate tradition, the mummy of prince Joseph
> and the theater.
>   . . .
> mickiewicz is limited *słowacki is an incomprehensible gibberish.*

Even at this early stage Polish futurism distinguished itself from the Italian
model—a distinction that became deeper with time. While the famous Italian
futurist manifesto of 1909 attacked cultural tradition in the name of new technological civilization, the Polish futurists rebelled not only against old culture
but against new civilization as well. In *Gga* there is not a trace of the rapture over

GGA

pierwszy polski almanach
poezji futurystycznej. dwumiesiecznik prymitywistów.
warszawa. grudzien 1920.

anatol stern
— muza na czworakach. —
aleksander wat
— fruwajace kiecki. —

The cover and title page of *Gga. The First Polish Almanac of Futurist Poetry*

g g a.

i polski almanach futurystyczny.

Druk „Wasniewski" Marszałkowska № 116

technology so characteristic of the Italian futurists. The city and all technological inventions are repudiated with all other products of civilization: *"we destroy the city.* all mechanism—airplanes, tramways, inventions, the telephone. In place of them, primitive means of communication."

An excellent example of primitive means of communication is the word *Gga* in the title of the manifesto, an onomatopoeic sound in Polish that imitates the honk of a goose and is in itself a declaration: "let's open the eyes. then the pig will seem more enchanting to us than the nightingale, and the gga of a gander will ravish us more than the swan's song." The sentence is primarily directed against the sentimentalism and moodiness of the poetry of the Young Poland group but the choice of a pig and goose rather than a racing car or airplane has other implications. Polish authors called themselves "primitivists," and rather than dignity and seriousness they chose "simplicity, vulgarity, gaiety, health, triviality, laughter." The sound *gga* suitably sets the tone of youthful gaiety and aggressiveness for the whole manifesto—a tone more in the spirit of dada than of futurist declarations: "gga. gga. gentlemen fell out into the arena of the world, brandishing its double *g,* it shouts *aa, aa*—this is the mouth of that wonderful and vulgar beast, really a muzzle, a muffler, or snout." Thus the airplane or automobile of Italian futurism is replaced in its Polish version by an animal, and technology is replaced by jocular primitivism. Here we are clearly in the world of dada, of joyful ebullience, childish games, and nonsense: "we praise reason and this is why we reject logicality, this limitation and cowardice of the mind. Nonsense is wonderful in its untranslatable content which brings out our creative breadth and power." Also dada, not futurist, is their dislike of violence and war—"wars should be waged by fists. slaughter is not hygienic"—as well as the treatment of politics as a joke: "we understand the social system as the rule of genuine idiots and of capitalists. it is a terrain most fertile in laughter and revolution." To see laughter as a principle of art and literature also has its source in dadaist tradition. *Gga* states: "art is only that which gives health and laughter."

The very wording of these statements alludes to the 1909 manifesto of Marinetti, and implies a direct opposition to some of its basic tenets.[7] Czesław Miłosz has commented that the term "futurism" applied to the group of Polish poets that includes Stern and Wat is a misnomer, and he considers the movement as basically dadaist. Aleksander Wat discusses the same problem in his memoirs: ". . . Everything fell under the name of futurism, although this movement has little in common with classical futurism. The name was the least appropriate, and even though we changed it into neofuturists and so on, it really wasn't that. Undoubtedly the greatest influences were on the one hand Russian futurism, Mayakovski, and especially Khlebnikov, and, on the other hand, dadaism. In a way it should be reduced to dadaism."[8] From Italian futurism the movement took primarily elements of negation, that is, elements shared by futurism with such diverse movements as dada and even surrealism. The positive postulates of Marinetti's futurism were either ignored or rejected. The cult of the machine, which was taken seriously by Marinetti and his followers, became a joke in Polish futurism: "Love electrical machines, marry them and beget Dynamo-children—magnetize them and educate them so that they grow up to be mechanical citizens."[9] As Wat remarked, in the context of Polish reality in 1920 the machine was an exotic and decorative element in futurist poetry. In a country as backward as Poland in the 1920s, the machine was by no means a part of everyday experience, but something rare and unusual, "We treated the machine like those dandy Negroes treat trousers—they carry them thrown over the shoulder." [10] The praise of civilization and with it the machine, so typical of Italian futurism, appeared in Poland later, in the program and poetry of the Cracow Avantgarde.

Nor were the young Polish poets seriously preoccupied with the various aesthetic notions of Marinetti concerning syntax, the use of adjectives and verbs—with the one reservation, however, of Marinetti's famous call for "words at liberty," which was immediately seized by the Warsaw futurists precisely because for them it incarnated anarchy and freedom. Polish futurists saw an open door to total permissiveness in Marinetti's call: "The notion that words can be at liberty, that words are things and that one can do with them whatever one pleases this was an enormous revolution in literature, it was a revolution similar to—let's say—Nietzsche's 'God is dead.' Because all of a sudden words are at liberty, one can do anything with them. And this gave us incredible dynamism." [11]

At the same time, Polish futurists interpreted the phrase "words at liberty" in their own particular manner. Inspired by Marinetti, Wat and Stern proclaimed in their manifesto that poets should treat words as objects and not as vehicles of meaning: "Words have their weight, sound, color, their shape, THEY OCCUPY A PLACE IN SPACE. these are the decisive values of a word. the shortest words (a sound) and the longest words (a book). the meaning of a word is of secondary importance and does not depend on the concept ascribed to it. they must be treated as sound material USED NONONOMATOPOEICALLY." If the concept of words as "sound material" probably had one of its sources in Marinetti's "words at liberty," the rejection of onomatopoeia once again sets the Polish futurists in opposition to the Italian, and brings it closer to the Russian futurists, whose influence on the Polish poets was considerable. For Marinetti, onomatopoeia was an essential poetic tool, yet it is basically a mimetic device, and the reproach of simplistic realism had already been made against this concept of the Italian futurists by Guillaume Apollinaire. [12] It was repeated by Jasieński and other Polish futurists. Marinetti's "words at liberty" also implied a rejection of syntax—an implication that futurists entirely disregarded. With the exception of Czyżewski, there is very little loosening of syntax in Polish futurist poetry and, even when words slip into nonsense, the only constructive element that remains is the syntax.

The Second Stage: Under the Banner of Life

The manifesto *Gga* was written in 1920 in Warsaw by Stern and Wat. A year later, futurists from both Warsaw and Cracow presented a united front by publishing what is known as the first futurist *jednodniówka.* It contained four manifestoes that were different in tone, style, and attitude from the dadaist *Gga.* [13] They not only betrayed different authorship but, more important, gave Polish futurism new scope and established a second direction in which it developed. It has been established that at least three out of the four manifestoes were written by the Cracow poet Bruno Jasieński. Although he was the same age as his Warsaw friends, Jasieński

Cena mk 30

JEDNODŃUWKA FUTURYSTUW

mańifesty futuryzmu polskiego

wydańe nadzwyczajne

na całą Żeczpospolitą Polską

KRAKUW   czerwiec   MCMXXI

DO NARODU POLSKIEGO.

MAŃIFEST

w sprawie natyhmiastowej futuryzacji żyća.

An excerpt of the title page of *The Manifestoes of Polish Futurism*
and the manifesto by Bruno Jasieński

MAŃIFEST

w sprawie poezji futurystycznej.

BRUNO JASIEŃSKI.

seems to have been a more mature and less impulsive man. He had a very organized, critical mind, and it is not surprising that he was the author of the first history of Polish futurism, the essay mentioned earlier, whose lucidity, impartiality, and objectivity are striking if one considers that it was written by an active participant of the movement only a year after its last manifestation, and that he was only twenty-two years old. In 1921 he showed the same critical ability and gift for synthetic thinking. While much of *Gga* is emotional and adolescent, the manifestoes of Jasieński are rational, mature, well thought out and organized, and their argumentative power is much greater. Jasieński did not concur with the dadaist tendencies of the first manifesto and considered its primitivistic credo an anachronism. He later admitted that the manifestoes he wrote were not discussed and established beforehand by all the Polish futurists, but rather they were an attempt to make the ideological and artistic position of the group known and accessible to the public. The manifestoes traced only the most general lines of Polish futurism, "the most general plane on which we could all be contained without resorting to individual amputations." [14]

Jasieński's manifestoes situated Polish futurism in a specific historical moment. They considered the importance of the movement both in the context of the political, social, and cultural world crisis and in the context of the particular moment in Polish history: "The world war, together with a huge shift of entire states, social strata and nations, entails a great shift in values. The result is a cultural crisis, the scene of which today is all of Eastern and Western Europe. In our country this crisis is manifest in a particularly acute and specific form. A century and a half of political slavery has left a hard and indelible imprint on our whole physiognomy, psychology, and production."

Futurism is presented as a response to this historical moment and as an attempt to keep pace with rapidly changing reality. The manifestoes speak of a "new man" and call for the organization by all Polish society of "a common fruitful effort in the direction of an immediate, profound, fundamental and lasting futurization of life which reaches to the roots." The ambition of the futurists was no longer an isolated reform of art, but a radical reconstruction and reorganization of life. Although the manifestoes discard all that is declared to be dead in tradition, including romantic messianism and "the stale mummies of mickiewiczes and słowackis," the spirit of adolescent contrariness that dominated the tone of the 1920 manifesto *Gga* is absent. Rather than accuse Polish romantic poetry of gibberish and narrowness, the 1921 manifestoes unexpectedly praise this poetry as a model to be followed, a poetry that is profoundly national, tied to its own time and "written with the blood of billowing life itself." The word *life* was the key word of Jasieński's manifestoes and was also the new banner of Polish futurism. The striking feature of the 1921 manifestoes is the presence of social concern, which is clearly the new orientation of futurism and its desire to participate actively in life. Both life and art are seen above all in their social aspect, the role of poetry and the poet is entirely defined by social considerations. Jasieński saw the end of an era as the end of certain social structures: "The life of the intellectual classes goes through a slow period of degeneration and neurasthenia." His tone is occasionally that of communist political propaganda. The new social awareness differentiates Polish from Italian futurism even more than the earlier primitivism of Stern and Wat, and brings it closer to Russian futurism, whose ties with the communist revolution were strong.

The concept of the artist participating in contemporary life also had a social orientation, for the poet, like every other member of society, is to be useful and productive. The difference between art and nonart entirely disappears; technology is an art together with painting, sculpture, and architecture. Everyone can be an artist as long as he, too, participates in the creation of a new reality—"we call upon all artisans, tailors, cobblers, furriers, and hairdressers to create new clothes, hairdos and costumes never seen before. We call upon technicians, engineers, and chemists to discover new, unprecedented inventions." The role of art is to be universal, democratic, and directed at the masses. The manifestoes accuse nearly all contemporary artistic movements such as cubism, expressionism, and dada of being past their time and cut off from the public. *Gga* had already introduced the concept of art as action, of an art for the crowds whose main attributes are outwardness and universality. The theater was to give way to the circus, music consisted of knocking several bodies against each other, and painting was to leave the canvas and be applied to everyday objects. The 1921 manifestoes ignored some of the dada elements of these proposals but picked up their basic tenets, developing them into a new concept of revolutionary art. Art should not be confined to concert halls and museums because the majority of people cannot afford to go there. The call "Artists onto the street!" translates this desire to make art accessible to the working masses: "Flying poetoconcerts and concerts in trains, tramways, cafeterias, factories, cafés, in public squares, railways stations, halls, passageways, parks, from the balconies of houses, etc. at every time of day and night."

The manifestoes betray Jasieński's background as well as his firsthand acquaintance with Russian futurism. Jasieński spent between 1914 and 1918 in Russia as a student in the Polish gymnasium in Moscow and witnessed the years of Russia's greatest social and artistic turmoil. The experience left a strong imprint on the young poet—his manifestoes, poetry, prose, and his entire life was a reflection and consequence of this experience. The influence of Russian futurism can be seen in the poetry and ideas of other Polish futurists as well, but in no one was it as intense and far-reaching in its consequences as with Jasieński.

Toward a Futurist Poetic Program

The manifestoes did not propose a comprehensive poetic program, but they indicated certain new, interesting possibilities for poets to follow, many of which were to become characteristic of all future Polish avant-garde poetry. The most general demand made of poetry was that it be new: "No one in 1921 can create and construct as it was already done before him. Life flows forward and does not repeat itself. Each creator is obligated by all he has found + this new marvelous leap that every artist must perform into the void of the universe. *Art is the creation of new things. . . .* Every artist is obliged to create new, unheard-of art that he has the right to call by his name."

These formulations recall Guillaume Apollinaire's famous essay, "The New Spirit and the Poets," written in 1918 and read by many Polish futurists. Akin to

Apollinaire, also, is the recognition of surprise as the essential element in modern art: "Art must be unexpected, permeating everything and crashing . . . a deluge of marvels and surprises." Rebelling against "the ghetto of logicality" and attracted by "the fabulous unexpectedness" of life, the futurists called for "rapid associations of things apparently distant in bourgeois logic; the shortcut between the two summits—a leap through the void and a *salto mortale.*" The stress on newness, surprise, and unexpected associations was common to all avant-garde artistic and poetic movements, but the manifestoes also contained an element that is specifically Polish. This element is the stress on the constructive aspect of a poetic work, and the demand for an "iron" composition and economy defined as "a minimum of material with a maximum of achieved dynamics." Calling this concise structure "futurist," the manifestoes introduced the concept of synthetic art and motivated its necessity by the tempo of modern life:

> Contemporary man is occupied for eight hours by his professional work. He has the remaining four hours in the day for eating, practical interests, sports, entertainment, social life, love, and art. For an average contemporary man between five and fifteen minutes a day falls to art alone. This is why he has to receive art in capsules especially prepared by the artists, cleansed ahead of time of all superfluousness and given to him in completely ready, synthetic form. *The work of art is an extract. Dissolved in the glass of the everyday it ought to color it all with its own tint.*

The presence of constructivist tendencies in the futurist manifestoes is surprising, because they seem inconsistent with the generally free and negative spirit of the movement. Aleksander Wat explained the evolution of futurism from antipoetry and antiliterature toward increasingly constructivist attitudes as a result of the maturing of very young poets, and the gradual development of a "taste for poetry."[15]

Without denying the validity of Wat's explanation, it is plausible to see Polish futurism's constructivist orientation as a result of its curious association with formism. This supposition is confirmed by the inclusion of an essay on poetry written by the leading formist theoretician, Leon Chwistek, in the last futurist publication, *Knife in the Stomach.* Chwistek's essay is an attempt to explain and justify the new poetry objectively. It reflects the formist belief in the autonomy of art and it transposes the formist concern with problems of visual artistic form into poetry. On the basis of the relationship of the form of a sentence to its meaning, Chwistek distinguishes among four types of poetry—primitivist, realistic, impressionist, and futurist. These four types of poetry reflect the progressive removal of poetry from logical sense, and its gradual approach to the empty sound of words that Chwistek compares to the sound of murmurs. At the same time, poetry moves further and further away from questions of truth and falsehood, and approaches the domain of purely formal issues: "It is obvious that the striving of poetry to separate itself from science and other disciplines foreign to art must direct poetry toward those elusive terrains where we do not yet have the pure music of murmurs, but which are already foreign to the problematics of truth and falsehood. We can call this striving *Formism* in poetry."

The essay is an interesting application of formist theories to poetry, but its presence in a futurist publication demonstrates the enormous confusion in the futurist poetic program. The theories of Chwistek were in direct opposition to the futurist demands for poetry concerned with everyday problems and accessible to the masses. The formist distinction between form and meaning, and the hierarchization of art on the basis of its relative proximity to what another formist Stanisław Ignacy Witkiewicz labeled "pure form," was completely alien to the spirit of futurism. The particular character of formism, which was a closed artistic school interested in the establishment of new artistic theories, was in opposition to the futurists' orientation toward life and of art actively participating in it. In the *New Art*, a magazine published in Warsaw in 1921 and closely connected with futurism, an editorial spelled out the disagreement between futurists and formists: "We do not break with ideological content in art as do the advocates of Polish formism. Because the work of art becomes universal and democratic only as a result of the world outlook and confession of faith of the artist."[16] But despite this repudiation, the *New Art* included the formist Chwistek on its editorial board as well as the future Avantgardist and constructivist, Tadeusz Peiper. The heterogeneity of poetic theories and proposals in futurist publications reflects their poetic immaturity— lacking a poetic program of their own, they tolerated and occasionally even adopted the theories of others. This is especially true of the formists, who were not only their elders but, more important, the only other artistic group in Poland at the time interested in the creation of new artistic and poetic language. The critic J. J. Lipski has also drawn attention to a common philosophical source that futurism shared with formism as well as with expressionism, to which it is usually contrasted.[17] This common source was Bergsonism, and the conviction of the superiority of intuition over cognitive intellect. In large part Bergson's influence explains the irrational and instinctive bias of futurism, which can also be found in formism. In addition, Lipski sees in Bergsonism the main cause of the opposition between the two currents of the Polish poetic avant-garde in the 1920s, futurism and the Cracow Avantgarde.

The futurists associated with the formists as early as 1918, and despite obvious differences and the separation of their activities in practice, there was never a formal break between the two. Although their association was paradoxical in view of their respective attitudes, it was not altogether surprising when considered within the artistic and cultural atmosphere of Poland at the end of World War I. What united the two groups was above all their opposition to the cultural status quo, to the romantic as well as postsymbolist tradition ("Moderna") in art and literature and they were united also by the desire to initiate what could be generally called "the new art." As the futurists matured the differences became more important than the similarities, and by 1923 Jasieński wrote unsparingly about his earlier formist friends:

The formists made on me the impression of a medieval guild of searchers for the new form. Separated from the street by the glass of their ateliers they solved the painterly problems that arose, one after another, as one solves mathematical equations—with the stubbornness of a stone and the certainty of one's truth. And behind the glass window Polish life was rolling past, it struggled in its postwar fever and hit its head against a wall, chased into labyrinths of dead-end streets, life was tangled, motley, tongueless.[18]

Several years later Leon Chwistek adopted a similar tone when he wrote about the dissimilarities of the two movements:

During several years the formists succeeded in throwing handfuls of the joyful folly of the highest art upon Cracow, and the jauntiness born of greatness. This pastoral ended as a result of the interference of poets. As long as it was a matter of pure art the inhabitants of Cracow were patient, but *Knife in the Stomach* frightened and froze them. A violent reaction began and the devotees of conventional mediocrity, forced for a long time into silence, latched onto it with both hands. The formists were abashed and started to look for a discreet retreat from the burning edifice.[19]

The constructivist tendencies of the futurists remained a matter of theory and were not seriously or consistently picked up in their poetry, they had to wait until Tadeusz Peiper and the poets of the Cracow Avantgarde to be fully developed and explored. However, their mention by the futurists was symptomatic of an awareness, or maybe only a feeling, that the stage of pure negativism was finished. Although these constructivist tendencies seemed to indicate the direction the new Polish poetry was to follow, the poetic doctrine of constructivism was too foreign to the temperament of the futurists for them to adopt it seriously: "We, outsiders in life with all our scandals, protests against society, and purposely teasing society, we were really an anti-literature."[20] When the youthful rebellion and negativism was over, the futurists did not side with any new aesthetic doctrine but chose another path, that of political involvement. This seemed more consistent with their initial impulse, which was rebellion directed not only at certain artistic and poetic modes and conventions, but more generally at all traditional social, ethical, and cultural values.

Politics and Futurism

If Polish futurism as an artistic movement died sometime between 1922 and 1924, the paths followed by three of its more important participants in the years after the dissolution of the group curiously prolong the history of the movement into the next two decades. Around 1924 Jasieński, Stern, and Wat turned to socially committed poetry and, even more important, to political action. In 1924 Jasieński and Stern published a joint volume of poetry characteristically entitled *Earth to the Left (Ziemia na lewo)*. In their introduction the two poets declared their hatred for bourgeois culture and saw their volume as the first poetry in Poland "devoted to the man of the masses, this hidden hero of history."[21] Both poets extensively translated Mayakovski, and in 1927 Stern published another volume, *Race to the Pole (Bieg do bieguna)*, which contained many poems, particularly the long poem "Europa," that were saturated with social and political content. Jasieński went further, and aside from writing became involved in direct political action—he associated with Polish Communists and published articles on Marxist philosophy and revolutionary tactics in a communist newspaper. In 1925, Jasieński left for

Paris where he wrote his lengthy and tendentious poem, *The Lay of Jakub Szela (Słowo a Jakubie Szeli)* about the leader of a peasant uprising in Galicia in 1846. In France Jasieński organized a politically oriented theater among the Polish miners there, and wrote a novel that quickly became world famous, *I Burn Paris (Palę Paryż)*. The novel was an answer to a story entitled "Je brûle Moscou," by the French writer Paul Morand. Jasieński, who was a member of the French Communist party, published his novel in installments in the communist newspaper *L'Humanité.* Expelled from France because of the violent political character of his book, Jasieński emigrated to the Soviet Union in 1929. There he continued his literary and particularly his political activities until his arrest in 1937. He died in 1939 in a prison camp near Vladivostok.

The story of Aleksander Wat, though less flamboyant, is equally significant and exemplary. In 1922 Wat stopped writing futurist poetry and with the exception of a small volume of philosophical parables *Unemployed Lucifer (Bezrobotny Lucyfer)* published in 1927, he did not write a single literary work until 1957. Wat explained his inability to write creatively as the impossibility of reconciling what was aesthetically acceptable with communist ideology and approach to art. Since he considered that the only ideologically acceptable literature was "socrealism" but at the same time rejected it aesthetically, Wat chose what Shklovski and the LEF group in the Soviet Union had chosen before him—not literature, but fact and propaganda. In 1928 he organized and edited the first communist literary magazine in Poland, the *Literary Monthly (Miesięcznik Literacki),* which gathered around it a Marxist group of writers. The magazine was extremely popular and influential among Polish intellectuals and writers with leftist sympathies. As editor of the *Literary Monthly,* Wat turned against his own futurist past. In an essay evaluating and synthesizing Polish futurism, Wat accused it of being socially and politically regressive, as well as being still under the sway of symbolism. The opinion of its protagonists that it was antibourgeois was false, according to Wat, and its anarchism was misleading. Polish futurism in fact "was a crooked mirror in which Caliban looked at himself with disgust." [22] Later Wat admitted that his change of attitude and his rejection of the nihilism, despair, and cynicism of his dadaist stage was a matter of conscious choice. Communism and the editorship of a communist magazine provided him with a purpose and a cause as well as what he called a *vita activa:* "Not only to interpret, but with one's own hands to change the world." [23] Wat edited the *Literary Monthly* between 1929 and 1932, but by 1936 he severed his contacts with communism completely. From the perspective of thirty years later—in 1968—during which he had experienced five years of Soviet camps and prisons, Wat saw his relation to communism as demoniac and the *Literary Monthly* as a *"corpus delicti* of degradation, as the history of my degradation in communism and by communism." [24]

The engagement of the three most prominent futurist poets in political action and the close association of two of them with communism throws additional light on Polish futurism. However, the interpretation is open to controversy—both Anatol Stern and Aleksander Wat wrote about futurism nearly fifty years after the movement, and they offer two entirely different interpretations of its social and political significance. Stern maintains that from the very beginning the movement was distinguished by acute social awareness: "Polish futurism was an unambiguous advocate of social revolution."[25] Speaking of the collapse of the old moral and social order at the outbreak of the first World War, Stern wrote: "We were fully aware of it . . . when in 1918 we came out with a rebellious protest against the masquerade of social appearances, and against the passéist poetry that represented it." Stern denied the anarchistic nature of the futurist rebellion in Poland and dissociated it from similar tendencies in Italian futurism or in dada. The account by Aleksander Wat, written almost simultaneously with that of Stern, differs from it considerably. While Wat also stressed the futurists' awareness that the old world was finished and that a total change was necessary "no matter how, what, and where,"[26] he thought that the leftist sympathies of the futurists were vague and stemmed from an intellectual and emotional need for renewal rather than from a deliberate programmatic choice. The futurists' feeling that an "earthquake" had occurred might have been connected as much with the Russian revolution as with the reading of European catastrophist literature—"The catastrophist atmosphere was very vivid in Europe at that time, it was Spenglerian before Spengler." However, for the Polish futurists the feeling of catastrophe was far from tragic, unlike the deeply felt catastrophism of the poets of *Żagary* in the 1930s. Partly because of their youth, partly because the threat of fascism or Soviet communism was still absent, the catastrophe seemed promising to the Polish futurists, "the crumbling of the world into ruins *à la longue* gay ruins . . . a subject for spiritual happiness because it was just possible to build something new; it was a big unknown, a journey into the unknown, there were great expectations. . . . If something breaks down so thoroughly from the base, there is room for anything and everything. It was the joy that everything is permitted. And in this sense maybe even the word futurism has a meaning." Contradicting Stern's statements, Wat offered a skeptical evaluation of the importance of the movement in which he himself was an active participant. According to him Polish futurism was socially and poetically of no consequence and interesting only if taken philosophically since "it was the only platform, the only group (of young high school kids, why, we were just finishing high school!) that said, everything is permitted. Of course, by analogy and not because of social interests—I maintain it with all certainty. Neither I, nor Stern, nor Czyżewski, nor early Jasieński. We were socially and politically cynical."

The documentary value of these two contradictory evaluations of Polish futurism should be taken with reservations. It is difficult to agree with Stern about the serious revolutionary intentions of early futurism—his own poetry contradicts this interpretation. On the other hand there might be some exaggeration in Wat's affirmation of the social cynicism of the futurists, especially since Jasieński's 1921 manifestoes had a definite social orientation.[27] At the time Wat wrote his memoirs he hated his communist stage and tried to present it in such a way that he cut off its roots in his own personal development, to isolate it in order to reject it. The sufferings inflicted on him by the Communists more than justify his attitudes. Wat wrote his account of futurism in France and America, but despite his personal bias he had resurrected a more convincing image of the movement and unlike Stern he did not feel any immediate political pressure. His stress on the adolescent character of Polish futurism contains much truth and is confirmed by the early

futurist writings. Considering the development of Polish futurism from this perspective, we see the passage of the futurists from early rebellion to later political
involvement as a passage from youth to maturity. At the time of their literary
debuts in 1918 and 1919, the age of the futurists ranged between seventeen and
nineteen, with the exception of Stanisław Młodożeniec and Tytus Czyżewski.[28]
Stern was born in 1899, Wat in 1900, and Jasieński in 1901. By 1924 these poets
were past the age of adolescence. What at eighteen was youthful rebellion became
channeled at twenty-four into political opposition; the dadaism of the futurists
underwent a characteristic evolution. Pure negation is difficult if not impossible to
maintain as a permanent attitude because it implies total resignation and fatalism.
Man always gropes for faith and meaning, and the young futurists must have felt
after some time that their own nihilism and cynicism were burdens difficult to bear.
As Wat affirms in his memoirs, "There was only one alternative for a man who did
not believe in God, this was Communism."[29] The conversion of the Polish futurists
to communism, the path from pure negation to social idealism and political involvement, was not an isolated case in the history of the European avant-garde. It
also happened to the dadaists and surrealists in France, Switzerland, and Germany,
and to the futurists in Russia.

Aleksander Wat's realistic observation casts great doubt on Stern's claim of
the futurists' political perspicacity, their devotion to the cause of the revolution
at the very onset of the movement. In the light of Wat's statement it seems more
correct to consider the futurists' sympathy for communism not a result of their
political foresight but rather a result of the paucity of the choice. The Polish
futurists' sympathy toward communism rather than—for example—fascism, with
which the Italian futurists sided, has many reasons.[30] It can be explained by the
political situation of Poland. In a country tending toward militarism, the only opposition remaining—and the most radical—was communism. If the futurists wanted
to continue in their negation, they had to side with the political Left. There was
another element in their choice, the attractiveness of the concept of culture and
art proposed by communism: the difference between art or literature and action
disappeared. Poet and artist were active participants in history, those who shaped
it, Stalin's "engineers of the soul." Czesław Miłosz has described the attractions
and pitfalls of this attitude in *The Captive Mind.* Alekasander Wat himself admitted
to the appeal of this concept when he spoke of the *vita activa.* What is more, the
Polish futurists had a model to follow, that of the Russian futurists. It was difficult
to resist the example of Mayakovski, who visited Poland in 1927 and befriended
the futurists.[31] Among all the influences, that of Mayakovski and the Russian
futurists proved to be the strongest.

The Swan Song of Polish Futurism

The last collective publication of the Polish futurists was the poster-size leaflet
Knife in the Stomach published in 1921, that is, only five months after Jasieński's
manifestoes.[32] Its provocative, phonetically written title (which could be translated
"Nife in the Stumuk"), with its black humor, was matched by the equally provoca-
tive but less black subtitle borrowed from the manifestoes of the Zurich dadaists:
"We want to piss in all colors." In flamboyant language it proclaimed the death of

The futurist leaflet *Knife in the Stomach*

KRYTYKA

nieśmiertelny tom futuryz (o sterne)

bruno jasieński.
mięso kobiet

helena buczyńska.

ALEKSANDER WAT.
PŁODZEŃE.

tytus czyżewski.
transcendentalne panopticum

figury z wosku

anatol stern
Kosmiczny nos

elektryczny genjusz panopticzny

elektryczny napoleon

mickiewicz panopticzny

medium zahypnotyzowane

dyrektor panopticum

wszystkie elektromaneikiny

publiczność i maneikiny

dyrektor publiczność maneikiny

jaz:

pierwszy elektromagnetyczny

poeta i malaż

tytus czyżewski

aleksander wat
namopańik barwistanu

nosang

rewolucyjny nos!

stanisław młodożeńec.
KINO

Pathé frères

wszystko jest.

Pathé frères

nieprawda — neprawda

ŃE?!!

Pathé frères

stanisław młodożeńec.

O O
bombaj
twierdza

bombaj

bomb

leona hwistka
"wielość żoczywistości"

leon hwistek
o poezji

PRONASZKO I WITOS

MY I PRASA.

traditional art and the victory of futurism: "the sluggish swine of Polish art, stabbed with a knife in the stomach, began to roar. a lava of futurism spewed out through the hole." The leaflet was almost entirely devoted to futurist poetry and contained contributions from each of the five futurist poets. The choice of poems and their interesting typography made the diversity that characterized the futurist group disappear, and Jasieński saw *Knife in the Stomach* as the first and last collective answer of Polish futurism. The illusion of unity lasted at least for the life span of the poster itself.

The diversity of attitudes and the even more diverse poetic styles of the Polish futurists gave rise to many discussions. It was pointed out even by the futurists themselves that the lack of a uniform poetics, or poetic theory, was responsible for the small impact futurism had on the development of Polish poetry.[33] Polish futurism never created an artistic or poetic school and its collective activities remained limited to a few provocative performances and ephemeral leaflets. Although they stirred public opinion at the moment, they were soon forgotten. Even poets who were barely a generation younger than the futurists, like Czesław Miłosz, did not read their poetry or manifestoes. In addition, all the Polish futurists wrote futurist poetry for a very brief time, sometimes no longer than two or three years. Most of them were beginning poets who were still looking for their poetic style and identity. None of them created either qualitatively or quantitatively a significant body of poetry and by the time they had matured as poets they were no longer futurists. However, seen from a historical perspective, futurism was a distinct movement and reflected a distinct state of consciousness. In his vivid appraisal of Polish futurism, Bruno Jasieński described it: "There was a city of Polish consciousness and there was a handful of partisans who wanted to conquer it. They were like people who gathered on a square to count their forces, to arm themselves and think out a plan. And they called the square: Polish Futurism. And now they disperse into the city— each one along his own street."[34]

But the lack of uniformity added to the interest of the movement and its multifariousness. Using a less martial metaphor than Jasieński, Polish futurism could be described as a kaleidoscope or mosaic in which each piece of glass or tile is of a different color, but when put together they project a single gleam and form a single image. It is interesting that no one of the five poets could be considered as more representative of futurist aesthetics than any other, and no one of them wrote poetry entirely contained within futurist poetics, whether we take Russian or Italian futurism as its model. The work of each poet was a curious mixture of various elements—both foreign and native Polish—and in each case the formula was different. For example, Czyżewski came closest to the aesthetic postulates of Italian futurism, but he combined them with the exclusively Polish theory of formism. Jasieński on the contrary seized on the social and revolutionary aspect of futurism and in this he closely followed the version of Russian futurism best represented by Mayakovski. Młodożeniec concentrated on linguistic experiments. Stern injected humor into Polish futurism and gave it its air of youthfulness and provocativeness. And finally Wat combined the destructive nihilism of dada with a creative interest in the irrational sources of poetry.

TYTUS CZYŻEWSKI

Tytus Czyżewski stands out from the rest of the group of Polish futurists: he was older, and he was a painter as well as a poet. Twenty years older than Stern, Jasieński, and Wat, he belonged to a different generation and his futurism was of a different brand. Czyżewski alone was close to Italian and not to Russian futurism. He was influenced by its poetics, but not by its political implications. He did not have the Russian experience of Jasieński and Młodożeniec, and he was too old for the Dada extravagances of the Warsaw futurists. Czyżewski studied painting in Paris and was well informed about Western European artistic and literary movements; he was probably one of the very few Polish poets of his time who had a firsthand acquaintance with Italian futurism. When the first futurist manifesto by Marinetti was published in *Le Figaro* in 1909, Czyżewski was in Paris, and considering the tremendous uproar this manifesto provoked in Parisian artistic circles, it is not difficult to assume that Czyżewski immediately became familiar with its content. However, even if the source of most of Czyżewski's ideas, themes, and formal experiments can be traced to the poetics of Italian futurism, his use of these theories was always highly individual. Marinetti's proposals attracted Czyżewski, but in adapting them to his own ends they underwent a transformation that often negated the original point of departure.

In Czyżewski's poetry the influence of futurism was complemented and counterbalanced by his association with formism. Known as a formist painter, his adherence to the group of formist artists preceded his association with the futurist poets. Czyżewski's background as a painter had a twofold impact on his writing— first, it is reflected in the strong visual quality of his poetry, both in his extensive use of colors and shapes, and in the typography and drawings he incorporated into his poems. Second, his strong sense of composition reflects formist theories about the preponderance of form over content. He said of himself: "I accepted the name of a Futurist which was bestowed on me as I once accepted (in absolute earnest) the name of a Formist. I must declare that all names apply to me indirectly and transitorily."[35] It is interesting that Czyżewski not only successfully bridged the gap separating formism and futurism but, with his concern for composition, he provided a connection between futurism and the constructivism of the Cracow Avantgarde.[36]

The most striking resemblance between Marinetti's poetics and Czyżewski's attitudes is that both associate the machine with instinct. In both poets, technology is seen as an outburst of primitive instinct, and is presented in opposition to the long tradition of Western rationalism. The cult of matter joins with the cult of the irrational; it was a great rebellion against the Cartesian *homo sapiens* as well as against literary sentimentalism. In a manner similar to Marinetti, Czyżewski proposed the machine and the animal as two models for the artist: "We will be brothers to animals and we will learn from them *instinctive art,* we will love machines because they are our sisters, and animals because they are our teachers and brothers."[37] Calling himself "the first electromagnetic poet and painter," one who has overcome tradition and sentimentalism, in "Transcendental Panopticon" ("Transcendentalne panopticum") Czyżewski boasted of creating art equal to his models:

I enter   life   I create
a sea   of electrons   storms
in   my   brain
I give art   and   hypnolaws
of animal nests
of electro-mediumistic instinct.

wchodzę   w życie   tworzę
morze   elektronów   burz
w   mym   mózgu
daję sztukę   i   hypnoprawa
zwierzęcych gniazd
elektro-mediumicznego instynktu.

However, these apparent similarities to Italian futurist manifestoes are misleading for Czyżewski's attitude toward the machine as well as technology in general differed greatly from that of Marinetti. Far from worshipping the machine and extolling its perfect beauty, far from endowing it with life and considering it as an ideal poetic object, Czyżewski almost always treated it humorously, both in his poetry and in his manifestoes. Where there is solemnity and exaltation in Marinetti's writings, in the Polish poet there is humor and irony. Czyżewski took Marinetti's ideas and transformed Marinetti's passion into intellectual play. The exalted tone and bombastic style of Marinetti were entirely foreign to Czyżewski, who adopted a tone much closer to that of the dada manifestoes; it is probable that many of his proclamations were written tongue in cheek. The cult of the machine, taken so seriously by Marinetti's followers, becomes a joke with Czyżewski: *"Love electrical machines, marry them and beget dynamo-children—*magnetize them and educate them so that they grow up to be mechanical citizens."[38] In one of Czyżewski's poems an enormous marble phallus undergoes a transformation into a huge electric light bulb, then becomes a dynamo phallus, and it almost seems to be a parody of Marinetti's identification of sexuality and technology.

However, the frequency of certain themes typical of Marinetti's futurism indicates that the movement left a strong imprint on Czyżewski and contributed to the formation of his own aesthetics. This was especially true of his poetry, which to a certain extent was an individual interpretation of Marinetti's poetics. Czyżewski's ideas about poetry, which are scattered in introductory notes and prefaces to his own works, can be seen as original conclusions drawn from Marinetti's poetics, in particular his concept of "words-in-freedom" and the abolition of syntax. Czyżewski thought that the foremost task of poetry and prose was to liberate the word "from the logical slavery of sentence and syntax," and he saw both Marinetti and Apollinaire as the first poets to have initiated this process.[39] Czyżewski wanted to free the word both from its logical meaning and from its symbolical connotations, thus restoring its original autonomous value—its value primarily as a sound but also as a graphic sign. "The word in poetry and prose has a realistic meaning and is autonomous in relation to other words situated next to it or even occasionally connected to it by a logical interpretation of thought.[40] The autonomous value of a word is distinct and separate not only from its logical, conceptual value, but from its onomatopoeic associations as well. When speaking of the sound or aural value of a word, Czyżewski excluded onomatopoeia and instead emphasized sounds that were used suggestively without being imitative, as in the poetry of primitive peoples, the war or funeral chants and wedding songs of African Negroes. Czyżewski's interest in the suggestive, incantatory power of words and his indifference to onomatopoeia separates him from Marinetti and brings him closer to Apollinaire, whom he greatly admired and whose arguments against onomatopoeia were strikingly similar to his own.

In his poetry Czyżewski attempted to achieve this autonomy of words by loosening syntax and juxtaposing words without syntactical connections. He called this process "anarchization": "If we take for example a certain number of words and by means of what I call anarchization unite them, giving them an autonomous and suggestive meaning, endowing them in a context (a sentence) with a smaller, or greater, logical or imaginative meaning, we will bring it close to the fundamental meaning of the word, as poetry."[41] This anarchization divides the words of a poem into groups of analogical words and sentences, a procedure that according to Czyżewski gave meaning and unity to the poem as a whole and made it similar to a living organism, despite the superficial illogicalness of words and phrases. One of Czyżewski's earliest attempts at this type of poetry was included in the collection entitled *The Green Eye. Formist Poetry, Electrical Visions (Zielone oko. Poezje formistyczne, elektryczne wizje)*.

The Eyes of the Tiger

Black vertical lines
Yellow greenness the sea
                    The hum of purple
Chi chi
Cry of the monkey
Blue stripes of green
Azure   yellow   purple   palms   a cloud
Cry of the bird of crimson
                    hi hi
On slate paw he pads
                    Quietly
Huge green   *eye*
Bloody green eye   the other
Of the monkey Chi-chi
Of the parrot hi hi
                    The green eye
Mass that is yellow-green
Purple all around
The heart of the monkey trembles
The mystery draws blood
                    Green eye

Palms hum The rhododendron waits
                    Butterflies fly
Immobile the eye watches
Purple-green
                    And that *other*
                    Green *eye*
Fear drowses
Of the monkey shi-shi
Of the parrot hi-hi
                    Green eyes
Is it already night   is it already day
                    Is it a dream
Is it fear—   is it hypnotism
Palms   Silence   Twilight
Monkeys   Butterflies   Parrots
Chi-chi hi-hi chi-chi
                    THE GREEN EYE

                Oczy tygrysa

Czarne pionowe linie
Zół̇ta zieleń morze
                    Szum fioletu
Czi czi
Krzyk małpy
Niebieskie pręgi zieleni
Błękit   żół̇ć   fiolet   palmy   obłok
Krzyk ptaka purpury
                    hi hi
Na sinej łapie stąpa
                    Cicho
Olbrzymie zielone   *oko*
Krwiste zielone oko to drugie
Małpy Czi-czi
Papugi hi hi
                    Zielone oko
Masa zielono-zół̇ta
Fiolet w krąg
Drży małpie serce
Tajemnica puszcza krew
                    Zielone oko
Palmy szumią Rododendron czeka
                    Motyle lecą
Nieruchome czuwa oko
Purpura-zieleń
                    I to *drugie*
                    Zielone *oko*

Strach drzemie
Małpy szi-szi
Papugi hi-hi
      Zielone oczy
Czy to już noc   czy to już dzień
      Czy to sen
Czy to strach — czy to hypnotyzm
Palmy Cisza Zmrok
Małpy Motyle Papugi
Czi-czi hi-hi czi-czi
     ZIELONE OKO.

The poem is about animal instinct, and through an arrangement of colors, sounds, and words it communicates rather than describes the fear of a monkey at the approach of a tiger. Not only does the choice of subject bring it close to futurism, but it is also an interesting example of Czyżewski's concept of words-in-freedom as well as anarchization: throughout the poem words and short phrases are juxtaposed with very few syntactical transitions such as conjunctions, prepositions, punctuation, or even inflections. In keeping with Marinetti's theories, the use of adjectives and verbs is very restrained—most of the verbs imply immobility ("waits," "watches," "trembles") and increase the tension, the sensation of fear reproduced by the poem. Only two verbs imply motion ("pads" and "fly")—the ominous padding of the tiger and the free flight of the butterflies effectively oppose the motionless terror of the monkey. The sounds of the monkey *(chi-chi),* of the parrot *(hi-hi)* and of fear *(shi-shi)* are only vaguely onomatopoetic, and rather than imitate the animal sounds, create an atmosphere of primeval nature and pure instinct. Their value is above all suggestive, and they are instrumental in heightening the tension of the poem. In this respect, the function of the sounds has an importance equal to that of all the other words in the poem, to which they are related by suggestive rather than explicit analogy. At the same time the sounds are distinct from the other words and have an important compositional purpose: they are distributed in the poem as signposts marking certain stages in the progression of the "action," and their accumulation at the end of the poem marks its climax. It is necessary to stress that for Czyżewski anarchization did not mean anarchy, and the adoption of words-in-freedom did not mean abandoning composition. In Czyżewski's poetry the formist is always visible behind the futurist.

The use of colors in the poem is similar to the function of the sounds, they are not imitative of reality but suggestive in a manner that recalls Rimbaud. From the realistic point of view the choice of colors is totally arbitrary: the sea, for example, is referred to by four different colors, black, yellow, green, and purple. While the choice reveals a painter's sensitivity to color, their arrangement betrays a formist for whom the overriding principle is that of composition. Leon Chwistek discussed Czyżewski's painting and remarked that it is based on visual perceptions—the same could also be said of Czyżewski's poetry. He went on to say that the painter did not directly reproduce these perceptions but instead created what Chwistek described as "a particular milieu" that results from the reciprocal relationships of shapes and colors in the painting.[42] Czyżewski's poems are similar to the compositions he created as a painter: real objects are arranged in a manner different from that in which they are perceived, although they are still recognizable. Colors, sounds, and sentences combine into interesting formal patterns that are neither nonsensical nor abstract and that, without being naturalistic, are strongly rooted in reality. Czyżewski took a conciliatory position in his discusssion of mimetic versus abstract art. He saw himself as an artist who creates his own image of reality through abstract formal means, without denying reality nor turning away from it. He did not identify with reality, nor was he a detached spectator and observer, but out of reality he created his own world. Czyżewski denied the possibility of pure abstraction in either poetry or painting and believed that the artist's individuality and creativity manifested themselves in the arrangement of the different elements in a work of art, that is, in its composition.

Czyżewski's preoccupation with form and his desire to achieve a poetic composition in which traditional syntax would play a minimal role led him to experiments with typography. Of all the Polish futurists he explored typographical effects in his poetry in the most thorough and most imaginative manner, which can be attributed to his visual sensitivity as a painter, although the initial impulse might have come from Marinetti. The typographical arrangement of "The Eyes of a Tiger" is still somewhat timid and consists mainly of isolating and emphasizing certain key words, but in later poems Czyżewski was much bolder. Kazimierz Wyka underestimated and misjudged Czyżewski's typographical experiments when he referred to them as "mechanical and graphic toys," the creative value of which is questionable.[43] Their significance and innovation can be seen more clearly if they are considered as substitutes for syntax rather than as purely visual decorations. The role of typography in Czyżewski's poetry is to provide connections and relations between words. The title of "Hymn to the Machine of My Body" is very futuristic, but the poem is semihumorous and represents one of the two different types of typographical design used by Czyżewski.

The syntax of the poem is reduced to a minimum, and the terms for human organs are juxtaposed without syntactic connection against terms designating various parts of a complex electrical system. The typographical arrangement of words suggests the possibility of two different readings, one vertical and one horizontal, and thus of different syntactic connections. This possibility, however, is misleading; grammatically as well as logically the poem permits only the horizontal reading, moving from left to right. Thus the syntax comes in, so to speak, through the back door. Czyżewski the formist was not ready to take his futurist experiment to its furthest development and consequence. The typography in this poem also has another role: the poem is an example of Czyżewski's notion of words-in-freedom and is composed predominantly of nouns. The "action" of the poem, curiously, does not take place inside the text but outside it, as a result of the typography, which is the true source of the dynamism of the poem.

The effect of "Hymn to the Machine of My Body" is made by the unusual arrangement of words on the page, but Czyżewski occasionally introduced graphic design as well as drawings into his poems. The most extravagant example of this kind of experiment is "Mechanical Garden" ("Mechaniczny ogród").

Hymn to the Machine of My Body

blood
stomach
they pulsate
coils

pepsin
heart
they beat
of my

blood
blood
strained
intestine

brain

cables to my veins
twisted wire conductor
to my heart
battery
have pity on me
my *heart*
dynamo-heart
electric lungs
magnetic diaphragm
of the belly

one   one   one
my heart beats come
electric heart one

transmission belt
of my *intestines*
two   two   two

have pity on me
one two

the telephone of my brain
dynamo-brain
three   three   three
one   two   three
the machine of my body
function turn
live

Hymn do maszyny mego ciała

krew
żołądek
pulsują
zwoje

pepsyna
serce
biją
mych

krew
krew
natężone
kiszek

mózg

kable do moich żył
skręcony drut przewód
do mego serca
akumulator
zmiłuj się nademną
moje *serce*
dynamo-serce
elektryczne płuca
magnetyczna przepono
brzuszna

raz   raz   raz
bije moje serce wraz
elektryczne serce raz

transmisyjny pasie
moich *kiszek*
dwa   dwa   dwa

zmiłujcie się nademną
raz dwa

telefon mego mózgu
dynamo-mózgu
trzy   trzy   trzy
raz   dwa   trzy
maszyno mojego ciała
funkcjonuj obracaj się
żyj

Mechanical Garden

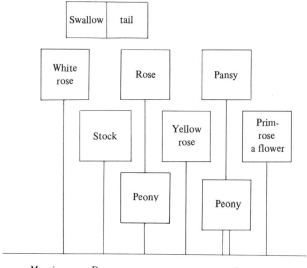

Swallow | tail

White rose

Rose

Pansy

Stock

Yellow rose

Prim-rose a flower

Peony

Peony

    Morning   Dew   Roses
  sun   sun flowers   in the distance mountains
  butterfly   swallowtail   yellow roses
    the grass laughs   sun
      laughs   and   I and my hope

Mechaniczny ogród

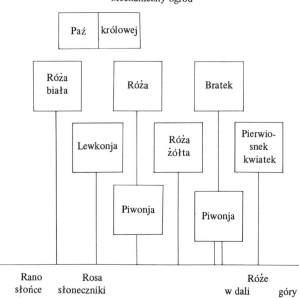

Paź | królowej

Róża biała

Róża

Bratek

Lewkonja

Róża żółta

Pierwio-snek kwiatek

Piwonja

Piwonja

    Rano   Rosa   Róże
  słońce   słoneczniki   w dali   góry
  motyl   paź królowej   żółte róże
    trawa się śmieje   słońce
      śmieje się   i   ja i moja nadzieja

Despite the geometry of the design, the typography has a mimetic quality that makes this poem a distant cousin of Apollinaire's *Calligrammes*. The stemmed squares containing the names of the flowers resemble flowers growing in a garden, and the two-compartmental box with the name of a butterfly suggests its wings. But aside from mimesis, the typography has a compositional function—as in the previous poem it acts as syntax and paradoxically it binds the words into new relationships no less determined than those with syntax. It provides connections as well as visual unity. It is typical of Czyżewski to associate the mechanical with the natural world and the geometrical design stands for one while the verbal texture represents the other. The two parts are separated by a horizontal line, with the lower part acting as a commentary on the graphic design of the upper. In a way the commentary detracts from the poem's formal purity, but at the same time it broadens its expressive power as a whole by endowing it with a personal emotional content. The harmony of the arrangement of the upper part corresponds to the emotional tone of the lower; both suggest happiness and hope.

"Mechanical Garden" is an example of the more ambitious artistic intentions behind Czyżewski's use of typography and his desire to use such devices to translate and enhance his own personal vision. In Czyżewski's poetry, typography and graphic design are abstract and formal, but they are primarily a means for self-expression, a means that came naturally to a painter. In one of his poems Czyżewski included abstract drawings and called them his "dynamopsychic stages."[44] This was not a simple "juggling with forms," but (to paraphrase Wyka and to polemicize with him) a method closer to his nature, a spontaneous method that the eminent critic unjustly refused to consider as "natural" in all of Czyżewski's futurist poetry.[45]

The futurist poems, though significant, were only a part of Czyżewski's poetic output. Much of his poetry, in subject matter and treatment of language, remained outside futurism. This is true of *Lajkonik in the Clouds (Lajkonik w chmurach*, 1930), which is about the folklore of the Cracow region, his poems about Spain and, most important, his famous *Pastorals (Pastorałki*, 1925), which is the basis for Czyżewski's poetic reputation among many Polish critics and which Kazimierz Wyka considered to be the poet's only truly original and lasting contribution to Polish poetry. Although a discussion of the *Pastorals* as well as other nonfuturist poetry of Czyżewski is outside the scope of this chapter, Czyżewski's shift from futurism to folk tradition for inspiration is significant, since it conforms to the pattern of evolution of all the Polish futurists mentioned earlier.[46] The critic Jan Józef Lipski has given a perceptive interpretation of Czyżewski's evolution, which he saw as a way of counterbalancing his futurism, as "a pure expression of utopian nostalgia for the world of pastoral without electricity or uranium. This world of the Polish mountain peasants' imagination is for him an opposition to and refuge from the world of contemporary technological civilization, which fascinated as much as frightened Czyżewski."[47] As Lipski suggests, Czyżewski is interesting not for his primitive longing but rather for the confrontation and coexistence of these two opposite attitudes, both on the philosophical and the poetic level. Although the tradition of folklore provided a balance to the futurist fascination with modernity, without Czyżewski's futurist experiment his poetry would have been incomparably and irretrievably poorer in its interest, range, and diversity.

BRUNO JASIEŃSKI

There could scarcely be a greater contrast than the futurism of Bruno Jasieński and that of Tytus Czyżewski. It had a different origin, followed a different course, and only for a span of a few years were the two close enough to create the illusion of belonging to one movement. If Czyżewski was above all an artist, art for Jasieński was not an autonomous domain but part of life itself, and more particularly an instrument in the social struggle. Czyżewski was attracted to futurism because its aesthetic theories opened new artistic possibilities, and he abandoned futurism when he had exhausted these possibilities in his own poetry. Jasieński saw futurism as an artistic corollary of social revolution, as the first step on the road to complete revolution and was only secondarily interested in futurist poetic theories. He abandoned futurism when he found other more efficient outlets for his social activities. The sources of Czyżewski's futurist poetic experiments are to be found in Marinetti and the poetry of Apollinaire, but the futurism of Jasieński—in both its poetic and social aspects—originated in the Russian movement and in particular in the model established by Mayakovski. Mayakovski's commitment to the revolution, his concept of poetry as an instrument of the revolutionary cause, his poetic temperament, which made him "the least interested, among the leading Futurists, in questions of craft and technique," and even his cynicism, individualism, and megalomania—all strongly attracted Jasieński and provided him with an example to follow.[48] Jasieński's poetry shows the influence of the great Russian poet in its subject matter, its rhythm, language, and in its emotional tone.

But the example of Mayakovski was not the only factor, nor even the most important one that shaped Jasieński's approach to futurism and to poetry in general. His interest in the social revolution and his passionate devotion to its cause was above all the result of two influences: his father, and his stay in Russia between 1914 and 1918. Jasieński was born in a small village where his father was a local physician. Disinterested and devoted to the poor, his father treated his profession as a social mission, and according to Jasieński's biographer he left a legend behind him that is alive today in the province where they lived. The attitudes of the father must have contributed considerably to shaping the sensitivity of the son. His stay in Moscow, between the ages of thirteen and seventeen, was when Russia was in the grip of its monumental social upheaval. The enormity of the event, even more impressive when seen through the eyes of an adolescent, irrevocably and unambiguously settled the dilemma—as old as art itself—of life versus art. For the sixteen-year-old Jasieński, the poetic revolution of Russian futurism must have appeared pale and abstract in comparison with the real, terrible, but at the same time fantastic drama that was taking place on the streets of Moscow. At the age of twenty, with all the impulsiveness of adolescence and yet with absolute sincerity, Jasieński expressed his impatience and announced his break with the entire aesthetic tradition in poetry. In a poem starting with the provocative and rebellious statement, "I am tired by language" ("zmęczył mnie język"), Jasieński broke away from the tradition in which he had grown up, and he proposed his own concept of poetry to which he was to remain faithful until the end of his life:

> O Italian, Russian, French brothers,
> so enormous in your pathos!

O you who are beloved, close to me, dearest—
I have all of you up to my ears!
. . . .
Poetry! Mistress of elegant gentlemen!
Anemic, nervous, pale masturbators!
Away! Today I want to praise the black vulgar rabble,
. . .
I will create for you a new art, the art of black cities.

O bracia włoscy, rosyjscy, francuscy,
tacy ogromni w swoim patosie!
O ukochani, najdrożsi, bliscy —
mam już was wszystkich po dziurki w nosie!
. . . .
Poezjo! Utrzymanko eleganckich panów!
Anemiczni, nerwowi, bladzi masturbanci!
Precz! Chcę dziś sławić czarnych, ordynarnych chamów,
. . .
Stworzę wam sztukę nową, sztukę czarnych miast.

In fact, Jasieński did not have to create this "new art" since it already existed; he described it in the prologue to his "Song of Hunger" ("Pieśń o głodzie")—it was the poetry of the everyday events printed daily in "long black columns" of thousands of newspapers. It was the poetry written by the city with its own "rhythm, pulse, and blood," the new "gigantic poetry": "the only one. twentyfourhoursaday. continually new. / which acts on me like a strong electric current" ("jedyna dwudziestoczterogodzinna. wiecznie nowa. / która działa na mnie, jak silny elektryczny prąd"). In comparison with this living, raw poetry of life, all other poetry was ridiculous. Jasieński banished the poets from his "un-ideal" republic not because they were dangerous but because they were useless: "poets, you are not needed!" ("poeci, jesteście niepotrzebni!").

There was only one path remaining for poets and that was to assume the role of mediators between readers and reality.[49] In the contemporary world man is assailed everyday by a multitude of signs and messages that cross over his head:

Entangled in the clamorous, colorful crowd,
in the enormous, black city a small, pale man,
hears the unceasing hum of multilingual words,
an array of crookedly crossed cries—the blades and clanging

["Morse"]

Wplątany w rozkrzyczany, kolorowy tłum,
w olbrzymim czarnym mieście mały, blady człowiek,
słyszy słów różnogwarych nieustanny szum,
szyk skrzyżowanych krzywo krzyków — kling i klangor

["Morse"]

The role of the poet is to be like a Morse code transmitter that, in the chaos of noises, in the complex system of the signals of life, detects the real message. The concept of the poet as transmitting station belongs to futurist aesthetics; it is a proposal of an entirely new model of poetry that breaks away from the romantic and symbolist tradition of personal lyricism. Jasieński's new art is more radical than Marinetti's aesthetic theories or the poetry of Czyżewski since it reduces creativity to mechanics and poetry to a dry record of "naked" events, facts, and objects. But this poetic ideal is in contradiction to Jasieński's own poetry, both because of its highly emotional and "unmechanical" tone and because of its strong tendency to the grotesque. The disparity between intent and realization was due to the disparity between poetry and life, to the very specificity of the creative process. As a critic observes: "The creation of poems out of 'objects' and 'events' is impossible. Whenever Jasieński tries 'to think a problem through to the end,' he arrives at grotesque and nightmarish visions."[50] One of the most interesting examples of this kind of distortion is "TeeeTH" ("ZemBY"):

—A Rhapsody—

Cold. Stiff. Swollen.
With eyes coated by enamel,
Which glows at night,
When right behind the wall someone sick is passing away.
Strange.
Like a fairy tale
For small well-behaved children
On long winter evenings,
When behind the window
Snow
Falls and falls enveloping the terrain
With its weird white monotony.
And from the half-open doors of seething bars
Puffs of steam come out in bursts—
From every corner.
From black brothels,
From underground
Unevenly,
Jerkily
Are chattering
TeeeTH . . .

And those,
Which have small sadness in them,
Sharp—drawn out—grating
The teeeTH of an ugly pock-marked prostitute,
Who returns home in the morning
Chilled through and untouched

Like a dog,
With the insistence of the one who didn't find a client,
Somewhere under a fence,
Waits for the returning guests of others,
For their vicious advances . . .
And the wind pinches her calves
Lustful and sticky.
And from somewhere deep, from the inside,
Comes a dry unpleasant knock
Of chopped bones.
Higher and lower.
Do—Re—Mi—Fa—Sol . . .
Like strange ghostly scales
With a single returning refrain,
Which an old, demented professor of solfeggio,
Sings in the salon of a dying lady
Fast, uneven
Rickety arpeggios
Flow over with a long dragging train.
. . . . . .

At the concert in a crowded hall
A pale nervous musician
Dances with his fingers on the keyboard
The wild gavottes of Chopin's waltzes
And everywhere he hears the rhythm
The chatter— the chatter— the chatter,
Which comes out from his fingers,
Which interweaves with his fingers,
Even, monotonous, sinister,
As if all the TeeTH in the world
Were ringing together . . .
And in a paroxysm of fright
He slams the terrible keyboard,
Which also has chattering
Rickety teeeTH . . .
And he suddenly sees in the crowd, towering upward,
In long galleries which run in an arc
Through lorgnons, feathery headpieces and hats,
From a niche of the boxes on the parterre
In the smile of a mistress in décolleté
The shining TeeeTH of a PANTHER.

— Rapsodia —

Zimne. Sztywne. Obrzękłe.
Z oczami powleczonymi szkliwem,

Co w nocy świeci,
Kiedy zaraz za ścianą ktoś odchodzi chory.
Dziwne.
Jak bajka
Dla małych, grzecznych dzieci
W długie zimowe wieczory,
Kiedy za oknem
Śnieg
Pada i pada, zasnuwając teren
Swoją dziwaczną, białą monotonią.
A z półotwartych drzwi kipiących barów
Buchają kłęby —
Ze wszystkich kątów.
Z czarnych lupanarów,
Z suteren
Niejednostajnie,
Urywanie
Dzwonią
Z e m b y...

I te,
Co mają w sobie jakiś smęt malutki,
Ostre — przeciągłe — zgrzytliwe
Z e m b y brzydkiej ospowatej prostytutki,
Co wraca do domu nad ranem
Zmarzła i nietknięta
Jak pies,
Z natręctwem takiej, co nie znalazła klienta,
Gdzieś pod parkanem,
Czekać na cudzych wracających gości,
Na ich zjadliwe zaczepki...
A wiatr szczypie za łydki
Obleśny i lepki.
A skądś głęboko, z wnętrzności,
Idzie suchy, nieprzyjemny stuk
Siekanych kości.
Wyżej i niżej.
Do — Re — Mi — Fa — Sol...
Jak dziwne, upiorne gamy
Z jednym powracającym refrenem,
Które śpiewa w salonie konającej damy
Stary półobłąkany profesor solfeggia,
Przelewają się długim powłóczystym trenem
Szybkie, nierówne,
Rozklekotane arpeggia
· · · · · ·

Na koncercie w natłoczonej sali
Blady, zdenerwowany muzyk
Tańczy palcami po klawiaturze
Dzikie gawoty Szopenowskich walców
I słyszy wszędzie ten rytm
I stukot – i stukot – i stukot,
Co mu wychodzi spod palców,
Co mu się w palcach przeplata,
Równy, monotonny, złowrogi,
Jakby dzwoniły naraz
Wszystkie z e m b y całego świata . . .
I w paroksyzmie trwogi
Zatrzaskuje straszną klawiaturę,
Która ma też stukające
Rozklekotane z e m b y ...
I widzi nagle w tłumie, piętrzącym się w górę,
W długie, półkolem biegnące kruźganki
Poprzez lorgnony, egrety, rajery
Z niszy parterowej loży
W uśmiechu wydekoltowanej kochanki
Błyszczące z e m b y PANTERY.

Far from being a mechanical recording of events, the poem is closer to a cruel fairy tale or a nightmarish vision. It is a grotesque symphony of human teeth that perform strange barcaroles, "rickety arpeggios" and "ghostly scales." Under the influence of this savage music, the artist—who is the pianist of the poem—transforms Chopin's waltzes as he plays them into "wild gavottes," he becomes frightened by his own art and interrupts the concert. It is characteristic that Jasieński's artist is a performer and interpreter rather than a creator, he is a transmitting apparatus whose play, like the poem itself, is supposed to be the transmission of life, but its own menacing clatter drowns and destroys the harmony of the music. What is meant to be transmission becomes in the process of playing and writing—in the moment of creativity—an interpretation, and life itself is transformed to the point that it becomes fantastic. If Jasieński's pianist destroys the harmony of art by listening to the rhythm of life, the poet in turn—this time unintentionally—distorts this reality in the transmission. Life is transformed into art rather than vice versa, and the circle art-life-art closes in on itself. Jasieński is no more in control of his own creative impulse than the pianist, and his poetry is as much the result of his unconscious artistic instinct as his controllable conscious will. Jasieński himself was aware of this particular mechanism of his own creative process, and he described it in the introduction to his fantastic novel, *The Legs of Isolde Morgan (Nogi Izoldy Morgan,* 1923): "Every problem becomes macabre if we want to think it out to its conclusion. Let's try to think for an hour about the house which we pass every day without noticing it, and this house will slowly grow for us into ghastly dimensions."[51] The critic Edward Balcerzan believes that this process is a reflection of a general law of the attraction of opposites as much as a particular poetic vision that belonged to Jasieński. Consequently, theoretically and philosophically opposed artistic movements such as expressionism and futurism can show amazing similarities. Just as deformed matter in an expressionist work often starts to live an autonomous life, the futurist cult of matter, carried to its extreme, can transform itself into pure mysticism—

> The degraded "spirit," "humiliated" by matter, can be reborn in that very matter and impose a new, unexpected and almost "mystical" meaning upon it. As a result of these mutual identifications, Jasieński's futurism was at times indeed an expressionism. The expressionist effects were born not from an insufficiency of the futuristic quality, but on the contrary from the "overcharge" of a work with futurist consciousness.[52]

In Jasieński's poetry the grotesque operates on two levels, stylistic and thematic. It permeates his imagery ("a dry unpleasant knock / Of chopped bones," "in the smile of a mistress in décolleté / The shining TeeeTH of a PANTHER"), and it is also a function of the situations the poet selects to describe. The world of Jasieński's poetry is that of the metropolitan underground: murky dark corners, brothels, disreputable night bars, poverty-stricken rooms. It is a world of prostitutes, madmen, sexual perverts, and innocent victims, a large modern city in which suicide alternates with rape, and death with accidents, as in the poem entitled "City" ("Miasto").

> A steady rain pelts down.
> It spits water against the window panes.
> A policeman walks, walks on the corner,
> Every time he stops—he listens . . .
> Nothing.
> The windows have lowered their shades.
> There, in the hotel,
> A light is burning all night.
> Someone is sick.
> They have sent for a doctor.
> Through the window you can sometimes see a slim brown-
> haired woman.
> The whole first floor is dark, dead-silent . . .
> On the third floor a small light—
> An older man has lured there a seven-year-old girl
> and rapes her on a chair.
> The child has wide-open eyes . . .
>
> The policeman is walking on the corner
> Back and forth. Back and forth.
> And looks in the black windows.
> From behind a corner a thief spies on him.
> It is raining.
> They are getting wet . . .

Deszcz tnie miarowy.
W szyby wodą pluje.
Chodzi, chodzi na rogu posterunkowy,
Co się zatrzyma — nasłuchuje...
Nic.
Okna zapuściły story.
Tam, w hotelu,
Światło całą noc się pali.
Ktoś chory.
Po doktora posyłali.
Przez okno widać czasem wysmukłą szatynkę.
Ciemny, głuchy cały parter...
Na trzecim piętrze światełko. —
Starszy pan zwabił do siebie 7-ioletnią dziewczynkę
I gwałci ją na fotelu.
Dziecko ma oczy szeroko rozwarte...

Na rogu posterunkowy chodzi
Tam i na powrót. Tam i na powrót.
I patrzy w czarne okna.
Zza węgła podpatruje go złodziej.
Deszcz pada.
Mokną...

The fascination with the morbid, criminal, and sensational side of life is so prominent in Jasieński's poetry that it verges on obsession and is more an expression of the poet's psychology than his declared futurist "interest in life." The source of his descriptions was often not personal experience but probably the literature on the subject, especially Russian literature from Dostoevski to Mayakovski, with which Jasieński was familiar.

Jasieński's desire to bring poetry close to life affected both the subject matter of his poetry and its language. In an attempt to de-poeticize the language of poetry, he used the style of daily newspaper reports as a model. A good example of this is the following poem:

Morgue

They came in a black closed ambulance.
(It was evening . . . an autumn evening . . .
Mud—spleen—reverie . . .)
They carried out something heavy, covered by canvas.
They put the stretchers on the stones.
Everything was done deftly.
A lamp illuminated them with bright white light.
It was silent . . . Rain sang in the gutter . . .
Horses shuffled their hooves . . .
(. . . Something's happened . . . Something's happened . . .)

A few bystanders stopped.
They looked. They asked questions.
Brief words were heard.
A short, broken conversation
Carried on in a staccato undertone . . .
. . . 25 years old . . . A prostitute . . .
. . . with mercuric chloride . . .
They lifted the stretchers. They went in to the vestibule.
(Rain was falling . . . drops were beating on the roofs . . .)
One led the way with a flashlight.
(. . . Dance of shadows . . .)
They carried it down on sticky, worn steps
To a huge, vaulted cellar.
Stretchers stood in a row.
Something black flitted past . . . vanished . . .
Perhaps a rat? . . . Perhaps a shadow from the street? . . .
One carried the flashlight.
He stopped.
They put it against the wall.
They loudly blew their noses.
They left.

A key rasped in the lock . . .
Still the quiet, distant voices . . .
Still the steps becoming hushed, going up . . .
(. . . As she thinks . . . as she thinks . . .)
Then a rumble on the pavement behind the gate . . .
And nothing . . .
Silence . . .
Darkness . . .
They left her ALONE, completely ALONE . . .
Alone, and to the side.

The stretchers stood in a row, motionless, covered.
One leg after another.
A pair of greenish eyes glinted from the corner . . .
One . . . A second . . .
They stared for a long time, searching . . .

Something rustled on the wet stone floor . . .
. . . .
Above, lamps were burning on the street.
On the sidewalk a drunken worker dragged himself past,
Eternal argonaut on the oceans of streets.

Cars raced along the street with the whistle of sirens.

Morga

Przyjechali czarną, zamkniętą karetką.
(Był wieczór... jesienny wieczór...
Błoto — spleen — zapatrzenie...)
Wynieśli coś ciężkiego, nakrytego płachtą.
Postawili nosze na kamienie.
Robili rzecz zwinnie.
Lampa oświetlała ich jasno, biało.
Było cicho... Deszcz śpiewał w rynnie...
Konie człapały kopytami...
(... Coś się stało... Coś się stało...)
Przystanęło kilku ciekawych.
Patrzyli. Pytali.
Dolatywały pojedyncze słowa.
Jakaś rozmowa urywana, krótka,
Prowadzona ściszonym staccatem...
... 25 lat ... Prostytutka...
... sublimatem ...
Podnieśli nosze. Weszli do sieni.
(Deszcz padał... krople tłukły o dach...)
Jeden świecił im z przodu latarnią.
(... Taniec cieni ...)
Ponieśli w dół po lepkich, wyślizganych schodach
Do ogromnej, sklepionej piwnicy.
Nosze stały rzędem.
Coś czarnego mignęło... przepadło...
Może szczur? ... Może cień z ulicy? ...
Jeden świecił latarnią.
Przystanął.
Postawili pod ścianą.
Wytarli głośno nosy.
Wyszli.

Klucz zgrzytnął w zamku...
Jeszcze ciche oddalone głosy...
Jeszcze kroki cichnące na górę...
(... Jak myśli ... jak myśli ...)
Potem turkot po bruku za bramą...
I nic...
Cisza...
Ciemno...
Zostawili SAMĄ, zupełnie SAMĄ...
Samą jedną na uboczu.

Nosze stały szeregiem nieruchome, nakryte.
Noga przy nodze.

Z kąta błysnęła para zielonkawych oczu ...
Jedna ... Druga ...
Wpatrywały się długo, badawczo ...

Coś szeleściło po mokrej kamiennej podłodze ...
. . . .
Na górze paliły się lampy.
Chodnikiem wlókł się jakiś pijany robotnik,
Wieczny po oceanach ulic argonauta.

Ulicą świstem syren ścigały się auta.

The poem alternates between two types of discourse. While the essentials are given in a rapid, telegraphic, matter-of-fact, and informative style, in short but complete sentences, what could be called a poetic commentary adds information through unfinished sentences, sudden pauses, or insinuations characteristic of spoken language. This poetic commentary adds a subjective, psychological dimension to the poem and stands in sharp contrast to the dry, impersonal tone of the factual account. It acts like shadow that complements light and gives depth to the flatness of facts, indeed, it is the poetry that unexpectedly supplements life. To accentuate the difference between these two speaking voices, especially in the first part—since in the second part only the subjective commentary can be heard—Jasieński puts most of his "own" poetic comments between parentheses, implying a scale of relative importance of these two sources of information. However, despite this precaution the inclusion of the poetic commentary can be seen as a concession to purely artistic values on the part of Jasieński. As in the poem "TeeeTH," the poet counterbalances the reporter even in this grim and unpoetic story.

Jasieński's futurism was above all ideological, and the purely linguistic experiments that preoccupied poets like Tytus Czyżewski and Stanisław Młodożeniec occupy only a marginal place in his poetry. He attempted them, however, in a few poems, under the influence of such Russian futurists as Velemir Khlebnikov or Aleksei Kruchenykh. The poem "Springlike" ("Wiosenno") is an attempt to manipulate words as if they were objects, by playing with their semantic identity. The Polish text is

Wiosenno

genialnej recytatorce tego wiersza
p. Irenie Solskiej-Grosserowej
TARAS koTARA S TARA raZ
biAłe pAnny
poezjAnny
poezOwią poezAwią
poezYjne poezOSny
MAKI na haMAKI na sOSny
rOŚnym pełnowOSnym rAnem
poezAwią poezOwią

pierwsze
szesnastoLEtnie LEtnie
naIWne dzIWne wiersze
kłOSy na włOSy bOSo na rOSy
z brUZDy na brUZDy jAZDy bez UZDy
słOńce uLEwa zaLEwa na LEwo
na LEwo na LEwo na LEwo prOSTo
OSTy na mOSTy krOST wodorOSTy
tuPOTY koPYT z łoPOTem oPADł
oPADł i łoPOT i łoPOT i POT.

The first line contains the possibility of two different readings, either "taras, kotara, stara, raz" or "Taras, ko, taras, tara, raz." Although only the first reading has any meaning, the isolation of the "S" justifies the second reading as well. The typography of "koTARA" also suggests that the identity of a word is relative, since it can contain other words or parts of words (ko-tara), and thus is open to different meanings and capable of designating different objects or realities. A mere typographical trick is able to reveal these different possibilities inherent in words. The capitalization of the "A" in *panny* (girls) reveals *Anny* (the plural of the feminine name Anna), the word *sosny* (pine trees) contains *sny* (dreams), *hamaki* (hammocks) contains *maki* (poppies), and so on. In discussing this poem Edward Balcerzan speaks of the words being like balls in the hands of a juggler, appearing and disappearing under the very eyes of the reader; they are like "an illusionistic 'box' hiding another word."[53] The accumulation of words with similar sounds, highlighted and emphasized by their capitalization, has a similar effect and suggests affinities between words that are semantically unrelated. This phenomenon has been described by another critic as "false etymology," because "the similarity of the phonetic structure of the words creates an impression of etymological affinity."[54]

In "On the River" ("Na rzece") Jasieński experimented with what is known as *zaum* or transrational language:

> na rzece rzec ce na cerze mrze
> pluski na bluzki wizgi
> w dalekie lekkie dale że
> poniosło wiosłobryzgi

The effect of this first stanza depends primarily on the phonic similarity of the words within each line. The first word of the line introduces the sounds, which are then repeated in various combinations, using assonance and rich consonance. The sounds change from line to line, each one establishing a new pattern. It is significant that the words in Jasieński's poem are not nonsense words, or pure sounds, as in the *zaum* poems of Kruchenykh, for example, and the poem as a whole contains a meaning, even though it would be difficult to pin it down exactly, line by line and word by word.[55] Generally speaking the first stanza alludes to a trip on a river by boat, the splash of oars *(pluski, wiosłobryzgi),* the dying sound of words *(rzec ce na cerze mrze),* the faraway distance *(dalekie dale).*

Jasieński's unwillingness to isolate the purely phonic qualities of language or to abandon meaning for sound are symptomatic of his approach to language and poetry in general. He was alone among the futurists in stressing the semantic value of words: "The word is a complex material. Aside from its sound content it has another symbolic content which it represents and which should not be destroyed because of the danger of creating a third art, no longer poetry but not yet music."[56] For Jasieński, poetry was above all a carrier of a message, not an art for and in itself. The only poetic reform he proposed and adopted was that of phonetic orthography, which from the artistic point of view was insignificant but which had an ideological motivation since it brought poetry closer to everyday spoken language. In Jasieński's poems, phonetic orthography often acts as a coverup or "futurist dressing" for traditional form, for many use traditional versification and some explore even more intricate and rare verse forms such as the hexameter.[57] It is interesting that all the most programmatic and futuristically "rebellious" poems of Jasieński—those contained for the most part in *Shoe in the Buttonhole (But w butonierce)*—use traditional poetic forms, while the few poems that experiment with form, such as "Springlike" and "On the river," are conventional in subject matter. This phenomenon can be explained by Jasieński's attitude toward futurism. Since he believed formal problems were not very important, the poems just quoted were merely lip service paid to the futurists' experiments with language. On the other hand his programmatic poems, because of their nature, dispense with all experimentalism. Jasieński wanted to declare his attitudes and views in a straightforward manner, and traditional versification best suited his purposes. At the age of twenty, when most of his programmatic poems were written, Jasieński did not yet have an original poetic style at his disposal, hence he reverted to ready forms.

Jasieński's break with futurism in 1923 was a logical consequence of his social and artistic attitudes. From the beginning of his association with the movement, he saw its role not so much in the creation of new poetic forms as in the struggle for a new *future* world. His increasing involvement in social activism after 1923 could justifiably be seen as the continuation of his futurism, and yet the poet himself separated the two and considered the year 1923 as a dividing line between his futurism and the period of his new "social consciousness."[58] This new consciousness eventually led Jasieński out of the literary domain altogether, and into the world of action.

STANISŁAW MŁODOŻENIEC

Stanisław Młodożeniec once described his own contribution to the first poetry reading of Polish futurists in Cracow as "a bit of peasant freshness enlivened by the zeal of novelty."[59] The statement is an accurate characterization of his own poetry and a precise judgment of its place in Polish futurism. It also encapsulates extremely well the twofold nature of his poetry, which is its most salient feature. From the beginning Młodożeniec's poetry followed two different though not necessarily opposite directions, folk and futurist experimental poetry. Both tendencies were already present in his first volume *Lines and Futurines (Kreski i futureski,* 1921), and they continued to develop simultaneously in subsequent volumes with the only change being the relative proportions of the two types. In his first volume the poems of futurist inspiration outweighed the peasant poetry, while in later volumes the peasant themes became more and more prominent, the experimental verse receding and eventually disappearing. Of the four volumes of poetry that Młodożeniec published between 1921 and 1939, only *Sunday (Niedziela,* 1925), is entirely inspired by peasant themes, and yet, even though futurism is absent on the ideological level, it penetrates the linguistic textures of this volume as well. *Future-scales and Future-scapes (Futuro-gamy i futuro-pejzaże,* 1934) was the last one to maintain a connection with futurism, and the last one to "marry"—in the words of its author—the old with the present. And although Młodożeniec never denied his connections with futurism (on the contrary, he always emphasized them) after 1934 he purposely narrowed his poetic world to the one that can be seen from "the peasant's dike." [60]

Paradoxically it was Młodożeniec, the futurist who was the most rooted in peasant life and concerns, who was at the same time the author of the most programmatically futurist poems, of the most radical experiments with language. Several of his early poems repeat the main tenets of the futurist manifestoes, the rejection of the past and tradition, optimism, pacifism, enthusiasm for the present, attraction to the city, and modern technology:

> Enough of walking according to old floors,
> and carrying the head bent under the ceiling—
> the fallow unwalked-on land of the world is beautiful,
> and the sky is to be scythed with the nose—
> . . . . . .
> Time is preparing for its wedding.
> Dare only to look,
> open the eyes like saucers—like glass bubbles—look:
> on the amber turret of Eiffel
> an automobile dances with a tank—
>
> ["world and wind"]

> Dosyć już chodzić podług starych podłóg
> i pochyloną głowę pod sufitem nosić -
> piękny jest świata nieschodzony odłóg,
> a niebo na to, by je nosem kosić -
> ....
> Czas się do ślubu swego sposobi.
> Tylko się spojrzeć odważcie - -
> bałuszcie oczy - jak szklane bańki - patrzcie:
> na Eifla bursztynowej baszcie
> tańczy automobil z tankiem - - -
>
> ["świat i wiatr"]

The form of these poems is also programmatically futurist, and similar to a manifesto. In keeping with the futurist poetic program Młodożeniec abandoned the traditional, personal form of address in his futurist poems, and in his own way tried to

The jacket of Bruno Jasieński's
Shoe in the Buttonhole

The cover of Stanisław
Młodożeniec's *Lines and Futurines*

The cover of
Earth to the Left
by Anatol Stern
and Bruno Jasieński

realize the goal of poetry for the masses, or poetry that both speaks in the name of the collectivity and addresses that collectivity. Also futurist is the tone of these poems, the "raised voice" and even shouting, which prompted a critic to compare Młodożeniec's poetry to ideological agitation:[61]

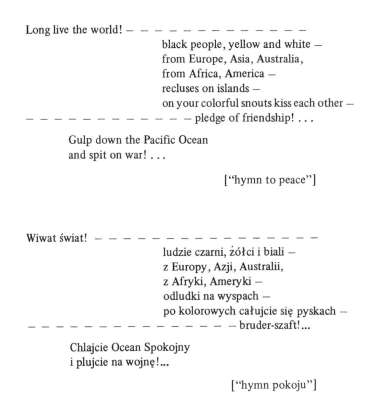

Long live the world! — — — — — — — — — — — — — —
　　　　　　　black people, yellow and white —
　　　　　　　from Europe, Asia, Australia,
　　　　　　　from Africa, America —
　　　　　　　recluses on islands —
　　　　　　　on your colorful snouts kiss each other —
— — — — — — — — — — — pledge of friendship! ...

　　　Gulp down the Pacific Ocean
　　　and spit on war! ...

　　　　　　　　　　　["hymn to peace"]

Wiwat świat! — — — — — — — — — — — — — — — — —
　　　　　　　ludzie czarni, żółci i biali —
　　　　　　　z Europy, Azji, Australii,
　　　　　　　z Afryki, Ameryki —
　　　　　　　odludki na wyspach —
　　　　　　　po kolorowych całujcie się pyskach —
— — — — — — — — — — — — — bruder-szaft!...

　　　Chlajcie Ocean Spokojny
　　　i plujcie na wojnę!...

　　　　　　　　　　　["hymn pokoju"]

And yet it would be only partly justifiable to classify Młodożeniec's early poetry, even his most programmatic poems, as unconditionally futurist or as a kind of futurist ideological agitation. For behind Młodożeniec's raised voice, some doubt can be sensed about the object of his agitation. Although his early poetry contains a number of slogans and some of the paraphernalia of futurism, it is nevertheless entirely lacking in the pompousness and exaltation typical of Marinetti or of the poets of the *Switch,* to whom it has a certain superficial resemblance. Like all the other Polish futurists, Młodożeniec kept a distance from his own futurism, which was more loud than profound, more programmatic than sincere. In "Express" the metaphoric train of the new times rushes headlong, blindly and at great speed, without direction or goal:

and where to?
    you don't know?
    and how am I supposed to know about it?
well—priest—fortuneteller of goals, where are we going? . . .

a dokąd?
    ty nie wiesz?
    to skądże mam ja o tym wiedzieć?
ej — księżę — wróżbiarzu celów, my dokąd? ...

The poem ends with the word "blindly" *(na oślep),* repeated three times in three consecutive lines that are printed vertically and sideways, as if foreboding a catastrophe:

NA OŚLEP
NA OŚLEP
NA OŚLEP

In Młodożeniec's poetry the naive futurist enthusiasm for modern technology is toned down by doubt as to its purpose. The inclusion of poems on peasant themes with their down-to-earth realism and tragic accents in the futurist volumes *Lines and Futurines* and *Future-scales and Future-scapes* undermines the credibility of his futuristic optimism. The volume of poems *Squares (Kwadraty,* 1925) proves that such "decadent" feelings as sadness, suffering, spleen, and melancholy were not entirely foreign to the author of the playful "futurines."

Futurist ideology found expression in relatively few of Młodożeniec's poems but experiments with language inspired by futurism are characteristic of his early works. It was in these experiments with words and sounds that his futurist and peasant poetry blended together. Młodożeniec's linguistic experiments followed two directions, the formation of neologisms and the exploration of sound effects, especially onomatopoeia. The programmatic poem "XXth century" ("XX wiek") that introduces the collection *Lines and Futurines* is a good example of the first tendency:

it's sprung — summerrushes through autumnness whitesnowing.
— CINEMATOGRAPH   CINEMATOGRAPH
                 CINEMATOGRAPH . . .
nightingaling whisperofforests calorwavely are carusoing.
GRAMOPATHEPHONE   GRAMOPATHEPHONE
                 GRAMOPATHEPHONE . . .
a kimonoeyed yokohama love you from europe
— RADIOTELEGRAM   RADIOTELEGRAM
                 RADIOTELEGRAM . . .
espaniel with laydis parleying with sarmatian
ESPERANTISTO   ESPERANTISTO
                 ESPERANTISTO . . .

I dewarsaw I comet I sunreach
AEROPLANE   AEROPLANE . . .
I uniletter the babblomania.
                                          – STENOGRAPHY . . .

zawiośniało – latopędzi przez jesienność białośnieże.
– KINEMATOGRAF   KINEMATOGRAF
                              KINEMATOGRAF . . .
słowikując szeptolesia falorycznie caruzieją.
– GRAMOPATHEFON   GRAMOPATHEFON
                              GRAMOPATHEFON . . .
iokohama – kimonooka cię kochają z europy
– RADIOTELEGRAM   RADIOTELEGRAM
                              RADIOTELEGRAM . . .
espaniolę z ledisami parlowacąc sarmaceniem
ESPERANTISTO   ESPERANTISTO
                              ESPERANTISTO . . .
odwarszawiam kometuję dosłoneczniam
AEROPLAN   AEROPLAN . . .
zjednoliterzam paplomanię.
                                          – STENOGRAFIA . . .

The poem is a humorous futurist manifesto that fulfills simultaneously ideological and poetic functions. The technological revolution goes hand in hand with the poetic revolution, and Młodożeniec not only enumerates new technical inventions but immediately illustrates their impact on language and poetry. These new inventions—the phonograph, radio, airplane, telegram—are matched by neologisms that are poetic inventions in language, but which are created by two rather mechanical methods. One joins two words *(białośnieże, szeptolesia, latopędzi)*, a procedure resembling linguistic hybrids designating new technological inventions (the cinematograph, radiotelegram, gramophone, or phonograph). The second method changes the grammatical identity of the word. Most frequently nouns and adjectives are used verbally, with the addition of verbal prefixes and endings *(zawiośniało, słowikując, caruzieją, odwarszawiam, kometuję, dosłoneczniam, zjednoliterzam)*, reflecting the futurist desire to substitute dynamism of action for static poetic description. The humorous "Futurobnia" (the title could be approximately translated as "Futurofacture") is a tour de force of these procedures, and all the words without exception are neologisms with the same two methods used in "XXth century." It would be a mistake, however, to consider Młodożeniec's play with word formation as a serious or consistent attempt to renovate poetic language, as he used this type of neologism in only a few poems, and always in a playful, humorous context. In the poem just quoted he referred to it as "unilettering the babblomania" *(zjednoliterzam paplomanię)*. It is interesting that all the neologisms in the lower case lines of the poem are based on native Polish words, and—what is more significant—on words that refer to nature (spring, sun, snow, forest, nightingale), not to civilization. Despite its attraction the technological world remained foreign to the poet, and the only world he felt free to change, transform, and reinvent was the world of nature, his native realm.

The most extensive experiments of Młodożeniec with language were explorations of sound effects, in particular alliteration and onomatopoeia. His poetic imagination was predominantly auditive and he considered poetry closer to music than to painting. Unlike painting, which is visual, poetry like music "organizes into concrete shapes the reality that is heard."[62] Młodożeniec believed that the return of poetry to its origins, to song, was the characteristic and renovating trend of modern poetry and that this auditive aspect of poetry was the basis for its social function and its participation in collective life. "In this breath, in this collective rhythm, is the whole novelty and importance of today's poetry."[63] This is why Młodożeniec considered declamation to be the only proper form of communicating poetry, that what is important for the reader is hearing and not reading. "Printed poetry—the book—is barely a skeleton, the musical notes that have to receive all the richness of artistic means of expression—that is, the voice rhythm, and occasionally even singing—in order for poetry to speak to us properly."[64] The use of alliteration and onomatopoeia is so widespread in the poetry of Młodożeniec that occasionally the reader has the impression that only the affinities and contrasts between sounds of words define the direction of a poem's development. In the poem "Summer" ("Lato") the sequence of words is entirely determined by their sounds. Each word in the poem has a sound relationship to the word that precedes or follows it:

```
. . . pstro  . . . . . . . . . . . . . . . . . . . . . . . . . . .
      pstrawo  . . . . . . . . . . . . . . . . . . . . . . . .
      pstrokato  . . . . . . . . . . . . . . . . . . . . . . .
      . . . . . . . . . . . . . . . . . . k10 krople kolorów
      l . . . . . . . . a . . . . . . . t . . . . . . . . o

. . . białe  . . . . . . . . . . czerwone
      zielone . . . . . . . . . . . lila
      szale  . . . . . . . . . . woale
      falbany perkalem falują . . . . . szaleją
      . . . . . . . . . . . . . . . . . . . . . . . w alejach
```

The first stanza is built on a progression of sounds leading from the word *pstro* ("in bright colors, colorfully") to the word *lato* ("summer"). *Pstrawo* ("brightish") and *pstrokato* ("in a medley of colors") not only repeat the sounds of *pstro* but their suffixes introduce the vowel *a* and the consonants *w, k,* which are picked up by the words of the fourth line, *krople kolorów.* The fourth line introduces the consonant *l,* and by repeating the vowel *o* in a quick sequence (krople kolorów) leads in the fifth line to the climactic word *lato,* which ends the first stanza. The soft and open sound of *lato* contrasts with the harshness of *pstro,* a contrast that determines the slowing movement of the first stanza: the allegro and staccato of the first three lines contrast with the lento and legato of the last line, and the impression of the colorfulness of summer is superseded by a sensation of heat, slowness, and languor. The typography of the stanza reflects the same movement with the word *lato* spread out over the whole fifth line. This word defines the sound pattern of the second stanza, with its emphasis on the open vowels *a, e,* and *o,* and the liquid *l,* sounds that are suggestive of the lightness and frivolity of summer. The progression of sounds in the second stanza is marked by similarity rather than contrast, and alliterations based on *a, l,* and *e* are built up until the literal and metaphorical frenzy of the last line *(szaleją).* These first two stanzas are characteristic of the whole poem, which continues to develop in the same manner.

Młodożeniec frequently combined sound effects with typographical effects and thus—like Czyżewski—appealed simultaneously to the auditory and visual sensitivity of the reader. However, his typographical experiments were considerably less inventive than Czyżewski's, for he limited himself to a single typographical device, the printing of certain interior vowels or consonants in capital letters, to emphasize certain sounds. A good example of this device is entitled "The World" ("Świat"):

Nie ma lUdzi ani zdArzeń - chodzą sAme kOła
białe kOła -
czarne kOła -
koła dOokOła

Czyjeś rĘce wyciągniĘte - nogi chwiEjnie błĄdzą
i stĄpAją -
i szukAją
w wiecznych kOłach błĄdzą

Wiry płAszczyzn zataczAją kręgi - - -
niEskończOne
niosą głOwy -
trwożne twArze -
światy niEskończOne
Dzień zasYpia w fałdach nOcy - z nocy siĘ wylĘga
cień się kArmi -
mlekiem świAtła -
światło ciEń wylĘga

Nie ma grAnic świat i człOwiek - ani nAwet kAmyk
któż to rzUcił -
w serce świAta -
w ludzkie sErce kAmyk?

idą lUdzie i zdarzEnia - wody wiEcznej kOła
białe kOła -
czarne kOła -
koła dOokOła.

There are no peOple nor evEnts—the whEEls alOne walk
white whEEls—

<pre>
                  black whEEls—
                          wheels all arOund
        Somebody's strEtched hAnds—the legs unstEadily wAnder
        and tAke a stEp—
                          and sEarch
                          and wAnder in Endless circles
        WhIrls of sUrfaces form cIrcles— — —
                          InfInIte
        they cArry their heAds—
                  feArful fAces—
                          InfInIte worlds
        Day falls aslEEp in the fOlds of the night — hatches
                          Out of the night
        shadOw fEEds—
                  on the mIlk of lIght—
                          lIght hatches the shadOw

        Neither the wOrld nOr man have bOundaries—nOt even a stOne
        whO threw—
                  intO the heart of the wOrld—
                          intO the human heart the stOne?
        _
        peOple and Events gO—whEEls of etErnal water
        white whEEls—
                  black whEEls—
                          wheels all arOund.
</pre>

Młodożeniec expresses the philosophical theme of the poem, that time is infinite and so is all existence, on three levels—semantic, visual, and auditory. The traditional and hackneyed metaphor of time as an ever-turning wheel, as ever-running water, is expressed through the device of capitalized vowels, with a double effect. It is visual, since the shape of the capital vowel *O* simulates a circle, and it is auditive, since the vowels suggest limitlessness and indefiniteness when read aloud. Even an object like a stone and a sound such as *kamyk* lose their definite, specific character when the word is spelled *kAmyk*—the emphasis on the vowel *A* entirely changes the sound value of the word by weakening the strength of the circumscribing consonant *k*. The emotional content of the poem—the feeling of anxiety, and the sense of wandering without direction—consequently acquires through typography and sound texture the concreteness and literalness of objects.

The linguistic and typographical experiments of Młodożeniec were attempts to make literal illustrations of the verbal message of the poem, greatly reducing their poetic value and interest. A critic observed that they lead, paradoxically, to a kind of supernaturalism, "Overcoming 'indirect' description (through the meaning of words), they brought this poetry close to maximally direct description (through asemantic sounds), to a kind of 'phonographic' reproduction."[65] Młodożeniec's tendency toward visual and especially auditive mimesis led him to explore the effects of onomatopoeia to their extreme limits, not only in his futurist poetry but also when he dealt with peasant themes. "Moscow" ("Moskwa"), one of Młodożeniec's best-known poems, is composed almost entirely of onomatopoeic words:

```
– – – – – – – – – – – – – – – – – – – – – –
– – – – – – – – – – – – – – – – – – – – – –
– – – – – – –tu–m – – – – – – – – – – –
– – – – – – – – – – czy–m tam? – – – – –
– – – – – – – – – – – – – tam – tam TAM
TU–M – – – – – – – – – – – – – – – – –
tam–tam TAM – – – – tam–tam–tam TAM
– – – – – – – – – – – TU–M – – TU–M
czym–m tam–tam?... tam–tam?...
                                czym–m tam?
TAM – M?... TU–M? – – – – – – – – – – – –
– – – – – – – – – – – – – – – – – – – – –
czyli–m tam?...        jeżeli–m tam to i tu–m
– – – – – – – – – – – – – TU–M – TU–M
a i tam – – – – – – – – – – – – a i tu–m
– – – oj – ja JJAJ – – – – – – tam – tam –
– – – – – – – – – – – – – – – – a i–tum
to–m i tam i tu–m – – – – – – – – – – – –
– – – – – – – – – – TU–M – m – m – m –
– – – – – – – – – – – – – – – – – – – – –
```

The sounds *tum* and *tam* imitate the ringing of bells, and their alternation suggests the swinging of the bell's clapper, a swinging that corresponds psychologically to the poet's hesitation as to where he belongs—to the world of "here" or the world of "there." However the alternative is only apparent and the similarity of *tum* and *tam* indicates that their semantic opposition does not exclude the possibility of reconciliation on another plane. At the end of the poem the opposition is indeed overcome, both on the psychological level—since being "there" means also being "here" —and on the artistic level, because the existence of the poem depends on the harmony of opposites and on the harmony of the bells it imitates.

"Moscow" is interesting not only as an example of Młodożeniec's use of onomatopoeia and his artistic extremism, but it also indicates the poet's ambivalence toward the two worlds with which he identified. The poem's title points to one of these worlds, the Moscow where by accident and against his will he found himself at the age of nineteen, swept up by the retreating Russian army in 1914. He spent the next four years as a student at the Polish Gymnasium (a pretext to avoid Russian military service) which had numerous psychological and artistic consequences. The "here" of the poem is Poland, and more precisely the world of the poet's youth, the village Dobrocice, "the beloved country," and "the entire native world" to which he constantly returns in his poetry. It is difficult to decide how profound his feeling of being split between these two realities was because apart from the poem just quoted Młodożeniec rarely referred to his "Moscow experience." Throughout his life he remained mysteriously silent about his four years in Russia,

yet the weight of that experience must have been significant and his first acquaintance with futurism must date from that time. Like Jasieński, Młodożeniec could
not ignore either the social or the artistic revolution that was taking place in
Russian life and poetry. However, he was four years older than Jasieński and he reacted differently to the same experience. As he had already developed strong literary inclinations, the future author of *Lines and Futurines* was attracted more by
the poetic than the social revolution. Judging from some of his poems in which revolution is associated with the violence of untamed elements and with a feeling of
chaos and fear, the spectacle of the Russian revolution must have frightened and
estranged Młodożeniec more than it fascinated him. This is why the only positive
traces of the Russian experience are to be found in his poetic ideas. Inspired by the
linguistic experiments of the Russian futurists and especially by their concept of
the word's autonomous existence as sound, Młodożeniec applied those ideas to his
own poetry and used them for his own solutions.

In a sensitive essay on Młodozeniec's poetry, the critic Tomasz Burek sees in
the Russian experience the key to the poetic duality of Młodożeniec—"If the village of Dobrocice is the father of Młodożeniec's poetic vision, the Moscow of 1917
is its mother." [66] The distinctive characteristic of his poetry is that these two experiences are not in opposition, but instead complement and mutually illuminate.
Compared to Czyżewski and Jasieński, Młodożeniec's peasant poetry did not mark
a change or stage in his poetic development, but was from the very beginning an
integral part of his poetic personality, representing his desire to express to the
world what was forever the most vivid, the closest to his heart. And yet his adherence to futurism was so strong that futurist experiments penetrated the linguistic
texture even of his peasant-oriented poetry. Curiously it was Stanisław Młodożeniec, whose voice was the quietest in the loud and provocative proclamations of
the futurists, who experimented with poetic language in the most radical manner,
and who also remained faithful to futurist inspiration for the longest period.
Młodożeniec wrote futurist poetry for thirteen years—from 1921 to 1934—and although he simultaneously wrote poems on peasant themes, in no other Polish poet
was futurism alive for so long.

The cover of
Anatol Stern's *Futurisias*

ANATOL STERN

The poetry of Anatol Stern represents a facet of Polish futurism that can best be described as the biologism, the provocativeness and humor of adolescence. It is the dada youthfulness of futurism, an outburst of joy and instinct, a loud reaffirmation of the world of matter and biological forces. Stern's early poetry in the volume *Futurisias (Futuryzje,* 1919) is full of unbridled spontaneity and impetuosity, of sexual desire and erotic dreams. The young poet bursts with joy, youth, health, and energy:

> Although my knees hurt in bad weather
> I am light, an animal and healthy.
> With a razor I clip the airy pagoda
> Of bamboo turquoise and dreams.

["Sun in the Belly"]

> Choć łamie w kolanach na niepogodę
> Przecie jestem jasny zwierzęcy i zdrów.
> Brzytwą podcinam leciuchną pagodę,
> Z bambusów turkusów i snów.

["Słońce w brzuchu"]

In *The Naked Man Downtown (Nagi człowiek w śródmieściu,* 1919) nakedness is a gesture of provocation but also of liberation—liberation from culture, from civilization and morality. The freedom of the natural man replaces traditional authority, and the naked body of a youth takes the place of the old monuments of national heroes and bards:

> Walking down a black street, I feel: slabs burn
> My feet through the tough leather soles,—
> And someone searching for the body, with a wet hostile hand
> Tousles me clumsily, tears all the seams of my clothes.

> And there I wander naked, giving my slender body
> To the sticky gaze of the surrounding lamps,
> Until I climbed a pedestal and had the wonderful whim
> Of turning into a bronze statue.

> Ulicą idąc czarną, czuję: płyty parzą
> Stopy moje przez twarde skórzane podeszwy, –
> I ktoś ciała szukając, mokrą ręką wrazą
> Szarpie mnie niezgrabnie, ubrania wszystkie drze szwy.

> Oto błądzę już nagi, smukłe swoje ciało
> Poddając spojrzeniom lepkim lamp naokół,
> Aż dopóki przecudownie mi się nie zachciało
> Sposągowieć bronzowo, wdarłszy się na cokół.

[Nagi człowiek w śródmieściu, 1]

Other poems in the collection propose that the moral ideals of suffering and purity be replaced with the ideal of pleasure, that love be replaced with sex, and Isolde with the prostitute Villevi. It seems as if poetry was both a sublimation and an outlet for the young man's overflowing energy. Futurism, with its rejection of tradition —both in art and in morality—and with its unreserved glorification of youth and instinct, perfectly corresponded to the frame of mind (and body) of the boisterous, sensual, twenty-year-old poet. With adolescent verve Stern proclaimed his own "Book of Wisdom" in which the primitive spontaneity of animals took the place of intellect or the thoughtfulness of a homo sapiens:

> Why are people wise
> Why do people think?
> . . . .
> I want to bray like a donkey
> I want to leap like a cow.

> Czemu ludzie są mądrzy
> Czemu ludzie myślą?

> Chcę ryczeć jak osioł
> Chcę skakać jak krowy.

The opposition of the natural impulse to the intellect is as much in the spirit of adolescent rebellion as it is in the spirit of dada or futurist opposition. The sexual fantasies so prominent in Stern's early poetry have a similar double source, they are both dada gestures of provocation and adolescent dreams. The poet's wishful thinking, his boastfulness about presumed sexual exploits, are unmistakable marks of his youth and a continuation of the games of childhood. The new roles played by the poet of a Chinese emperor, a Mauritanian sage, a medieval knight, and the exotic countries where his erotic adventures take place are the next step after playing cowboys and Indians.

> When with solemnity, once a year,
> I come out from my pagoda shimmering with pearls
> These girls with a gleam in the eye
> Fly down from everywhere as if for mating.
>
> ["Meeting"]

> Kiedy uroczyście, raz do roku,
> Wychodzę z perłowolśniącej swej pagody,
> To dziewczęta z blaskiem w oku
> Zlatują się zewsząd, jak na gody.
>
> ["Spotkanie"]

At the same time the ironic tone and the realistic, unclimactic endings of these fantasies indicate that the games were not played in earnest. A sentence or stanza, usually placed at the end of the poem, punctures the ephemeral and quixotic adventures like a balloon. Their purpose is not so much the gratification of desire as downright mockery of conventional love poetry, as in "Carmine Lassitude" ("Karminowe znużenie"):

> Permit me—my dear—before I hang myself
> By twining around my neck the thread of your hair,
> Before my silky death to console myself a little
> By passionately pinching you on your strong calf.

> Pozwól — moja droga, — że nim się powieszę
> Okręciwszy wkrąg szyi twego włosa nitkę —
> Przed jedwabną śmiercią nieco tym się pocieszę,
> Że gwałtownie uszczypnę cię w twą silną łydkę.

Here the parody is a result of the mixture of two mutually exclusive poetic styles, of lofty idealism and low realism, that represent two very different mental attitudes (suicide and "consolation," hanging oneself and pinching, the image of silky hair and of a strong calf). The same opposition of high and low style occurs in many of Stern's metaphors. Such bold combinations as "the skies on a platter" *(niebiosa na półmisku),* "the sun in the belly" *(słońce w brzuchu),* or "hearts on frying pans" *(na szklanych patelniach skręcały się serca)* perform a double function: they humorously downgrade the high poetic style and they "democratize" all reality by promoting commonplace objects to the rank of "high" poetry. In the first case their function is parodistic, in the second they fulfill the futurist goal of introducing everyday reality into the poem.

Even the use of nonsense has a parodistic effect in Stern's poetry. In a poem entitled "conversation of lovers" ("rozmowa kochanków") parody results from a clash between the title and the content of the poem:

> ? ? ? ? ? ? !......   *czyżby, czyż?* ...
> a, a, ak, agh, akh !!!!   twe czyż ćwierka
> bee dlin. mm   jak z świerku czyż
>   bu lu "lu bu" fr!
>   bu lu lu "lu lu bu" fr fr frfrfr !!
>   *kizia*
> milusieńki kukusieńki kusieńki sieńki
> malutenka kulusieńka pienka — cieńka — enka
>   *mimi* ba — mm mm *w*!!
>   kr trh. (ń ń...) wr! *wrr*
>   aa

[*Romans Peru,* część III, "ucieczka"]

With the rejection of conventional concepts of love and wisdom went rejection of accepted canons of beauty. Stern presented his ideal of feminine beauty in the poem "The Women of My Dreams":

it tells me nothing, the pink venus of botticelli
leaning out from the round half-shell of the ocean!
I scoff when the herd of flat women in front of her
turns to ashes in admiration—mumbling banners

the beauties of raphaels leonardos rosettis
this frail maid from whom you, boy, beg favor . . .
I demand different dimensions! different colors from those!
seeing yours I seethe, porter of the beautiful earth

foreign to me are these splendors! hot like summer
the skin of women teasing with the velvet of greengage plums
if I am to praise someone—then it will be the big-bellied
girl who fights the humming wheat with her sickle

. . . .

I do not praise those bodies of frail shapes
whose lures have to be drawn with the lightest hand!
I worship clumsy forms and heavy ovals
and I sing broadhipped splendidly breasted women!!

Kobiety wyśnione

nic mi nie mówi różowa wenus botticella
wychylająca się z okrągłej oceanu konwi!
drwię sobie gdy się przed nią z zachwytu spopiela
stado płaskich kobiet — bełkoczących chorągwi

rafaelów piękności leonardów rosettich
to wątłe dziewczę którego — chłopcze — łaski błagasz...
innych żądam rozmiarów! barw innych nie tych!
widząc wasze pienię się pięknej ziemi tragarz

obce mi te wspaniałości! gorące jak lato
skóry kobiet drażniące renklod aksamitem
jeśli już mam kogo sławić — to tylko brzuchatą
dziewkę co swym sierpem walczy z szumnym żytem
. . . .
nie te sobie ciała o wątłej linii chwalę
których najlżejszą ręką się kreśli powaby!
ja wielbię formy niezgrabne i ciężkie owale
i śpiewam tęgobiodre pysznopierśne baby!!

The impatient, loud tone of the poem reads like a futurist manifesto and brings to mind Marinetti's vituperative comparison of museums to cemeteries. However, it is not the futurist consciousness that is the most appealing element in the poem, but rather the eruption of an irrational element: futurist antitraditionalism is only a pretext for the outburst of exuberant sensuality. More captivating than the programmatic opposition of life and art, of a peasant girl and Botticelli's Venus, is the revelation of a new kind of eroticism, the earthly sexuality of naked biology—of clumsy but solid shapes, of bright unattenuated colors. Stern's exuberance is reflected in the language of the poem, in its extraordinary abundance of rich, sensual metaphors, which the critic Kazimierz Wyka has called "a lava of metaphors." [67] Their explosive effect is all the greater for being clad in a rigorous syntax and a form of classical rhymed verse, while the impatient sensuality is expressed only through the broken, dynamic rhythm.

In the early poems the biologism of the poet was always concealed behind a futurist pose and was used as a tool of parody or provocation, but in *The Angelic Boor (Anielski cham,* 1923) it came out into the open. In his best poems Stern's biologism, freed from programmaticness and irony, is almost pantheistic in the way it engages the entire world. In the poetic universe of Stern all objects are endowed with biological instincts: the moon, like a he-goat, attacks the ewes who are the stars *(skacze na kozy gwiazdy/ wychudły srebrny kozioł rogaty),* a haystack with sticks in it suggests a raped girl *(dziewka— stóg siana a w stogu patyk),* and tramways amorously rub against one another *(bokami tarły się o siebie tramwaje dzwoniące).* In one poem the world is compared to a tavern where the sun, clouds, and earth join in a sexual orgy together with the poet. The following poem, which has been compared to Cézanne's *Bathers,* is a good example of Stern's biological eroticism:

Countryside

glistening women in transparent water
splashed each other with handfuls a shout and a splash and laughter rang out
scattered clothes wrinkled on the shore
and a gray cane of smoke went to the sky from above thatched roofs

then on horses crushed by the black disc of the sun
banging with heels in the copper of their bellies so they rumbled
the riders plunged in among the wet shivering bodies
which ran together into a single long sharp shriek

and the sweltering day slipped out like an eel
someone was wrenching loose swooning and hoarse from shouting—
the white slender palms of birch trees were swinging
and baobabs of lindens murmured something swarming with bees

Kraj

błyszczące kobiety w przezroczystej wodzie
pryskały na się garściami grał krzyk i plusk i śmiech
marszczyła się na brzegu rozrzucona odzież
i sina laska dymu szła w niebo z nad strzech

gdy waląc piętami w brzuchów miedź aż dudniało
na koniach przez słońca czarny przygniecionych dysk
wpadli między mokre trzęsące się ciała
które się zbiegły w jeden długi ostry pisk

i wyślizgnął się jak węgorz dzień upalny
ktoś wyrywał się omdlewał i od krzyku chrypł —
kołysały się białe wysmukłe brzóz palmy
i mamrotały coś pszczelne baobaby lip

Images assail both eyes and ears, the scene of the bathers is full of movement and accompanied by ringing sounds of shouting, of laughter. The atmosphere of eroticism permeates nature as well as people. The poem is marvelously dynamic. As well as being an expression of the author's biologism, it illustrates what might be called the kinetics of Stern's poetry: images move and change, they rapidly follow and overlap one another. The critic Stefan Gacki has described this quality of Stern's poetry extremely well: "Each poem intoxicates with a tropical atmosphere, an impatient broken rhythm (which Stern superbly manipulates), an orgy of sparkling bright colors. There is no static image, no sculpting of a frozen moment, everything flows, slips one behind another, jumps apart in order to create a new range of dynamic silhouettes." [68] The fluidity of Stern's manner of seeing recalls certain cinematic techniques—not surprising as film had always been one of the poet's special interests. As early as 1922 Stern wrote reviews of films, in 1924 he became editor of the magazine *Film News (Wiadomości Filmowe),* and a few years later he began to write film scenarios. In an essay significantly entitled "The Sources of the New Aesthetics," Stern argued that film techniques greatly influenced the evolution of modern poetry: "In the history of poetry the demarcation line is defined by the technological revolution, the history of the new poetry begins almost simultaneously with the history of film." [69] Stern considered the French poets Apollinaire, Cendrars, and Max Jacob to be the "apostles" of the new "kinetic aesthetics" in poetry, which he defined very broadly. He went beyond the identification of kinetics with the purely external movement of images, and for him the new aesthetics implied an entirely new vision of the world that manifested itself on all levels of expression: in the simultaneity of images, in the apparent disorder and unstable sequence of emotional content, in irrationalism, and in a changing rhythm that reflected the variability of poetic thought and lyricism. The features of the new aesthetic that Stern enumerated can all be found in his own poetry.

Stern's dynamic imagination was accentuated even further in poems that employed vers libre, which suited the naturally uneven rhythm of Stern's poetry exceptionally well. An interesting example of Stern's use of vers libre is the beginning of "The Conquest of Paris" ("Zdobycie Paryża"):

on the deep blue sky
grenades burst
with an open throat the earth drinks the blood
in a garden pregnant women with a smile
lean against ripe pomegranates

na modrym niebie
pękają granaty
otwartą gardzielą ziemia spija krew
w ogrodzie o dojrzałe granaty
opierają się z uśmiechem ciężarne kobiety

Stern's vers libre has been described as "syntactic" as the lines coincide with the syntactic units of sentences,[70] but this syntactic "correctness" is counteracted by the varying number of syllables in each line, which gives the poem its rough, broken rhythm. Similar contrasts occur in the rhyming pattern of the poem—regular rhymes are absent, and instead of harmony the sounds at the ends of lines create a jarring effect *(niebie-granaty-krew);* however, the poem is rich in internal rhymes *(pękają-opierają),* in assonances *(niebie-ziemia-uśmiechem),* and consonances *(granaty-kobiety),* all of which create an effect of harmony and sound cohesiveness. The contrast that occurs in the versification between syntactic order and broken rhythm, between harmony and cacophony of sounds, also defines the structure of the stanza and makes the poem dynamic. It is built upon the juxtaposition of two parallel but contrasting sentences, one referring to death, destruction, and war, the other to life, fertility, and birth. The parallels between earth and woman, the grenade and the pomegranate (which are homonyms in Polish, and give the poem an ambiguity the translation cannot render), blood and pomegranate juice, make the contrast between the two even more powerful. The political message of this poem against war is entirely a function of its poetic technique.

One of the elements Stern thought was characteristic of the "new aesthetics" was the irrational; he also believed it was an essential component of futurist aesthetics. In his preface to *Race to the Pole (Bieg do bieguna,* 1927) Stern wrote about futurism in the following manner: "My friends and I let into the poetic salon the untamed animal of irrationality which had been let out of the burrow of the subconscious and which, without any tact, broke and turned upside down all the nice rules of present poetics." In Stern's own poetry the irrational element is extremely important and accounts both for his stylistic peculiarities and philosophical attitudes. The cult of the irrational was intimately connected with his biologism, and both were in opposition to the idealistic concept of man, but while in *Futurisias* the opposition was narrowed to mockery at the idealistic concept of love, and biologism was reduced to sex, in *The Angelic Boor (Anielski cham,* 1923) both were put into a broader notion of what could be called a new humanism. In his mature poetry the praise of the irrational was transformed into the praise of the subconscious, seen as a source of man's creativity. The materialistic philosophy of futurism led many of its adherents, such as Czyżewski and Jasieński, to the concept of man as a machine. In Stern man is presented in opposition to the machine, as a creature marvelously and creatively irrational:

To the Worshipper of Machines

you say: look carefully this factory is the house
where the immortal machines hammer out TOMORROW
you say: you also are a machine only a machine—although
in many respects you yield to these iron angels
you advise me to observe how the shoulder of the hangar slopes upward
and the transmission belts of wide dreams
hum in this huge clear space no worse than in the head

yes only at a certain moment will you clearly see the difference
you will see a tiny difference between the machine and me
at the moment
when lying on the back
with difficulty I will stammer out from myself a large flask
full of mystic—yes!—a flask full of mystic suffering
and of scraps of lilac glances
and of the counters of the department store "SMITH & CO."
and words with a muffled R
and traveling salesmen eaten by moths
and exhausted children stoned to death by spools of cotton
and you don't know why

and you don't know why—
(o the black humus of creative disorder!
the classicism of the subconscious!!)
—of the mute cries
of this bridge made of desperately
wrung hands
which leads into detestable
—detestable?—
and full of the chirping of swallows, of the flight of gold crosses and clouds
infinity

this you will not see
in the most modern
American machine

Czcicielowi maszyn

powiadasz: spójrz-no uważnie ta fabryka to dom
w którym wykuwają JUTRO nieśmiertelne maszyny
powiadasz: i ty maszyną jesteś maszyną tylko — chociaż
pod wielu względami ustępujesz tym żelaznym aniołom
radzisz mi się przyjrzeć jak hangaru podnosi się ramię
a transmisyjne szerokich marzeń pasy
szumią w tej jasnej hali nie gorzej niż w głowie

tak tylko że w pewnej chwili ujrzysz wyraźnie różnicę
ujrzysz drobną różnicę pomiędzy maszyną a mną
w tej chwili
gdy leżąc na wznak
z trudem wykrztuszę z siebie wielką flaszę
pełną mistycznej — tak! — mistycznej pełną męki flaszę
i skrawków liliowych spojrzeń
i kantorów domu handlowego „SMITH & C-NY "
i słów ze stłumionym R
i zjedzonych przez mole akwizytorów

i ukamienowanych szpulkami bawełny wyniszczonych dzieci
i niewiadomo czemu

i niewiadomo czemu —
(o czarnoziemie twórczego nieporządku!
klasycyźmie podświadomego!!)
— niemych krzyków
tego mostu z rozpaczliwie
załamanymi rękoma
który biegnie w znienawidzoną
— znienawidzoną? —
pełną jaskółczego świergotu i lotu złotych krzyżów i chmur
nieskończoność

tego nie dojrzysz
w najnowocześniejszej
amerykańskiej maszynie

"Classicism of the subconscious" accounts best for the most striking and appealing
trait of Stern's futurist poetry, its peculiar combination of irrational impulsiveness
and the classical constraint of form.

There was a close connection between Stern's new humanism and his earlier
biologism and materialism. Both were reactions against the stifling idealism and
spiritualism of the preceding period, and both asserted that man was made not only
of spirit and soul but was above all a living organism, a body full of impulses and
natural instincts. The title poem of the collection *The Angelic Boor* is a proclamation of Stern's philosophy, and in it he protested both against the abstract Platonic
concept of man as idea and against the definition of man by moral and spiritual
categories, illustrated by the famous story of Diogenes the Cynic.

you
who sniffs the wind and searches for a man
look only look around
for the whole cosmos
is dripping with the living man!

philosopher lighting your way with a spy's flashlight
and waiting for the great guest in the barrel
why didn't you stop
in front of a simple cook
or before a street urchin bathing in the river?

["The Angelic Boor"]

ty
który węszysz pod wiatr i szukasz człowieka
spójrz tylko rozejrzyj się wokół
toż kosmos cały
żywym człowiekiem ocieka!

filozofie świecący szpiegowską latarką
i na wielkiego gościa czekający w beczce
czemuś się przed pierwszą lepszą
nie zatrzymał kucharką
albo przed ulicznikiem kąpiącym się w rzeczce?

["Anielski cham"]

Stern's biologism acquired a new dimension in *The Angelic Boor,* for even if he
continued to describe man as an animal, at the same time he saw him as a rival of
angels owing to the ennobling effect of labor:

WORKERS a stinking winged rabble
o steaming cattle more wonderful than angels!

ROBOTNICY śmierdząca uskrzydlona gawiedź
o parujące bydło cudniejsze od aniołów!

["Anielski cham"]

It is labor that accounts for the adjective "angelic" in the title of the poem, and it is
in labor that Stern saw the source of human heroism:

look then at this twoarmed idea
how it strains itself how it walks how it curses how it laughs
look at these indescribable movements of legs and shoulders
of hips and chests pushing the loads of heavy weights
. . . .
o incomprehensible hand steering the wheel
o marvelous labor of ten hard fingers!
like a volcano ever fruitful like a raging hero
is each of you—who rolls the recalcitrant cylinder of the earth!

spojrzyj-no na tę dwuramienną ideę
jak się wysila jak chodzi jak klnie jak się śmieje
spójrz na te nieopisane nóg poruszenia i barów
i bioder i piersi popychających ładunki ciężarów
. . . .
o niezrozumiała ręko kierująca sterem
o cudowna praco dziesięciu twardych palców!
jak wulkan wciąż płodzący jak szalejący heros
jest każdy z was — toczących oporny ziemi walec!

["Anielski cham"]

The materialistic humanism of Stern and his praise of human labor led directly
to social poetry. The social and political commitment that colored several poems in

The Angelic Boor found its strongest expression in the next volume, *Earth to the Left (Ziemia na lewo)*, published jointly with Bruno Jasieński in 1924. This volume is outside futurist inspiraton, although a logical outcome of this inspiration. *The Angelic Boor* brought to Stern an awareness of the social function his poetry was to fulfill, together with a realization of his own role as poet and a sense of belonging— both artistically and philosophically—to the European avant-garde. If in 1919 Stern's futurism seemed to be a spontaneous outburst rather than a consciously adopted artistic and philosophical attitude, by 1924 Stern had a sense of taking part in a common cause with other European poets and clearly established his parentage:

> come come to me friend
> both you cocteau and you mayakovski
> boccioni tzara
> and you and they
> all of you
>
> ["The World's Jumping Searchlights"]

> chodź chodź do mnie przyjacielu
> i ty cocteau i ty majakowskij
> boccioni tzara
> i wy i oni
> wszyscy
>
> ["Skaczące reflektory świata"]

Stern considered 1923, the date of the publication of *The Angelic Boor,* to be the ending of the futurist movement in Poland. In keeping with the basically dada character of his early futurist activities, Stern saw in Polish futurism a period of destruction, scandal, and provocation.

> As far as I am concerned, I stopped to consider myself worthy of the name of futurist the moment I noticed that people started a conversation with me peacefully, and that they did it without any obvious fear or disgust. Futurism died in me when I stopped being a riddle for myself, often a frightening riddle. I think of that time with regret, despite the conviction that its end was inevitable. Because futurism was a period of destruction preceding a period of construction.[71]

The Angelic Boor and *Earth to the Left* brought partial answers as to what this constructive stage would be, but the swerving line of Stern's poetic path after 1924 proves that these answers were not definitive. As a poet of antithesis, his poetic evolution could be best described as one of antitheses, swinging like a pendulum between extreme positions, between the dada provocativeness and carefree playfulness of *Futurisias* (1919) and the philosophical humanism of *The Angelic Boor* (1923), between the socially involved, almost revolutionary tone of *Earth to the Left* (1924) and the religious, somewhat mystical tone of *Race to the Pole* (1927).

The cover of *The Immortal Volume of Futurisias*
by Anatol Stern and Aleksander Wat

ALEKSANDER WAT

Aleksander Wat's temperament was the opposite of Anatol Stern's, his closest
futurist associate and, briefly, his friend. The futurism of Wat, like Stern's, was
oriented toward dada, but Wat found in dada an aspect that Stern was oblivious
to, its nihilism and tragic overtones, not its humor, provocativeness, and playfulness. Neither of the two poets shared the futurists' enthusiasm for modern civilization and its most spectacular achievement, the "machine"—an enthusiasm that
gave futurism its optimism in distinction to the negative, anarchistic dada. In
Stern's poetry, however, dadaist provocativeness and rebelliousness were counterbalanced by humor and vitalism, both of which entailed an attitude that was essentially positive, but the negativism of Wat was complete, lacking a grace that could
attenuate or counteract it. There is another distinction between the two: Stern was
the poet of instinct and the biological side of human nature, Wat was the poet of

intellect and culture; Stern's dispute with the idealistic tradition concerned man's basic nature, Wat questioned the value of all the ideals and achievements of the human mind and spirit.

The main work of Wat's futurist period is the long prose poem, *I on One Side and I on the Other Side of My Pug Iron Stove (Ja z jednej strony i Ja z drugiej strony mego mopsożelaznego piecyka)*, published in the autumn of 1919 (and inscribed with the date of 1920). *The Stove* was both a farewell to literature and an outlet for the poet's disillusionment and frustration. Many years later, Wat described his emotional state at the time of writing *The Stove:* "The Stove . . . had for me other goals: of psychotherapy, or rather of the psychoanalytic confession of a disturbed and frightened soul preparing itself for death. For a long time I had the intention of committing suicide as a *poète maudit* at the latest before the age of 25, which seemed to me the last barrier before moral degradation." [72] A passage in *The Stove* renders the young author's mood in a more poetic way:

> I don't know what to do with the night? The day passes
> like pearls, like colorful shells its taste scatters . . .
> And the night? . . . What to do with night which torments
> the chest. Whether to jump like a fish through the window
> and flower the brain beautifully with the pavement . . .
> Nights are eternal and never, never pass. Well. Fold
> and hide yourself in its rolls of parchment.

> *Nie wiem co czynić z nocą? Dzień mija jak perły, jak*
> *muszle barwne osypuje się jego smak . . .*
> *A noc? . . . Co czynić z nocą która trapi pierś. Czy*
> *rybą skoczyć oknem i skwiecić mózg pięknie brukiem.*
> *Noce są wieczne i nigdy, nigdy nie mijają. Cóż. Złóż i skryj*
> *się w zwoje pergamentów.*

The two epigraphs to *The Stove* reflect the same frame of mind. One, a quote from medieval Latin, alludes to death, and the other, from Baudelaire's preface to the *Paradis artificiels,* describes the romantic image of a lonely dark poet that must have appealed to Wat's sensibility and feeling of desolation at the time. [73]

In its composition, tone, and language, Wat's work is reminiscent of Arthur Rimbaud's *Illuminations* and *Une Saison en Enfer.* Rimbaud's precocity and intelligence, his moral skepticism and negation of religious values, his disdain of literature, and his unusual destiny—all of these were attractive and congenial to the Polish poet. The image of Rimbaud, "the 'sentimentally educated' silly young boy" accompanied Wat during the entire period of writing *The Stove,* and allusions, both direct and indirect, to the great French poet are numerous in the poem. The example of the nineteen-year-old Rimbaud writing his last poetic works in which he passes verdict on religion, morality, and literature must have prompted the eighteen-year-old Wat to write his own "literary testament."

Wat's disillusionment and sense of moral degradation were not the result of experience but of extensive reading. "A funny eighteen-year-old Warsaw Faust, I re-

belled against books, against ten or so years of life in books; I wanted to 'live.'" [74]
His work betrays a philosophical background and knowledge of history, literature,
and mythology amazing for an eighteen-year-old, even if we take into consideration
that he was a student of philosophy at the time. When writing about his adolescence, Wat mentioned his avidity for reading; at the university he surprised his
professors with his thorough knowledge of Schopenhauer, and his reading included,
among others, the complete works of Kierkegaard, which he read in German. The
feeling of decadence and of an impending "earthquake" also came from his reading
of European catastrophist literature. Wat's intellectual precocity had its negative
reaction, and his young sensibility could not bear the bitter lesson of suffering and
cruelty given by literature and history. After a period of depression, during which
his high-school classmate Anatol Stern jokingly called him "Buddha-Zarathustra,"
Wat rebelled by becoming a futurist. He identified his nihilism and his loss of faith
in the possibility of a future European civilization with dadaism and futurism.
"Polish futurism, dadaism, was at this point of contact with the philosophy of
despair, the impossibility of future existence, of the whole *mal de vivre*. . . . I suffered very much then . . . and I went through a rebellion against this suffering,
against pain." The rebellion prompted Wat to write, and *The Stove* was a reaction
against "all that ballast of pain of the world, all the despair . . . the feeling that it
cannot be this way any longer." [75]

    The Stove could be called an enormous nonsense poem in prose. Its composi-
tion is a mosaic made of short disconnected pieces, each one absurd if considered
by itself but acquiring meaning as the fragments gradually build up, not so much to
form a coherent whole as to communicate, through recurring themes and motifs,
the oppressive feeling of the end of civilization. In Wat's poem the collapse of civilization is not caused from without, by some cataclysm, but from within by its own
degeneration:

> The withered swarm of wethers is enchanted by the
> smoke of cigarettes. The vendors of the evening newspapers will take
> possession of Sesame. Angels meditate on the radiance of
> paradise from the colorful footlights and my yellow vest
> in the resounding crucible of the seedy cabaret. My dear
> Symparanekromenoi, let us retire into serious and dignified
> silence. Do you hear how in the corner of a closet a louse
> has been crunched under the fingernail of a raving god?

> Zwiędły rój skopców zachwyca się dymem papierosów.
> Sezam przygarną sprzedawcy gazet wieczornych. Aniołowie
> rozmyślają nad rajskim blaskiem kolorowych kinkietów i mojej
> żółtej kamizelki w huczącym tyglu tingltanglu. Drodzy moi, sym-
> paranekromenoi, oddalmy się w poważną dostojną ciszę.
> Słyszycie, jak w kącie szafy pod paznokciem oszalałego boga
> chrustnęła wesz?

The themes and imagery of degeneration, sickness, withering, exhaustion, impotence, and old age recur obsessively throughout the poem, referring to people

("moldy old women") as well as to objects ("musty basements," "pillars eaten by vermin," "sick alleys"), to nature ("scrofulous jasmines"), and to mythological gods ("exhausted Narcissus," "sickly Dionysus").

Man is struck by impotence:

> The flogged servant, a slave of Onan, met the
> thirteen-year-old Beatrice on his path, on the third degree of
> the Crooked Circle. Since it was dusk and with velvet
> duckweed it drove all bad weather and untimely curses
> away— he took her by her small fingers and led her to
> his crimson, solitary bed. But he was exhausted (im-
> potence furled his backbone and withered his hands),
> he turned his back to her.

> Biczowany rab, niewolnik Onanii spotkał na swojej drodze,
> na trzecim stopniu Krzywego Koła trzynastoletnią Beatrice. A że był
> zmierzch i odpędzał długą aksamitną rzęsą wszelkie niepogody i nie-
> wczesne klątwy—więc wziął ją za paluszki i poprowadził na swoje
> szkarłatne, samotne łoże. Lecz wyczerpany (niemoc zwinęła mu
> kręgosłup i zwiędłe ręce) odwrócił się do niej tyłem.

In another passage Wat speaks of "the humiliation of ripe pomegranates, which will be no longer (the ancient families die out). The young golden-haired king stricken with incurable disease" ("Upokorzenie dojrzałych granatów, których już nie będzie [starożytne rody giną]. Złotowłosy młody król rażony nieuleczalną chorobą").

Physical degeneration is merely a symptom of more general moral degradation. In *The Stove* Wat questions, and compromises, all the fundamental ideals of human-ity—love, morality, and religion. The legendary Isolde, symbol of love and purity, is ridiculed and presented as a willing, depraved participant in licentious orgies:

> From the moment the lame, festering Ivon implanted on
> her lips the oath of love and peace, royal Isolde was the soul and the
> wild paradise of lepers . . .
> To any deranged whimpering or desire to nestle someplace,
> she would give her luxuriant body. Then to the hungry she gave her
> breasts, milky as all the herds of the king of the white Flemings.

> Odkąd kulawy zaropiały Iwon złożył
> na jej ustach zakład miłości i pokoju, królewska Izolda była duszą
> i szalonym rajem trędowatych.
> kiedy skomlącym obłąkanym żądnym gdzieś
> się wtulić—oddawała bujne ciało. Tedy głodnym dawała pierś doj-
> ną jak wszystkie stada króla białych flamandów.

The ideal of love and purity is discredited not only in its profane version, but in its Christian counterpart—the licentiousness of Isolde is echoed by that of Saint Mary:

The Byzantine Virgin Mary and resurrecting Lazarus
flog each other among the sounds of orgiastic organs.
The shamelessness of her lipstick and the shreds of
her shoulders into infinity. And at bottom a pitifully
wild shudder—dance of love. From the unlit windows
will come an Angel with a lily of Annunciation.—Will
it be artificial?

Byzantycka Bogorodzica i Łazarz z martwychwstający
chłoszczą się śród dźwięków orgiastycznych organów.
Bezwstyd szminki i strzęp ramion w bezkres. A na dnie
żałośnie wściekły dygot—pląs miłości. Z nieoświetlonych okien
zejdzie Anioł z lilią Zwiastowania.—Czy sztuczną?

Nothing sacred escapes Wat's devastating nihilism, and *The Stove* abounds in
blasphemous passages. The moral degradation of man goes hand in hand with the
moral debasement of God. In Wat's poem God disintegrates both physically and
morally: with a swollen and watery body "he shivers from cold and loneliness"
("drży z zimna i samotności") or, when old, crippled, and stinking, he runs away
and threatens the world—which has become a witches' sabbath—with "suppurating
curses" ("śliniąc zaropiałe przekleństwa grożąc nam wściekle kulą i cuchnąc niemo-
żliwie"). According to Wat, religion is a sham, and those who do not know that it
is only a theatrical spectacle, that the actor playing God the Father goes mad and
the actor playing God the Son is drunk, are fools. Wat did not even spare Jesus,
who he claimed was transformed from a redemptor into a cynic who conceals his
vice and lives comfortably among men no better than savage troglodytes.

The stinking jaws of the troglodytes will vomit out a
swarm of injured curses. In a tavern a huge flax-haired
fellow sells for a glass of spirits the nipples of his mistress.
And from the obscurity of the third corner
Jesus Christ will come out, and cover the drunken company
with the smoke of a cigarillo.

Cuchnąca paszcza troglodytów wyrzyga rój skaleczonych
przekleństw. W szynku wielki białowłosy chłop sprzedaje za
kieliszek spirytusu sutki swej kochanki.
A z mroków trzeciego kąta wyjdzie Jezus Chrystus i za-
słoni dymem cygaretki pijaną kompanię.

All dogmas are undercut, all ideals negated. In a world of total moral dissolution,
the absolute is a "sexless whore" ("kurwa bezpłciowa"), and the only wisdom comes
from an awareness of one's own illusions.
Wat's poem is like a bag in which very different times, places, cultures, myth-
ologies, and religions are all mixed together. They are part of the same crumbling
world, and in wild pandemonium Christian saints meet Greek gods, prophets from

the Old Testament drink absinthe in contemporary San Francisco, the god Bashkir lives among Andalusian witches, and Trafalgar is a lake in Dante's hell. The confusion of cultural and geographical references was a form of rebellion for Wat, a manifestation of disrespect for the entire European cultural tradition. With the destructiveness and impatience of adolescence, Wat rebelled against this tradition and all the books that consecrated it but had in fact become records of human baseness and dissoluteness:

> Damn! In a last effort I tear away this whole disgusting cacophony of scribbling stalls where Bushmen Solveigs, Gypsies angels jews, prostitutes counts, bedbugs graveyards howl bite bleed squeak, idiotic grimaces hanging from the decayed walls of ancient baths, satanic Sodoms of bluish resounding glaciers and the rotten breasts of a miscarried ram's sky.

> Psiakrew! W ostatnim wysiłku zrywam te całą wstrętną kakofonię bazgranin straganów gdzie Buszmeni Solveigi, Cyganie aniołowie żydy, prostytutki hrabiowie, pluskwy cmentarzyska wyją gryzą krwawią piszczą, idiotyczne grymasy zwisające z spruchniałych ścian starożytnych łaźni, szatańskie Sodomie błękitniejących dźwięcznych lodowców i zmurszałych piersi poronionego kafarskiego nieba.

Wat's despair and rebellion went deeper than tradition, and the young poet probed the problem of identity. This question, what he called the *principium individuationis,* recurs in several passages in *The Stove:*

> I have declared myself the tsar of space, the enemy of the interior and of time.

> Having acquired the joyful science of the mask, I burned with a marvelous desire: to become part of space! But one time I became frightened by the bottomless crack which I saw just *beyond* the surface of the nose, when I looked at it with my right eye. Cursed crack, cursed principium individuationis, like a yellow jacket it frightens me, torments, lashes, twists, paralyzes.

> Ogłosiłem się carem przestrzeni, wrogiem wnętrza i czasu.

> Posiadłszy radosną wiedzę maski, pałałem cudowną żądzą: uprzestrzenić się! Lecz pewnego razu przeraziła mnie bezdenna szpara, którą ujrzałem tuż *za* powierzchnią nosa, gdym nań patrzał prawym okiem. Przeklęta szpara, przeklęte principium individuationis, jak żółty kaftan mnie przeraża, trapi, chłoszcze, skręca paraliżuje.

The "joyful science of the mask" is the possibility of changing one's own identity, the temptation of liberation from the constraints of one's personality. But change and liberation are denied to the poet and despite his desire to be the "tsar of space," that is of freedom, and despite his hatred of time and "the interior," or subjugation, he is in fact their slave and the slave of his own self.

The feeling of imprisonment contributed to Wat's suicidal tendency. The passage quoted earlier in which the young poet entertains the idea of death communicates also a sense of suffocation, or claustrophobia, at not being able to detach oneself from one's own image—"How terrible it is to meet one's own likeness at midnight" ("Jak okropnie jest w północ spotkać własny blady wizerunek"). The sense of being a prisoner of one's self also explains the title of the poem, which ends with a moving and powerful cry of despair:

> They wield the key to the abyss and the key to the sky.
> Which one will they use?
> . . . .
> I don't know if my brain and shape is a solid body, or a flat transsurface.
> But I see one thing: this, this: (a black) empty crack between, of the palm.
> It causes despair, it conjures up the spirit of the abyss which repulses you
> *away from itself.* (I see! the key to the abyss was used!)
> Idiot brutes trash son of a bitch.
> It is *I* burning in the inquisitiorial interior of my pug iron stove, it is *I* burning in the middle between me co-lying on one side of the stove and me in the same way on the other side of the stove. Hurr! I look at the ominous palms of this one on the one side and that one on the other side.
> On the one and on the other side *I* sit.
> It is *I* on the one side and *I* on the other side.

> Dzierżą klucz od przepaści i klucz od nieba. Który użyją?
> . . . .
> Nie wiem czy mózg i kształt mój jest bryłą czy pozapłaszczyzną płaską.
> Lecz widzę jedno: to, to: (czarną) pustą szparę między dłoni.
> Przyprawia o rozpacz, wywołuje ducha przepaści, który cię *odtrąca od siebie.* (Aha! użyty klucz od przepaści!)
> Idiota bydło drań cholera.
> To JA się palę w inkwizytorskim wnętrzu mego mopsożelaznego piecyka, to JA się palę wpośrodku między mną współleżącym z jednej strony piecyka a mną tak samo z drugiej strony piecyka. Hurr! Oglądam złowrogie dłonie tego z jednej strony i tego z drugiej strony.
> Z jednej i drugiej strony siedzę JA.
> To JA z jednej strony i JA z drugiej strony.

Wat's nihilistic attitude is also reflected in his use of language and imagery and in his predilection for nonsense and paradox. *The Stove* begins with a seemingly contradictory sentence, "Happiness loiters after us joyless essential necessary and golden" ("Szczęście szwenda się za nami bezradosne istotne konieczne i złote"). The description of happiness is paradoxical, happiness that is not joy but a necessity is unhappiness, and the attributes of happiness contradict each other ("joyless" and "golden"). The use of words is in fact purposeful; Wat's play with language, his stretching the meaning of a word until it means its opposite continues, on the plane of language, the process of negation and demasking that occurs on the plane of values and ideas. "Joyless happiness," "words thoughtless but profound," "the sad spring," "the warm coat made of morning shivers"—*The Stove* abounds in these paradoxical juxtapositions. In a section of the poem entitled "Rebellion" Wat advocates humility:

> REBELLION: Take a triangular stiletto and go to Lake Tanganyika. When you meet a pale cayman—greet him with a humble word of humility.

> BUNT. Weź sztylet trójgraniasty i pójdź nad jezioro Tanganajki. Gdy spotkasz bladego kajmana – powitaj go kornym słowem Pokory.

The absurdity of the advice is obvious, but is not the Christian virtue of humility in a world as brutal as that of alligators just as questionable as Wat's advice, which is patently absurd? The "rebellion" of the title might implicitly contain this question, but the simultaneous presence in the text of the two opposed concepts, of rebellion and humility, seems ridiculous and paradoxical. In a world where all values are false and deceptive, paradox is closer to truth than logic. The disintegration of semantic values is a sign of the disintegration of spiritual values.

A different yet similar principle underlies a procedure that is the main source of the nonsense and humor in the poem. A sentence develops logically until a word that is entirely out of place undercuts its meaning. For example: "In front of the statue bend your head and whisper the intricate Syrian incantation that you were taught by the mother of your shadow" ("Przed posągiem pochyl głowę i szepnij zawiłe syryjskie zaklęcie, którego cię nauczyła matka twego cienia"). The entirely fantastic "mother of your shadow" breaks down meaning and turns the sentence to nonsense. The effect is all the more powerful because Wat's syntax and grammar are irreproachable. Wat's absurd, clad in an iron syntactical structure, unexpectedly explodes from within. There is a clash between form and content analogous to the clashes taking place in the realm of values and ideals. Wat's sentences preserve all the appearance of logical discourse, but they are put in the service not of truth but of nonsense. "Because my spinal marrow hurt excruciatingly, I had my missing fingernails manicured by the sullen ladies of Biarritz thinking that it would help" ("Ponieważ mlecz mnie bolał niezmiernie, więc dałem brakujące paznokcie manikurować markotnym damom z Biarritz, myśląc że to pomoże"). The sentence is both grammatically and syntactically correct, and the causal relations between its clauses are accentuated by the use of the words "because" and "thinking that" ("ponieważ," "więc," "myśląc że"). The nonsense results from the lack of logical connection between the cause and the resulting action and is intensified by the paradox of having a manicure and the absence of fingernails. Wat described his procedure as "the ungluing of the syntax of poetic discourse both from logical and—more broadly—rational discourse. The connections of individual sentences, and within the sentences of words, made not on the basis of logical continuity or a plausible description, not even on the basis of psychological associations, but through the eruption or invasion of deep, dark words and content into the normal course of speech in the state of dimmed consciousness."[76] Wat also gave an interesting interpretation of this procedure, which was done "not to obscure the meaning, but on the contrary to throw a beam of light on things that are by their nature dark; thus not pure nonsense . . . not 'the reason of feelings,' . . . but on the contrary the feelings of reason—Spinoza's 'amor dei intellectualis.' "

It is interesting to compare Wat's disruptive use of syntax with the futurist "words at liberty," whose great revolutionary power Wat stressed in his writings. What attracted Wat in the concept of "words at liberty" was that words were treated like objects, but unlike the Italian futurists he preserved the syntax intact. Wat always operates with sentences and never with isolated words. Also, his play with language is always philosophically motivated, it is never pure nonsense. At a certain point in *The Stove* Wat repeats the same sentence three times, each with a different word order:

> D'INFINITE. The road is shown to the Magi from the sunrise.
> Shown from the sunrise is the road to the Magi.
> To the Magi from the sunrise the road is shown.
> Galgalat and Malgalat come sleep with me.

> D'INFINITE. Utorowana jest droga Magom od wschodu słońca.
> Utorowana jest od wschodu słońca droga Magom.
> Magom od wschodu słońca droga utorowana jest.
> Galgalat i Malgalat chodźcie ze mną spać.

The repetition of the same sentence in different syntactical orders has the appearance of trying for the best possible stylistic arrangement, but in fact it is a play with its meaning. It reveals the unexpected ambiguity of the statement, and seems to minimize the importance of meaning in favor of purely stylistic concern, form apparently prevailing over content—the poet treats words like toy blocks that he arranges and rearranges under our eyes, as if ignoring their meaning. But the last sentence reveals the intention hidden behind the stylistic game: it suggests that the bibilical story could be rearranged, the events could have taken a different course. What remains is a senseless game with words that could be played infinitely, as the title of the piece ironically suggests.

The breakdown of meaning is accompanied by the disintegration of words, of language itself. "They warm their numb fingers. Fingers, gers, fiiinfi fi-fi" ("Grzeją skostniałe palce. Palce, lce paap p pa-pa"). When stretched to its limits, language changes into incomprehensible gibberish: "I stamp my feet and squeak: tam tiu tju tua tm tru tia tiam tiamtion tium tiu tium tium" ("Drepczę i kwiczę: tam tiu tju tua tm tru tia tiam tiamtion tium tiu tium tium"). Sometimes the story degenerates into rhymed nonsense reminiscent of nursery rhymes: "The Marys celebrated the holiday of their name-day in a huge suburb of old men. They circled cried cuddled they whine whine whine. They tattle babble gabble" ("Marie sprawowały święto swoich imienin no olbrzymim przedmieściu starców. Kołowały płakały tuliły skomlą skomlą skomlą. Kają bają zapraszają"). In his memoirs Wat observed that the peasant rhymes and sayings of his peasant nurse must have contributed to his developing a taste for the pure nonsense that influenced his dada poetry. Occasionally

Wat would use nonsense for parodistic effect, which he directed mostly at the poets
of the Young Poland movement: "When out of amethyst distances you will spin out
the baldachin of your hands . . . I shall come to the meeting where, trembling
in tears and unconscious, you will surrender, will surrender, he (she) will surrender,
we will surrender, you will surrender, they will surrender" ("Kiedy z ametystowych
dali rozsnujesz rąk baldachim . . . wyjdę na twoje spotkanie, gdzie drżąca we
łzach i bez czucia się oddasz, ty się oddasz, on [ona] się odda, my się oddamy,
wy się oddacie, oni [one] się oddadzą"). The style and tone of the passage are
those of Polish postsymbolist poetry until the verb at the end triggers the school-
like drill of its entire present conjugation. The parody results from the clash between the flowery, intricate style of the beginning and the mechanical repetition
at the end; the climactic act of surrender changes into the anticlimax of grammar.
The style of *The Stove* is often reminiscent of Polish postsymbolist poetry, which
Wat had extensively read in his adolescence. It is the heavily ornamented and con-
voluted style identified in Poland with the movement "secesja" and related to the
French art nouveau, to the English Pre-Raphaelites. In Wat's poetry, however, there
is a contradiction between the style and the content, which is dadaist. Once again,
as with Wat's sentences, the effect is that of a clash, of an eruption of the style
from within. A pretentious, rhetorical, or highfaluting pose ends in dada nonsense.
    There are many passages in *The Stove* where nonsense is a result of the play on
sounds. For example, the Polish "Ja piękny jak niebieskie piękno pękniętego
antyku" (lit., "I, beautiful like the blue beauty of a cracked antique"). The pattern
of sounds in the sentence is organized around three groups: (1) *piękn - nieb -
piękn - pękn - an* (2) *ja - jak,* and (3) *tego - tyku.* Many of Wat's most striking
images derive from the play on sounds. In the following passage the play on words is
based on the similarity of sounds as well as analogy of meanings:

    AUTOPORTRET. Powieki i bez powieki, i bez, i bez, i poza.
    I poza dumała cicho i ciepło a rostąż ramp skalała nieme bezusty. I
smętne o ty! i ty kosujko wież chorych i klin bezwargich powiek.
    Sztylet bez powieki. Wieki bez powieki. Powieki bez powieki. Kto powie
czy, jako pawie, wie co wypowie.

A literal translation of this passage would not capture the sounds of the Polish
words, while an attempt to render these sounds would no longer be a literal translation. The literal meaning is:

    SELF-PORTRAIT. Eyelids and without an eyelid, and without, and with-
out, and beyond.
    And the pose brooded quietly and warmly and the nostalgia of the foot-
lights defiled the mute mouthlessness. And melancholic O you! and you little
blackbird of the sick towers and the wedge of the lipless eyelids.
    Stiletto without an eyelid. Centuries without an eyelid. Eyelids without an
eyelid. Who will say whether, like peacocks, he knows what he will say.

The whole poem is dominated by the sound of the word *powieki* ("eyelids"), and the notion of being without an eyelid *(bez powieki)*. These give rise to most of the other words in the passage, either through the analogy of sounds or analogy of meaning. The phrase *bez powieki* leads to the formation of the analogical words *bezusty* ("mouthless"), *bezwargi* ("lipless"), and the analogical images *sztylet bez powieki* ("stiletto without an eyelid") and *wieki bez powieki* ("centuries without an eyelid"). The last image is based on the close sound similarity of *powieki* and *wieki*. The word *poza* ("beyond"), which ends the first line, combines sounds of the words *powieki* and *bez,* and is also semantically related to the word *bez* ("without"). Its homonym *poza* ("pose") starts the second line. Sound associations also operate in the sequence *nieme bezusty. I smętne o ty! i ty kosujko.* The word *kosujka* is a neologism and has a very approximate association with a blackbird *(kos)*. The last line is entirely based on sound play and derives from the original word *powieki;* like a flash—in Polish—it unexpectedly lights up with meaning.

Just as Wat's text ignores the rational logic of discourse, his images defy the visual imagination. The following passage is composed of images that are neither visually plausible nor imaginable:

> HUNTING ON THE BOULEVARDS. Purple legends stroke the loins of July days swollen with desire. The sun pulls at melancholic "blue stockings" by the maenads. Juicy lilies which desire their own body whisper under the glare of sonorous but narrow shields. Liqueur chartreuse verveine and the hours do not want to pass and lie down unnoticed on the basalt whirlpools, wild in an adagio of perfumed purples.

> POLOWANIE NA BULWARACH. Fioletowe legendy głaszczą nabrzmiałe żądzą lędźwia lipcowych dni. Słońce szarpane przez menady melancholijne „błękitne pończoszki". Soczyste lilie żądne własnego ciała szepcą pod blaskiem dźwięcznych a wąskich tarcz. Likier szartrez werwena i godziny nie chcą ujść i kładą się płazem na bazaltowe wiry, obłędne w adagio perfumowanych fioletów.

Wat's images have little relation to visual perception, nor are they a result of intellectual labor; they are products of the imagination alone, but a special imagination that has a striking resemblance to the surrealist imagination and to fairy tales. The resemblance to surrealism is not accidental, and can be explained by *The Stove* being written in a manner similar to the automatic writing practiced by the surrealists. Wat has said, "I wrote *The Stove* in four or five trances, in January, 1919, with a fever of 102-103 degrees. And then, during the winter nights near an iron stove, after my return from eccentric bohemian wanderings, I would work myself into a state of trance in order to 'liberate my witches.' . . . Several years before André Breton but out of the same Freudian inspiration I came upon 'écriture automatique,' I called it a self-recording, an autosnapshot." [77] When analyzing his own automatic texts, André Breton noticed that their most striking feature was their wealth of fantastic images. [78] Wat's poem confirms Breton's observation; his images, even if unimaginable, are nevertheless extremely suggestive, and the reason seems to be that they originate in the subconscious. They are multilayered, and if their im-

mediate effect when read is of the absurd, they also contain deeper layers of sub-
liminal messages that are felt by the reader, though not immediately accessible.
The kinship of Wat's imagery to fairy tales stems from similar premises. The
popular imagination that finds expression in fairy tales is also a translation of the
subconscious. Adam Ważyk has pointed out the relation between the quality of the
absurd found in the poetry of Polish futurists, and the absurd encountered in fairy
tales: "It is enough to shake off our habits and we will see in the tale of Little Red
Riding Hood an absurd grotesque." [79] The following image from *The Stove* could
easily come from a fairy tale: "The errant knight tears out with a spear his own
heart and *sacrifices it to the Madonna* red, living, lapping" ("Błedny rycerz wyrywa
dzidą własne serce i *poświęca je Madonnie* czerwone, żywe, człopiące"). Its im-
probability, as well as the horror and cruelty it contains, is typical of fairy tales.
Wat's nonsense is terrifying in the same way that they are terrifying, and probably
its relation to reality is only symbolic. Just as animals speak in fairy tales, inanimate
objects scream in Wat's poem: "The shod legs of the tables rebelled, they howl"
("Podkute nogi stołów zbuntowały się, wyją"). All of *The Stove* is written within
the highly unrealistic convention of the fairy tale—a convention in which the im-
probable is real and the incredible is true. Totally fantastic, it disregards both logic
and verisimilitude And yet the very effectiveness of Wat's nonsense is precisely its
synthetic quality. Like a fairy tale, it represents the "exaggerated essence" and not
a realistic account of facts and events. The poetic vision of the disintegration of
the world comes from an accumulation of scenes and images that in their isolation
are completely absurd and grotesque.

I on One Side and I on the Other Side of My Pug Iron Stove is the opus magnum
of Wat's futurist period. He wrote very little poetry in verse form, and the best
known are his nonsense poems, which he called "namopaniki." They were inspired by
the *zaum* poetry created by the Russian futurist poet Velimir Khlebnikov. *Zaum*
was based exclusively on the sound value of words and consisted entirely of neologisms. Although *zaum* poetry is not translatable into normal language, the sounds
of the words invented by the poet have a relation to the sounds in normal language.
The effectiveness of *zaum* poetry comes from certain sounds and groups of pho-
nemes having emotional connotations in each language—they are felt to be either
sad or amusing, familiar or foreign, endearing or hostile. Owing to this suggestiveness of sounds in a given language, the poetry of *zaum* is not entirely meaningless.

The following passage comes from a poem by Wat entitled "Namopanik Barwistanu":

O barwy o baruwy – o raby barbaruw, barany herubuw
o barwicze o czabary – babuw czary, o bicze rabuw
o barwiasy o syrawy – o basy wiary, o bary ras!
o barwionki o barwoczy o barwiony o barwohi
o barwigie o barwalie o barwiecze o barwiole
o kroony barw!
    O krale koloruuw – o bawoły barw o każdyći barwoh kral w niebio-
paszńi – o każdyći barwoh kraluje nogahi na śmierćeży – takoh na
czarnoszczu kraluje wszem kolorom białość i po śmierćeży powendrujem
do oraju do ograju Barwistanu

All sounds in the first stanza are directly or indirectly related to the sounds of the word *barwy* (colors). In the first three lines the word *barwy* generates a number of neologisms whose sounds are transformed through consonance back into normal words, only they are phonetically spelled as if to prove the hidden semantic possibilities of the neologisms. And so *barwy, baruwy* are transformed into *raby barbaruw, barany herubuw* (slaves of the barbarians, sheep of the cherubs), *barwicze, czabary* into *babuw czary, bicze rabuw* (witchcraft of women, whips of the slaves), and *barwiasy, syrawy* are echoed by *basy wiary, bary ras* (the bass of faith, the shoulders of races). This curious two-way process is accentuated by the typographical arrangement of the lines, each divided into two parts by a dash with the neologisms on the left side, the words that derive from them on the right. In the fourth and fifth lines the word *barwy* is repeated eight times, each with a different suffix; the crescendolike repetition, which acts like a charm or enchantment, ends with the climactic and rapturous exclamation, "o kroony barw!" The feeling of delight and growing ecstasy is also communicated by the repetition of *o*. The stanza has ring composition, and the word *barwy* both begins and ends it. The repetition in many different variations of what is essentially a single basic word, *barwy*, suggests the unusual versatility of this sound, which is similar—since the poem is about colors—to the versatility and potential wealth of the color white, source of all colors. This interpretation is confirmed by a sentence in the next stanza, *kraluje wszem kolorom białość* ("whiteness reigns over all colors"). The stanza is thus a translation into sounds of the remarkable optical phenomenon of the prism, through which white generates the delightful richness of the rainbow.

The last stanza explores the expressive possibilities of archaic language. It combines neologisms with forms characteristic of the older common Slavic (*każdyci, kral,* the ending *oh* in *barwoh, takoh*). The use of archaic language goes hand in hand with the emotional atmosphere of this stanza that is dominated by images of death, in keeping with the spirit of the Middle Ages. Following medieval symbolism, Wat associates death with black and white, and like a medieval primitive painting the poem ends with a vision of the garden of paradise, full of colors, where the soul wanders after death.

It is symptomatic that Wat should have been attracted to *zaum* poetry, and it indicates his dislike of logical and rational discourse. The use of suggestive sounds in his *namopaniki* stems from the same premises as the use of paradox and nonsense in *The Stove*—both testify that Wat's source of poetry was situated deeply in the human subconscious and closely related to man's irrationality. As he remarked himself, however, his use of nonsense did not imply an anti-intellectual attitude but, quite the contrary, was the expression of his profound intellectualism. What Wat rejected was a common-sense rationalism that seemed inadequate for expressing either the real paradoxes of the world or the paradoxes of his own personality. He believed that "literature is connected with what is the least social in man, with what is antisocial and irrational. I thought it tragic, but I thought that such is the gist of literature."[80]

Wat's philosophy of literature largely explains why he abandoned poetry and in fact all creative writing after becoming involved in politics and communism. He became editor of the prestigious communist magazine *Miesięcznik Literacki* in 1929. In 1927 he wrote a collection of short stories entitled *The Unemployed Lucifer (Bezrobotny Lucyfer),* a work whose nihilism equals if not surpasses *The Stove.* After that Wat fell into a silence lasting thirty years, and his next work was a collection of poems published in 1957. In the words of Czesław Miłosz, "The moment Wat entered into a pact with History he stopped writing poems and stories, and in this his Muse turned out to be probably wiser than himself." [81] In the long run Wat's aesthetic sense proved to be wiser in its choice of silence than his rational mind, which chose communism, a commitment eventually leading to the poet's incarceration in numerous Soviet prisons. Wat's "muse" also prevented him from writing according to the prescriptions of socialist realism. His poetics were anti-Marxist and in conflict with his social and ideological views. The contradiction between the two sets of values proved to be insoluble, since what the poet considered to be aesthetically valuable was contradictory to Marxist and communist ideology, and what was compatible ideologically was not acceptable aesthetically. As he wrote later, "Humanity has to be built rationally. I saw the ugliness of socrealism, and I thought that there cannot be any other communist literature than socrealism, and therefore no literature at all." [82] In Wat, social optimism combined with poetic pessimism, and these two contradictory attitudes were the source of what he called "aesthetic catastrophism". Using his own prophetic words from the opening sentence of *The Stove,* this could be translated "joyless happiness."

2

THE CRACOW AVANTGARDE

THE SWITCH

The Period of Transition

As Polish futurism was coming to an end, a new group of poets formed in Cracow, to be known in the history of Polish literature as "The Cracow Avantgarde." Its strong orientation toward progress and civilization made it appear at first as a continuation of futurism, but in fact its interest in formal issues and its constructivism put it in opposition to futurism. Before these differences became crystallized, the futurists and Tadeusz Peiper, who was to become the main theoretician of the Avantgarde, collaborated in a short-lived magazine with the all-embracing title, the *New Art*. Two numbers appeared, in November 1921 and in February 1922, and they can be seen as a transition between futurism and the Cracow Avantgarde. The first editorial article stressed the elements common to both groups: opposition to the preceding movements of symbolism, impressionism and naturalism, the desire for new art to be innovative, the rejection of logic, and the search for a new kind of metaphor. The article also mentioned the importance of the formal elements in a work of art, and hinted that Polish "new art" was turning in a new direction. It is interesting that all the theoretical articles in the two numbers of the magazine emphasized the need for form, sharing the belief of Leon Chwistek that "All contemporary art develops under the sign of form."[1] At the same time, the poets who published in the *New Art* were almost without exception all futurists— Wat, Stern, Jasieński, Czyżewski—and their poetry was in contrast to the theoretical orientation of the magazine.

Similar eclecticism and hesitation, typical of a period of transition, characterized the first series of *Zwrotnica (The Switch)*, the magazine of the newly formed Cracow group. The *Switch* was published in two series, the first comprising six numbers published between May 1922, and October 1923; the second, published after a three-year interval in 1926 and 1927, also had six numbers. In addition to being "the forge of the Polish avant-garde" as some critics called it, the *Switch* opened its pages to many poets and art theoreticians whose premises were akin to those of the Cracow Avantgarde only in the most general way, often negative rather than positive: "We are united by that which separates us from others."[2] This artistic heterogeneity was especially true of its first series, where the overwhelming majority of authors belonged to artistic groups or movements other than the Cracow Avantgarde. The poet Tytus Czyżewski, the art theoretician and philosopher Leon Chwistek, the famous playwright and theorist Stanisław I. Witkiewicz, the sculptor August Zamoyski, were all associated with formism. The poets Stanisław Młodożeniec, Bruno Jasieński, Anatol Stern, and Aleksander Wat were futurists. The translations of foreign poets represented a similar diversity of poetic schools and styles, Vladimir Mayakovski together with Esenin, Blaise Cendrars with Tristan Tzara and Paul Reverdy. As for the poets who would become identified with the Cracow Avantgarde, there was only Peiper himself who published under two different pseudonyms, Jan Alden and Jan Badyński. Peiper, the founder and editor of the *Switch,* dominated it. It was owing to him that the *Switch* preserved a unity despite the diverse aesthetic attitudes of its various contributors; he was the soul of the magazine, the author of all its programmatic and most important theoretical articles. He also edited a considerable part of an important section of the magazine first called "Notes" and later "Courier," which contained critical reviews of poetry, art exhibitions, concerts, and theatrical performances, polemics with critics, and a chronicle of the most significant artistic, literary, and technological events abroad, justifying Peiper's claim that the *Switch* was "a window onto the world." Older than the majority of young poets who gathered around him, Peiper was already intellectually and artistically formed when they were still searching for their poetic identity. By the age of thirty Peiper had spent several years in Western Europe, particularly in Paris and Spain, where he came in contact with new European artistic movements. Italian futurism and recent French and Spanish poetry contributed essentially to the formation of his own poetic ideas; for Peiper the *Switch* was a necessary forum where he could introduce and expose his ideas, while for many younger poets it was the workshop of their apprenticeship. These poets—Julian Przyboś, Jan Brzękowski, and Jalu Kurek—would come into prominence with the second series of the *Switch.*

In an article opening the first number, Peiper defined the goals of the new magazine in the most general terms. The most important attitude uniting all its collaborators was a concept of the present, a word that appeared in the complete title of the magazine: *The Switch. A Magazine. Direction: The Art of the Present.* The railway switch was a symbol for the "switch toward the now." At another point Peiper clarified his notion of the *present,* which was not to be confused with *contemporaneity:* "Contemporariness is a calendar notion, the present is a physiognomical notion." The first implied all contemporary phenomena, while the second signified only those specific products and characteristics of contemporary times that gave them their particular "physiognomy" and foreshadowed the future. The article praised the new epoch, the "embrace with the present" that was inoculated with the "bacilli of modernity" and struggled for power, abundance, and joy. New sources of emotion, beauty, and imagination were contained in three of the components of modern life—the city, the masses, and the machine, which were to be points of contingency between the new contemporary reality—"the present"—and the new poetry. These general terms did not seem to go beyond the tenets of futurism, but as Peiper gradually revealed his aesthetic program in subsequent issues, it became apparent the two programs were diametrically opposed. Peiper repeatedly pointed out his disagreements with futurist aesthetics.

The First Formulations

In his essay entitled "The City, the Masses, the Machine," published in the second number of the *Switch,* Peiper shifted the emphasis from life to poetry itself. The city, the masses, and the machine were not important to him as subjects for poetry, nor were they embodiments of a new type of beauty, but they did contain elements that could revolutionize poetry. For Peiper the masses became the model of new artistic composition, human society was a structural model for a work of art: "The organic structure, best known from the functioning of society, will inspire artistic structure. The work of art will be socially organized. The work of art will be a society." The concept of organic structure was unique and original in the context of the general avant-garde tendency toward the loosening of poetic structure; it announced the constructivist tendency of the Cracow Avantgarde that was to become one of its most distinctive traits. It is also a good illustration that the important moment—the present—for Peiper was the moment of the adaptation of life models to poetry, and not their imitation. The point of departure was to be poetry and artistic considerations, not life, which is why Peiper separated himself from the futurist attitude toward the machine. According to him, the treatment of the machine as a fetish or perfect beauty implied a false approach to an aesthetic problem: "If the machine was only a deity, it would not merit the attention of art; if it were the most perfect beauty, there would be no need for art." Instead, Peiper spoke of the exploitation of the machine for purely artistic purposes—and long before Calder's mobiles or electronic music he wrote of the possibility of using the machine in sculpture and music.

If "The City, the Masses, the Machine" set the general philosophical framework for the Cracow Avantgarde, Peiper's next essay "The Metaphor of the Present," published in the third number of the *Switch,* contained the first declaration of its poetics. The essay immediately gained enormous popularity among young poets and provoked a vivid response from the literary critics. Peiper's essay was original not because it acknowledged the unusual prolifity or "blizzard" of images in contemporary poetry, but because it provided a motivation for them. Peiper stressed two aspects of metaphor, its economy, and its antirealism, that made it a particularly valuable poetic tool. He stated that the economy of metaphor, its reduction of all verbal material to a minimum—the omission of comparative sentences, of description, of even the adverb *like* (which Peiper compared to "the dull vanilla of literary cuisine")—reflected a similar economy of means characteristic of all domains of contemporary life, and in this way gave to metaphor the distinct stamp of the present. What especially appealed to Peiper was that this "modernity" of metaphor was not a function of its content but rather of its formal qualities, of "the artistic craftsmanship itself." The other characteristic of metaphor, its "antirealism" or

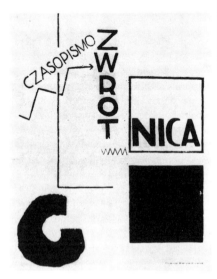

Covers for numbers
3, 4, and 6 of the *Switch*

distortion, was even more important for Peiper. He agreed with general critical opinion that the antirealism of a metaphor was in direct proportion to the distance between the notions it juxtaposed, but he proposed his own theory of its aesthetic motivation.

Peiper disagreed with the futurists, for whom metaphorical short cuts were the poetic corollary of the new sense of space and distance, produced in contemporary times by such technological phenomena as the airplane and radiotelegraph. He also disagreed with the critics who saw in the new metaphor a consequence of the impression or "skittishness" of the perceptions of modern man. In both cases Peiper objected to the naturalistic approach to metaphor and to poetry in general. For Peiper, the new metaphor had a purely artistic motivation and was a consequence of the need for antirealism. "The more distant and the less juxtaposable *in reality* the notions of a metaphor, the less descriptive the image. Metaphor built upon distant notions gives poetry its imaginative perspective." According to Peiper the very originality and uniqueness of metaphor lay in it neither describing nor imitating reality, but being a process of transformation. "By transposing notions into domains where they do not belong by nature, metaphor reshapes the reality of perceptions and transforms it into a new reality, a purely poetic reality." The emphasis was on the creative process itself; the result of its transformation—poetry—was qualitatively different from reality. Peiper's definition of metaphor stressed the divorce of poetry from reality, "Metaphor is an arbitrary act connecting concepts; it is the creation of conceptual relationships to which nothing corresponds in the real world." The break with the mimetic theory of literature was complete. In Peiper's definition, metaphor and by extension poetry had an autonomous character in relation to reality: it was connotative, not denotative. The emphasis was shifted from the problem of poetry and reality to the problem of the relation between poetry and the poet, or more precisely to the very moment of poetic creativity. The stress on the intellectual character of metaphor—its "conceptual relationships"—and on its "arbitrariness" underlined the poet's total independence and freedom with respect to reality.

On the philosophical plane Peiper saw the main value of metaphor in its leveling of traditional hierarchies, values, and emotions. It demonstrated all reality by putting traditionally "poetic" objects on a par with those of everyday reality. What Peiper found especially attractive in this process was the possibility of an aesthetic re-evaluation of reality as well as a philosophical rehabilitation of civilization, that reality made by man and opposed to nature whose slave he had been until quite recently: "Today's man has no reason to see in the sun anything more than a golden speckle; on the other hand he has the right to see in a trouser's button the mirror of his own greatness." Peiper's partisanship in the controversy of culture versus nature underlay all his aesthetic theories—he stood, an extremist, on the side of culture as opposed to nature, seeing culture as constantly evolving. Since this moment was the most advanced in time, he considered it the most civilized and sophisticated. This philosophical attitude was at the root of his profound disagreement with the strongest tradition in Polish literature, romanticism.

Peiper's cult of civilization provided a bridge between the Polish Avantgarde and positivism, but it also created a very misleading impression of kinship between the Avantgarde and Italian futurism. Peiper realized this and did not fail to clarify his position. The entire last number of the first series of the *Switch* was devoted to futurism, with Peiper defining his position and specifying his disagreements with no other avant-garde movement so thoroughly as he did with futurism. The affinities between Marinetti's manifestoes and Peiper's own ideas were deep enough to make him stress their differences. He admitted the importance of Marinetti as a revolutionary force that gave stimulus to all new art: "The victorious spell of Marinetti's words pushed the whole generation of today onto paths of innovation unknown for a long time. The daring that characterizes all the artistic endeavors of our times was born from the daring of Marinetti. He infused all of us with courage. He un-taught us the sterile admiration of works achieved in the past by others; he taught us faith in ourselves, and creative blasphemy. . . . This is his great historical merit." All the general ideas of futurism—bravery, movement, masculinity, action, will power, the battle with the past, the call for a new art—all these found an enthusiastic adept in Peiper. They were a valuable antidote against what he called the "lunatism" of the preceding period. Peiper believed that in Poland especially, futurism performed the useful function of distilling romantic values and clearing the atmosphere of false emotions, of artificial poses.

Yet Peiper's reservations about futurism, deeper and of greater artistic consequence than his agreements, outweighed his admiration. Peiper's main objection was that the basic postulates of futurism pertained to life and not to art, and its poetic reforms stemmed from the will to reform life rather than from genuinely artistic interests: "The concern with art itself, with purely poetic, painterly or musical values, is found with difficulty behind the curtain of their real thoughts." Peiper reproached Marinetti with sacrificing poetry to his philosophy, with sacrificing aesthetic to nonaesthetic values. According to Peiper it was the fascination with the world of matter, with "molecules and electrons," that led the futurists to deify the machine. Similarly the concept of dynamism, narrowly identified with kinetics, betrayed the wish to include the essential elements of modern life in art; even such purely poetic theories as "words-in-freedom" and onomatopoeia were mimetic and motivated by the wish to bring poetry closer to reality. Peiper, who was not interested in reality but in poetry, considered the destruction of syntax to be the destruction of a basic poetic vehicle, "because without syntax we can at best make an inventory of the world, but never will we be able to render the life of the world. Syntax is the apparatus which registers the relations that take place between phenomena, it is their linguistic reflection." Correlated with the defense of syntax was Peiper's defense of punctuation in poetry as a means of clarity and precision. Peiper's conservation of syntax was symptomatic of the aesthetics of the entire Polish avant-garde: both the poets of the Cracow Avantgarde and the Polish futurists constantly experimented with the problems of syntax, but they refined rather than rejected it.

Peiper's polemics with Marinetti were the most fundamental reappraisal of Italian futurism carried out in Poland, touching on all the philosophical, aesthetic, and poetic tenets of futurism, and sparing nothing. The essay proved that Peiper had analyzed all the theories of futurism to discover how profoundly incompatible they were both with his ideas on poetry and with his poetic temperament. His familiarity with the ideas of futurism made his arguments quite powerful and his criticisms pertinent. At the same time his polemics with futurism permitted Peiper to define and specify his own philosophy of literature and poetics—his own ideas were sharpened in the fire of battle.

The Constructivist Theory

The fullest expression of Peiper's poetics did not appear in the pages of the *Switch* but in a long essay published separately in 1925 and significantly entitled in Polish *Nowe usta,* literally "The New Mouth" or "The New Lips."[3] Although the philosophical approach remained the same as in his essay on metaphor, Peiper shifted his emphasis to the structure of the poetic work, opening his essay with the sweeping, provocative statement that "poetry is the art of beautiful sentences." The beauty of the sentence depended on the arrangement of words, on the artful sequence and association of concepts and images. The poem was a structure in which all sentences should be connected functionally to form a unity: "The plan of the arrangement in a poem should be visible like the plan of a railway station or a department store." Peiper rejected the traditional distinction between form and content. Since the design of the sentence and the poem as a whole predetermined its content, the reality the poet wanted to express was reshaped: "Subjective and objective reality undergoes a thorough transformation in a poetic sentence, and the more deeply this transformation reaches, the closer we are to the beauty of the sentence: nothing is more foreign to poetry than calling things by their name." According to Peiper, the distinction between poetry and prose was based on the indirectness of expression: "Prose names, poetry gives pseudonyms. . . . Poetry raises reality into the distinct world of the sentence, creating the verbal equivalents of things. The development of poetry consists in the fact that the verbal equivalent is more and more removed from the name of the thing." Instead of metaphor, Peiper introduced new and broader concepts of "pseudonyms" and verbal equivalents, but the principle of antirealism was the same.

Peiper believed that direct expression of feelings was contradictory to the essence of poetry. The romantic tradition that the poem was a reflection of the artist's soul and at the same time a work of art posed a dilemma for Peiper, because he believed these were mutually exclusive. For him the romantic ideal of poetry was the result of a false belief in the authenticity of the poetic word, a belief that word and feeling can be perfectly congruent. He argued that one cannot at the same time be truthful to reality and artistic, capable of moving the reader. To portray truthfully human emotions, feelings, and thoughts, the poet had to renounce his art; to disguise emotions behind verbal equivalents was the mark of good poetry. The "counterparts of feelings" *(odpowiedniki uczuć)* constituted proper poetic material.

Peiper called the type of poetry he proposed "emotionist," and distinguished it from associational poetry to which it had a certain resemblance, although the two types were built on opposing principles. "Emotionist" poems were constructed for their effect and were therefore independent of both subjective and objective reality, while associational poems closely followed the subjective reality of the poet. The poet's only aim—and limitation—was the specific emotional impact he attempted to make on the reader. In an ideal poem "the individual sentences would be linked not by the cohesiveness of the subject, but by the cohesiveness of the emotional effect." Peiper's reservations about associational poems stemmed from their concern with psychology rather than with artistic structure: "They rely on passivity, not on creative will; they are a collection and not a selection; they are not born from artistic premises, and this is why they cannot give birth to the poem." It was on these grounds that Peiper denounced the automatic writing of the surrealists as unartistic for if writing was simply a form of registration and did not entail selection or overall composition, it could not lead to a work of art. "The important thing is not the repetition of reality, in this case 'internal,' but the work, the poem. The important thing is not the direct spitting out of feelings or recording the natural sequence of images, but the organic poetic composition. One cannot put to one side the creative will which shapes the material of internal experiences according to artistic principles, which eliminates and composes."[4]

On the same premises Peiper rejected poetry in whose composition chance played a role. In this way he dissociated himself from most of the European avant-garde poetry that had followed Rimbaud's example in opening the gates to psychological associations and, after Apollinaire, allowed chance to play a role in the composition of a poem. In deep disagreement with the poetic practices of Dada and the surrealists, Peiper declared himself in favor of logic as the condition of any artistic creation—logic that, in his interpretation, did not entail a return to realism or naturalism.

Peiper's concept of poetry had its pitfalls. The most important was that paradoxically it opened the possibility for the dissolution of structure within the poem. The unity of experience or emotion in the poet had assured a cohesiveness to the poem, while total freedom with respect to inner and outer experience threatened it with chaos. Peiper realized this himself, "Feelings are not bricks; to check their resemblances is often like confronting two winds." The danger of structural anarchy was unacceptable to Peiper, who wanted the poem to be a hermetically closed entity with all parts logically motivated. As a practical solution to this problem, Peiper spoke on several occasions of "supports" that would give cohesiveness to poems, but rather than develop the notion, he gave as examples two of his own poems whose structure relied upon the use of rhetorical figures, and the idea of supports remained vague, unconvincing, and disappointing.[5] It is doubtlessly in response to the same problem that Peiper proposed his "system of blossoming." This was to serve as an example of poetic structure defined by logic and not by chance or random associations. In a "blossoming poem" an image or event are given by the poet in several developments, and each successive development of the initial image or event is more full and more ample than the one that preceded: "The poem would develop like a living organism; it would blossom like a bud in front of us. Already the first passage would contain everything that follows, the next passage would be the gradual development of the budding content of the first; in the last passage we would have in front of us a flower—already full and spread out." Peiper attributed great importance to this invention, and put great hopes in its future possibilities, but the blossoming system did not find followers among the Avant-garde poets.

To give poems an even greater sturctural cohesiveness and unity, Peiper retained such formal poetic devices as rhythm and rhyme. He rejected, however, the traditional musical function of rhythm and rhyme, and endowed them with a new literary and structural function, to provide a poem with formal supports, to serve as bonds, and to assure order and tightness. This is why they were subordinate to the sentence and its content and followed the conceptual divisions of the poem. According to Peiper, rhyme provided a firm skeleton, while the role of rhythm was to accentuate and expose certain words. Rhythm should influence the development of images in the reader's imagination; with the help of accents and pauses it should indicate the centers where images crystallize. Peiper thought there was no difference between rhythm in poetry and in prose since both served the same function. "The rhythm of a poem is beautiful when the concepts are beautifully distributed. If two words are well associated conceptually, by the same token they are well combined rhythmically. Beautiful rhythm is the trace of a beautiful course of words." Peiper found the monotony of traditional rhyme unbearable, and to counteract it he proposed the use of distant regular rhymes, that is, rhymes that are spaced over a greater number of lines than most traditional rhyme schemes permitted.

Peiper's aesthetic theory, which was adopted by the poets of the Cracow Avantgarde, was constructivist and dominated by the concepts of order and rigor. In the fourth number of the first series of the *Switch,* Peiper declared, "the *Switch* decided to be the organ of construction. It wants to be a scaffold for bricklayers." The poet was a manipulator of reality, an organizer. Despite his enthusiasm for modern civilization, Peiper had no reverence for reality—either past or present, old or new, external or internal, necessary or accidental. The poet was the supreme master and his only concern was the final product, his work. Poetry and art were not imitations but absolute creations. They formed new worlds, new logic, and a new order. It is characteristic that of all contemporary artists, Peiper felt the closest affinity with some of the cubist painters like Ferdinand Léger, and with the French purists Ozenfant and Jeanneret. Peiper considered Léger to be the most representative among contemporary painters, and the elements that he particularly appreciated in Léger's paintings were order, composition, and logic. Peiper found similarities to his own aesthetic ideas in the theory of purism, in its stress on novelty, logic, and precision. The ideas of purification, of the reduction of an object to its essential features in an artistic work, appealed to Peiper because it led to an art that was maximally autonomous and independent from reality. Like his own, the purists' approach to art was rational and left no room for irrational elements or chance.

If we were to look for the sources of Peiper's aesthetics, they could most probably be found in French symbolist poetry, in the theories of Stephane Mallarmé and in Spanish ultraism. During his stay in Paris before the outbreak of the First World War, Peiper became acquainted not only with the newest European poetry but also with the aesthetic theories of the recent past. Adam Ważyk has discussed Peiper's literary sources and suggested that Peiper read Mallarmé's *Divagations,* a new edition of which appeared in Paris in 1912. Ważyk also pointed to another influence on Peiper's aesthetics, the thesis of Rémy de Gourmont, popular among young French writers at the time, that the mind had the ability to break established conceptual relationships—this was his famous theory on the dissociation of ideas. It is possible to see here a source for Peiper's belief in the ability of the poet to establish arbitrary conceptual relationships, and for his definition of metaphor. Although Peiper usually concealed the sources of his aesthetic views, he inadvertently revealed one of them when he published an article on new Spanish poetry. It appeared in the *New Art* in 1921 soon after Peiper's arrival in Poland, before he had formulated his own theories or founded his own magazine. Peiper discussed Spanish ultraism and especially the poetry of Vincente Huidobro, who influenced his own theory. The elements emphasized by Peiper were those that later found their way into his own poetics—the concept of poetic craftsmanship, the literariness of poetry and its autonomy with respect to reality, the cult of the sentence, and juxtaposition as a compositional principle.

The Stabilization of the Group

The last number of the first series of the *Switch* came out in October 1923, and the first issue of the second series appeared in May 1926. The lack of a magazine of their own for three years did not hinder the poets of the Cracow Avantgarde from writing and publishing, and the years from 1924 to 1926 proved fruitful. The young poets associated with Peiper not only assimilated his ideas but published their first volumes of poetry: Julian Przyboś's *Screws* (1925) and *With Both Hands* (1926), Jan Brzękowski's *The Pulse* (1925) and Jalu Kurek's *Heat Waves* (1925). In 1924 Peiper himself published *A* and *Living Lines.* When the *Switch* resumed its second series its artistic position was established. The group began to be known as the Cracow Avantgarde and Peiper earned the nickname of the "pope" of the Avantgarde. The first series of the magazine had gathered together many writers who were artistically heterogeneous, but the second series was more uniform. The magazine also attracted several visual artists, especially those connected with Polish constructivism, and published reproductions and articles by such artists as Władysław Strzemiński, Syriusz Korngold, and Kazimierz Podsadecki.

The presence of the constructivists in the *Switch* was not surprising. A group of constructivist artists had formed in 1924 around the magazine *Blok,* and their articles made it evident that their aesthetic premises were strikingly similar to those of the Cracow Avantgarde. The programmatic article of the first number of *Blok* opened in the following way:

> We definitively liquidate the expression of personal moods, the manner of externalizing oneself which still exists in modernistic art.
> Art should not be the manifestation of the individualistic intentions of the artist, but the result of the effort of the collectivity whose worker and inventor is the individual artist.
> Diverging individualistic experiments must be replaced by a complete discipline and continuity of work based on canons.
> Instead of inspiration, aesthetic contemplation—a conscious formative will requiring clarity and precision of forms. The requirements of contemporary life put the problem of economy in the forefront.[6]

The constructivists from *Blok* and the poets of the Cracow Avantgarde shared the same concept of construction as a unity incorporating both form and content, the

The covers of issues 1 and 6-7 of *Blok*

same belief in the autonomy and distinctness of each art form, the same attitude toward the artist as worker, and the same concept of the creative process as a product of consciousness and will. Both stressed logic, precision, and construction as the essential elements of a work of art. Their collaboration in the *Switch* as well as in constructivist publications shows that the Polish avant-garde poetic movement was not isolated, but had its counterpart in the most original and powerful movement in the visual arts of that period. The constructivist tendency of Polish art and poetry in the twenties reflected "the spirit of the time" and filled a gap left in Polish art and literature by the nineteenth-century artistic heritage. What can be seen as a return to positivism was a justified reaction against the overwhelming romantic tradition.

Despite the apparent unity of aesthetic front in the second series of the *Switch,* there were signs of growing diversity in the Avantgarde group itself. They were of a twofold nature—on the one hand young poets once under the spell of Peiper had matured, and did not always comply with the orthodox poetics of their leader. They were just about to break with Peiper, to formulate their own poetics and follow their own paths. On the other hand a new problem emerged, that of the political identity of the group, its position on the pressing social and political issues of the day. In the late twenties and early thirties, the political stand and involvement of the writer came into the foreground of all discussions in the Polish artistic and intellectual community. The political diversity of the *Switch* drew many criticisms. Peiper was not only aware of the political differences among his collaborators, but from the perspective of time he saw in it the main reason for the lack of popularity of the second *Switch:* "Although a greater artistic unity existed among the collaborators of the second *Switch* than of the first, the political differences were greater.

They extended from communism to national democracy. Almost all the nuances of political color were represented, at least by their inclinations. . . . The magazine that united the representatives of different political leanings . . . made the most mobile element of the intelligentsia indisposed toward it."

The problem was not only the political diversity of the group, it was also what was seen as a lack of social involvement on the part of the *Switch.* The recurring criticism directed against Peiper and the Cracow Avantgarde was the reproach of formalism and aestheticism, a disinterest in content and in the social issues of the day. The problem of the social utility of literature in general, and of proletarian literature in particular, was posed over and over again by the writers and critics of the period. Due to new political and social pressures the orthodox position of the Avantgarde became untenable in the thirties. Peiper himself and all the other poets of the *Switch* gave in to this pressure by writing socially committed poems, and yet they never conceded that poetry should become a tool of political propaganda. Nor did they renounce their formal interests. The poets of the Cracow Avantgarde expressed their stand on the issue of committed poetry in several articles and interviews, the most significant of which was the lengthy essay "Art and the Proletariat" written by Peiper in 1929.

Peiper's point of departure was the assertion that every great artist is socially useful. This idea implied that it is not the subject matter but a spirit of commitment that gives poetry a social character. Just as the modernity of a poet does not depend on whether he writes about airplanes and machines but whether he has the spirit of modernity, so "the poet can speak of everything or anything he wants, if he is a social type his poetry will be of a social nature and will perform a social function." Although terms such as *modernity, social nature,* or *social type* are not precise, they can be understood in the context of Peiper's writings and to a large degree they were synonymous for him. A poet moved by the spirit of modernity and "the social type" are both artists who are interested in what happens in the life around them, not only on its surface but in all its undercurrents; such an artist by his very nature cannot be indifferent toward the problems of political and social life that are part of reality. It was on these grounds that Peiper defended the *Switch* as socially committed, although the commitment was not based upon political slogans.

The most original aspect of his views on the subject was his belief that form can be revolutionary not only in the artistic domain but also in the social domain. The formal achievements and innovations of a poet were more important than the subject matter of his works. "A literary work can proclaim the most social slogans, and yet their author might not be a truly social type, which the form of his work will betray. Different kinds of form reveal the degree of social commitment of the artist." The ideology of a poet is best revealed in his workmanship, in the formal means he employs: "It is obvious that a new manner of constructing a work of art, a new artistic order opposed both to the conservatism of inherited rules and habits, and to the anarchism of whims that are not subordinate to any directing will, can be realized only by a truly social type of artist." Peiper went so far as to distinguish between socialist and nonsocialist poetic forms, and shocked his contemporaries by calling his distant rhymes socialist. As early as 1923 Peiper had replied to a reproach that the *Switch* was not concerned with the struggle for the liberation of man: "The liberated man interests the *Switch* only insofar as he expresses himself in a liberated form."

Peiper never conceded that poetry could become directly involved in politics or that the poet could write political proclamations of propaganda. For Peiper the artist was above all an artist, and art, like politics, required complete devotion and dedication. He completely disagreed with the demand made by political activists and the Communists in particular that literature should be for the masses, that poetry could and would be read by workers. Such a literature would have to adapt to the intellectual level and tastes of the workers, just as children's literature adapts to the level and interests of children, hence it could no longer be true to itself and its own standards. The only valid standard of a work of art was its artistic value, and the proletarian consciousness was incommensurable with that value. Peiper defended his elitist position with his famous slogan that the new poetry was just for "the twelve." He went on, "I agree that my literature must at the present moment be incomprehensible for the masses, but I also want to draw attention to the fact that because the alphabet is not accessible to an illiterate person, one cannot for this reason question the social usefulness of the alphabet."

As in his polemics with futurism, Peiper's position about proletarian literature reflected his general philosophy of art. For him, each domain of art or life should be faithful to its essential nature, and each human product should fulfill its function to the utmost. Since the world of literature differs in function from the world of objects or politics, they must have different laws. If the goal of objects is their usefulness, and of politics its efficiency, then the goal of a work of art is to evoke artistic emotions. Most often these various goals are incommensurable with one another. The arts have their own autonomous demands and rules, and the curbing or renunciation of these is unacceptable from the artistic point of view.

Dissemination of the Avantgarde Movement

An account of the history of the Cracow Avantgarde would be incomplete without a few words on the activities of the group after the closure of the *Switch*. The group's cohesiveness ended with the second series of the *Switch*, but the sense of belonging to the Avantgarde community lasted much longer. The poets of the group made several attempts to sustain the cause of the Avantgarde as a literary and artistic movement. It was to continue the Avantgarde "front" that in 1929 Przyboś and Brzękowski joined the constructivist artists Władysław Strzemiński, Katarzyna Kobro, and Henryk Stażewski to organize a group known under the initials *a.r. ("artyści rewolucyjni,"* "revolutionary artists"). Because the group could not afford its own magazine it relied on leaflets called "communications." Only two "communications" appeared, one in 1930 and another in 1932. Printed in an innovative graphic design, they contained articles on both contemporary art and poetry, and poems by Brzękowski and Przyboś appeared next to reproductions of works by Strzemiński, Kobro, and Stażewski. The *a.r.* also initiated its own series of books, and among the seven volumes it published were collections of poems by Przyboś and Brzękowski. Its most impressive undertaking, however, was the establishment in 1931 of a sizeable collection of modern art, including works by Arp, Léger, Schwitters, Vantongerloo, Calder, and Picasso, in Łódź, the industrial city south-

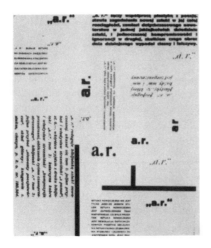

A page of the first "communication" of the *a.r.* group

The cover of the first issue of *l'Art contemporain—Sztuka Współczesna*

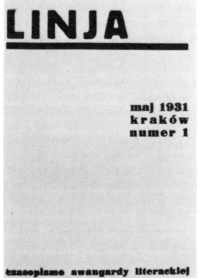

The cover of the first number of *Linia*

east of Warsaw. It was almost completely destroyed during the war. The last activity of the *a.r.* was the publication in 1936 of Brzękowski's theoretical essay, *Integral Poetry*. The formation of the *a.r.* group was remarkable primarily because it brought both poetry and the visual arts together to unify and strengthen the movement of the Avantgarde.

At the same time and with a similar impulse, Jan Brzękowski began the publication in Paris of a bilingual periodical, *Sztuka Współczesna–l'Art contemporain*. In addition to being a platform for both art and poetry, it was to be a bridge between the Polish Avantgarde and the avant-garde movements in the West. The magazine had three issues, which appeared in 1929 and 1930. All essays and articles were printed both in French and Polish, while the poetry was published only in translation, Polish poetry in French and French poetry in Polish. The range of poets and artists whose work appeared in *l'Art contemporain* was amazingly wide. Poems by the Polish poets Przyboś, Peiper, Kurek, Brzękowski, Czyżewski, and Ważyk neighbored those by Tzara, Desnos, Max Jacob, Arp, and Ribemont-Dessaignes; works by the Polish artists Zamoyski, Stażewski, Syrkus, and Strzemiński were next to those of Marcoussis, de Chirico, Masson, Mondrian, Balla, and Malevich, to name only a few. The essays on contemporary poetry and art also displayed great variety. A long essay by Brzękowski entitled "Kilometraż" ("Kilometrage," or "Mileage") was spread over all three numbers of the magazine and provided a general framework. It was an overview of the most important avant-garde tendencies, and aspired "to set a few posts designating the stages that have already been crossed." Brzękowski distinguished two basic tendencies in modern art, constructive and deformative: "Either the striving for concrete construction out of disconnected abstract elements, or the tendency toward the deformation of 'life' elements which has often reached the limits of the grotesque." He also discerned a third tendency, "literary symbolism" (with particular reference to the visual arts) that he evaluated negatively. He included in this third group such movements as futurism, expressionism, dada, and surrealism. The essay was intended to be—and to a certain extent was—a broad objective synthesis of modern art, but some of its statements and evaluations betrayed the strong influence of the aesthetic theories of the Cracow Avantgarde. Despite the inevitable bias of its editor, *l'Art contemporain* was an admirable initiative that for a short time fulfilled the role of a true international forum for Avantgarde art.

The continuing vitality of the Cracow Avantgarde was shown by the attempt of its poets to found a magazine in Cracow that would be a direct continuation of the *Switch, Linia (Line)* and its five numbers appeared between May 1931 and June 1933. Peiper refused to collaborate with the magazine. As Brzękowski lived in Paris and Przyboś in Cieszyn, Jalu Kurek became its editor. Although the ideological strength and artistic level of *Linia* could not be compared with the *Switch*, it was important in the history of the Cracow Avantgarde. Two essays in the first and second numbers, one by Kurek and another by Brzękowski, summarized Avantgarde activities of the past few years as well as reappraised the role and importance of the movement. The two authors differed significantly in their evaluations: while Kurek stressed the continuity between *Linia* and the *Switch*, Brzękowski considered the role of the *Switch* ("the laboratory of new ideas") to be finished.

He saw *Linia* as the next stage in the necessary evolution of Avantgarde aesthetics. "To proclaim the same ideas and to write in the same way as five or six years ago is not a proof of stability of convictions. Rather, it testifies to stagnation." Brzę-kowski also indicated which ideas of the *Switch* he considered to be outlived by time, "The city, the machine, metaphor, and poetic indirectness interest us already much less since they have become the property of all poets, and in them we exhausted the problems that were most interesting for us."

The next two numbers of *Linia* contained two more important essays, Przy-boś's "Form in the New Poetry" and Brzękowski's "The New Poetic Structure." Both concentrated on the problem of poetic construction and although they retained many of Peiper's ideas they diverged from his poetics by emphasizing the value of association as a possible method of construction. Przyboś realized the unorthodoxy of his attitude when he admitted that the use of association was motivated by his desire for maximum directness of self-expression and was therefore contradictory to the Avantgarde tenet of indirectness of expression. Przyboś stressed another aspect of associations, their value as a device that permits condensation of the content of a poem. Although Przyboś's definition of association did not exclude the demand for construction, his essay clearly indicated that his position on orthodox Avantgarde poetics had changed. Brzękowski's essay went further and openly opposed the postulate of construction, which he called an "outdated legend," and proposed to base poetic structure on much looser and more diversified principles than those recommended by Peiper. Like Przyboś he spoke above all of the importance of associationism. The two essays were significant because they indicated that the evolution of Avantgarde poetic theory and practice was away from the rigorous constructivism of Peiper—and it was unexpectedly approaching French surrealism, a movement most antithetical to the Cracow Avantgarde.

Linia was the last group venture of the Cracow Avantgarde, but despite their disagreements with Peiper, Brzękowski, Przyboś, and Kurek always identified with the Avantgarde until the end of their poetic careers. In this respect they were unlike the futurists. But even if not everything they wrote could be contained within the framework of Avantgarde poetics, they were and will remain in the history of Polish literature *the* poets of the Avantgarde.

TADEUSZ PEIPER

Although Peiper wrote voluminously on theory, he wrote surprisingly little poetry. Despite this disparity in volume, there is a very close correlation between Peiper's aesthetic theory and his poetic practice—indeed, the convergence between the two is so complete that it gives rise to the suspicion that either the theory was created to provide a commentary on the poetry, or the poetic practice was an illustration of the theory. Regardless of which point of view is correct, the interdependence of the two had important consequences for the evolution of Peiper's poetry, and was probably responsible for the deadlock that arose in it in 1929.

His poetry had two phases that corresponded to the two phases in his poetics. The two volumes of poems, *A* and *Living Lines (Żywe linie),* both published in 1924, belong to the first phase and share many of the themes of Peiper's early

A

1924

Napisał TADEUSZ PEIPER   Rysunkami ozdobił KISLING

The cover of
Tadeusz Peiper's *A*

The cover
of Tadeusz Peiper's
Six O' Clock! Six O' Clock!

theoretical writings published in the *Switch* and later included in the volume of collected essays *This Way (Tędy,* 1930). The second phase, represented by the major
theoretical work *The New Mouth (Nowe usta)* published in 1925, was given poetic
expression in the volume *Once (Raz)* that appeared in 1929, in fragments of unfinished narrative poems, and the last poem *For Example (Na przykład)* published in
1931. After this date Peiper wrote no more poetry. *Poematy,* the volume of his collected poems that came out in 1935, did not include any new poems, only revised
versions of poems written before 1931. Peiper wrote two plays, *Six O'Clock! Six
O'Clock! (Szósta! Szósta!,* 1925) and *Since He's Not There (Skoro go nie ma,*
1933), and two novels, *He Is 22 Years Old (Ma lat 22,* 1936), and *Christopher
Columbus, Discoverer (Krzysztof Kolumb odkrywca,* 1949). After World War
II Peiper was active only as a theater critic.

Thematically, many poems in the first two volumes of poetry are programmatic, and among these a large number could be described as autothematic. The
subject of "Eyes above the City" is its own genesis, and the poem illustrates Peiper's own creative process:

> At the summit of a factory chimney, the highest,
> I thought into a nest.
> I inhabited it together with my eyes,
>
> I live here as in a tower
> of cathedrals not yet erected,
> cathedrals of coal.
> Under the care of caressing pipes
> the hot smell of the labor and laughter of man
> rises toward me.
> The reverberation and chuckle I hear
> is a song in honor of the flesh of the earth.
> The smoke which flows around me
> is the victory of the soul of coal.
>
> I tear out my eyes;
> from the glass of curiosity I cut out wings
> and pin them to their sides;
> I take them in my hand,
> I throw them in the air;
> and my eyes,
> flying mirrors,
> circle above the city.

> Oczy nad miastem
>
> W szczyt komina fabrycznego, najwyższego,
> wmyśliłem gniazdo.
> Zamieszkałem w nim wraz z mymi oczyma
>
> Żyję tu jak w wieży
> niewzniesionych jeszcze katedr,

katedr z węgla.
Pod opieką pieszczących rur
wznosi się ku mnie
gorąca woń trudu i śmiechu człowieka.
Huk i chichot, które słyszę,
są pieśnią na cześć ciała ziemi.
Dym który mnie opływa
jest zwycięstwem duszy węgla.

Wyrywam oczy;
ze szkła ciekawości wycinam skrzydła
i przypinam im do boku;
biorę w dłoń,
rzucam w powietrze;
i oczy moje,
latające zwierciadła,
krążą ponad miastem.

The figurative nest from which the poet observes the industrial city is the product of his own mind ("I thought into" the nest—*wmyślić*—in the sense of "I projected myself into" it). Neither it nor anything else described in the poem has existence outside of the poet's imagination. Strictly speaking it is not even the imagination, since Peiper significantly used the expression "I thought in" instead of "I imagined." We are here witnessing a purely cerebral operation: the eyes that represent the senses are entirely subordinate to the intellect. In Peiper the senses are passive, only the poetic will pins wings on them. Closed in a tower, the poet needs the violent, symbolic act of tearing his eyes out and sending them into the world to see reality. The senses do not bring him sensations over which he has only partial control, as is the case with Baudelaire, for example—instead they are absolutely subordinate to his will, his visions are planned. The image of the tower further clarifies Peiper's attitude toward reality; despite his love for the present day and what is modern, Peiper was a poet in a tower, removed from reality and creating it within his own brain rather than perceiving it with his eyes. Also, Peiper realized that the reality about which he wrote did not yet exist ("cathedrals not yet erected"); the industrial reality of factories and mines was something of a fiction in the Poland of the 1920s and it still had to be imagined. The mining city and its accompanying images of reverberation, chuckling, smoke, smell, and laughter that rise toward the poet are only his own intellectual projection; it is not they that are the "song in honor of the flesh of the earth" because they do not yet exist. It is the poet who out of his own visions creates the song.

Peiper's concept of poetry as craft, and of the poet as craftsman, was reflected in his own poems by the recurrent image of the poet as a mason: "Mason on the scaffold, / how am I to dream, how am I to dream the world on a veil of roses" ("Murarz na rusztowaniu, / jak mam śnić, jak mam śnić świat na róż woalu") ("On the Scaffold" ["Na rusztowaniu"]). The key symbol in Peiper's poetry is the hand, which represents work. He believed that the creative process should resemble physical labor: "Words—give them to hands under custody." ("Słowa—dać je dłoniom pod straż"). Peiper elaborated a whole ethics of labor with both artistic and social implications. The opening poem-manifesto of the volume A is a call for physical work addressed to the whole nation. Paraphrasing a slogan used by politicians he said of Poland: "She was once from sea to sea, / today she must be from hand to hand" ("Była niegdyś od morza do morza, / dziś być musi od dłoni do dłoni") ("Postwar Appeal" ["Powojenne wezwanie"]). The "new man" is he who "has taken up residence in his own palm" (in the poem "City"), and the new poet is he who knows how to work with his hands: "The wind counts my fingers, pushes a hammer into my hand/ and pointing to the world, indicates the ovary of deeds" ("wiatr liczy moje palce, młotek pcha mi w rękę / i wskazując świat, wskazuje zalążnię czynów") ("On the Scaffold" ["Na rusztowaniu"]). In another poem of bizarre and almost surrealistic metaphors, a vein is described as carrying blood from the heart to the brain, finally to reach its destination, the hand, "the pink library of fingers" ready for action, for new words. In Peiper's last narrative poem *For Example*, the hands the protagonist sees in a tramway represent the whole of society and symbolize social conflicts.

Hands in the Tramway

Hands, hands, one hand, half a hand,
here on a basket a pale, emaciated hand,
there near the ceiling in a leather strap . . .
and here, in a glove, a soft little round wrist,
and there, in a sleeve, well, a hand-betrayal.
Not to see it! not to hear this cry of the hands!
Hands, hands, one hand, another hand,
fingers, fingers, fingers bent perpendicularly,
the back of the hand with pale blue veins,
and again this hand that is fleshy, meaty, soft,
and the one with a protruding vein as if battered on an anvil
and again another which wrings a glove,
no, not this one, that one, those thin fingers,
the hand on the basket, the hand of a faded woman,
yellow, fleshless, thickened joints,
the tip of the finger like a stump left after a battle.

Ręce w tramwaju

Ręce, ręce, jedna ręka, pół ręki,
tu na koszyku ręka wychudzona blada,
tam u sufitu w skórzanym orczyku. . .
a tu w rękawiczce przegub okrąglutki miękki,
a tam w rękawie, hi hi, ręka-zdrada.
Nie widzieć! nie słyszeć tego rąk krzyku!
Ręce, ręce, jedna ręka, druga ręka,
palce, palce, palce zgięte prostopadle,
wierzch ręki z niebieskimi bladymi żyłami,
i znowu ta ręka mięsista, mięsista, miękka,

i ta z żyłą wypukłą jakby obita na kowadle
i znowu ta co rękawiczkę łamie,
nie, nie ta, tamta, tamte chude palce,
ręka na koszyku, ręka wybladłej kobiety,
żółta, bezmięsna, zgrubiałe stawy,
koniec palca jak kikut pozostały po walce.

Many of Peiper's first poems settled accounts with the earlier literary movement, Young Poland. Peiper opposed their poetry of mood and feeling, and sought a new poetry of labor, of action—in place of the poetry of night, a poetry of daylight. The old accessories are either discarded or must serve new goals; the moon is no longer appreciated for its mystery, but for the light it gives:

> All night I walked through the city.
> From the blue ceiling I took off the moon
> and like a flashlight brought it down to earth.
> The poker of its light
> stirred up for me the shavings of day
> scattered on the street and buried in darkness.
>
> ["Among the Shavings of the Day"]

> Noc całą chodziłem po mieście.
> Z błękitnego pułapu zdjąłem księżyc
> i jak latarkę zniosłem go na ziemię.
> Kostur jego światła
> rozgrzebywał mi wióry dnia
> rozrzucone na ulicy i zasypane mrokami.
>
> ["Wśród wiórów dnia"]

Unlike most of the poets of Young Poland and even his own contemporaries, Peiper was a poet of the city, not of nature. His attitude toward the city was one of total approval, of appreciation of its particular life and beauty. Some of his descriptions of the city represent his best poetry.

Morning

> The dawn hangs on its first hours
> the gray sheet-iron of early light.
> Roofs glimmer,
> shadow on actions.
> The human shoulder still makes no movement, untouched
> by the nails of morning.
> The street sleeps, crushed under a cube of shadow.
>
> A moment, daybreak will drop, silver of the day swim
> across the city,

the man rises, looks at the world as at his son,
and with this
the city breaks into song, like a dreaming machine.

Rano

Rannych świateł szare blachy
rozwiesza świt na pierwszych swych godzinach.
Lśnią dachy,
cień na czynach.
Jeszcze nie drgnęło ramię człowieka,
                              nietknięte gwoździem rana.
Ulica śpi, sześcianem cienia przydeptana.

Chwila, brzask opadnie, srebro dnia przepłynie miastem,
człowiek wstanie, spojrzy na świat jak na syna,
a z tym
miasto się rozśpiewa, jak rozmarzona maszyna.

Peiper's ideological opposition to the poetry of Young Poland was expressed by the symbolic conflict of day and night, and was paralleled by a symbolic theme that runs through his poetry—the theme of man and woman, of poetry and love, presented in opposition to one another. For Peiper love and poetry were mutually exclusive, they were in irreconcilable conflict with each other. Poetry belonged to the world of day, action, and labor, love was associated with night, dreams, and passivity. Love was a prison, woman a "seamstress of dreams." Love was not inspiration but hindrance, the poet-worker cannot at the same time be a dreamer and lover and so chases woman away: "Go! Where they are building, the women wait behind the fence" (from "On the Scaffold"). In Peiper's poetry the god of work has replaced the goddess of love. Love is reduced to its physical aspect, and for man it is above all a physiological act, a moment of relaxation and release after the tension of a working day: "Love: / night in the shirt of silence after day in the harness of laurels" ("Miłość: / noc w koszuli z ciszy po dniu w uprzęży z wawrzynów") ("On the Scaffold").

But despite the apparent and almost programmatic opposition between love and poetry, the act of writing and the act of love are identified with one another in the poems that are the most intimate erotically. Many of Peiper's love poems are ambiguous and can refer either to love or to writing, to a woman or to a sheet of paper. The poem "Naked" is built upon this ambiguity, which is enhanced by the feminine gender of the Polish word for a sheet of paper.

Naked, in a cloud of bed-clothes, drawn into silence,
in the cradle of the night, night in the form of lips,
on the echoes of my words, works of black charm,
naked, on the echoes, when you will shine
a golden basin, pelvis, and in it the dust of pearls,
you, the sheet of paper which I will write on,

or perhaps before that I will throw it, kindling, onto the grate,
naked, glued into silence, be quiet and only steam.
More than your words I prize your whisper, the whisper of your body,
fragrance of your body, fragrance of slaughter and roses.

Naga

Naga, w obłoku z pościeli, wrysowana w ciszę,
w kołysce z nocy, z nocy o kształcie ust,
na echach słów mych, dzieł czarnego czaru,
naga, na echach, gdy będziesz błyszczała
złota miednica a w niej z pereł kurz,
ty, kartka papieru którą ja zapiszę
lub może wcześniej rzucę ją, podpał, na ruszt,
naga, w ciszę wklejona, milcz i tylko paruj.
Od słów twych wyżej cenię szept twój, szept twojego ciała,
woń twojego ciała, woń rzeźni i róż.

The poem reads like a love poem describing a naked woman until the sixth line,
where the poet addresses her as paper. There is an opposition between the passivity
of the woman and the sexual, active, creative force of the man; the woman is a passive receptor like the white and silent paper on which the man-poet will write his
words. She has no autonomy and is not even allowed to speak. The man's attitude
is ambiguous, and hesitates between rejection and destruction ("I will throw it . . .
onto the grate"), or creation and acceptance. The woman is both flesh, the cause of
defeat ("slaughter"), and an object of adoration (the "rose"). It has been noted
that Peiper's attitude toward love is ambivalent and oscillates between the two ex-
tremes of sanctification and degradation. His eroticism has been described as resembling the mystical tradition of the baroque, and also, paradoxically, an irrational
mixture of romanticism and modernism, "In the immanent poetics of Peiper, eroticism was a liberation of transcendence; in a world which was intentionally ration-
alized, ordered, and logically explainable, eroticism was the only possibility for the
liberation of 'mythical consciousness,' revealing what—to use Peiper's definition—was the 'the darkness of the subconscious.' "[7]
     Stylistically the most striking characteristic of the first two volumes of Peiper's
poetry is what he called the "blizzard of metaphors"when speaking of contemporary poetry. His metaphors are often farfetched and audacious, while reality is
twisted and distorted to fit the poetic image. The metaphors give the impression of
being painstakingly elaborated and they earned for their author the malicious
epithet of "the martyr of metaphors," and for his poetry the label of "metaphoritis."[8] Peiper's metaphors surprise because their motivation is entirely subjective.
Even the most imaginative reader has difficulty in perceiving the relationship of a
feminine leg to "the cruelty of sugar," or of a football to a "flying pantry of
sweets." Peiper's concept of metaphor excluded any realism—subjective or objective—and in its elaboration, the poet gradually removed it further and further from
the initial point of departure. By effacing the tracks of his work he created a metaphor that resists the reader's attempt to reverse the metaphoric process. Metaphor

acquires an autonomous life and is open to ambiguity. Karol Irzykowski pointed out the coded character of Peiper's poetry, describing it as a poetry with "a golden seal" similar to secret language.[9] The difficulty of Peiper's metaphors is aggravated because they are nonvisual and hard to imagine. One of Peiper's favorite procedures was to combine the concrete with the abstract. He either described a concrete object by means of an abstraction—a bird as "the red order of joy" ("Czerwony rozkaz radości"), the city as "a silence of shadow and purple" ("Miasto jest dzisiaj ciszą z cienia i fioletu")—or he made an abstraction concrete—the "pliers of love" ("obcęgi miłości") or "throats, the mines of fame of some poets" ("gardła, kopalnie sławy niektórych poetów"). The nonvisualness of his metaphors was intentional and consistent with his theory of the autonomy of each art—according to Peiper visual effects belonged to the domain of painting and not to poetry.

Another characteristic of Peiper's metaphors is the tendency of the metaphorical vehicle to outgrow the object to which it refers, particularly striking when Peiper writes about lungs as "the palace of vapor," fingers as a "library," or the arms as "chapels in meat." Contemporary critics spoke of the artificiality of Peiper's poetry, of the danger that a meager and trifling content was covered by a precious, ornamental style, and of the conflict between the frame and what filled it.[10] The preciosity and intricacy of his metaphors make his poetry surprisingly close to the mannerist poetry of the seventeenth century. The association is particularly relevant because he was a great connoisseur of Spanish baroque poetry and an admirer of Góngora, which explains in part why a large number of Peiper's metaphors refer to precious stones, gold, and silver. The dominant colors in his poems are white and silver, and the visual effects are almost always those of light, the glitter of metal, diamond, or crystal—"the silver of the day," "my walls of crystal," a "smile in gold." In a few poems Peiper compared himself to a goldsmith, his poetry to a piece of jewelry: "This day . . . if I set a sentence in it, / I would obtain a smile in gold" ("Ten dzień . . . gdybym dzisiaj wprawił weń zdanie, / otrzymałbym uśmiech w złocie") ("Letter" ["List"]). The concept of the poet as jeweler translates very well the precious quality of Peiper's poetry, and it also captures an important aspect of his creative effort, the honing of intricate metaphors.

The abundance of metaphors in Peiper's early poetry was responsible for the slack structure in many poems: "In the blizzard of complements, definitions and appositions coming one after another, the primary organizational principle disappears and the syntactical scheme of the poem is obliterated, becomes invisible."[11] The problem of structure was a thorny one in Peiper's theory; the author of *Nowe usta* thought he had resolved it in his own poems by resorting to rhetorical figures. The structure of his poems relied on sentences, and their composition was determined by the syntax, which in his poetry was the the main element of order. Peiper proudly asserted that almost every sentence in his first two volumes had a structure that until then had been unknown in Polish poetry. His early poetry vacillated between two styles, the descriptive and the rhetorical, with frequent overlapping of the two within a single poem. The following poem is a good example of the first type:

The Street

The street.
Two rectangles of brick over the rectangle of cement.
Hymn of the vertical.
Light slips through the tollgates of the roofs
to the thieves of day—punishment.
A tramway, peacock of tin, . . . gl-gl . . . gaggles its vanity.
Sun = only gasoline or vapor.
Man = bird of coal.

Ulica

Ulica.
Dwa prostokąty z cegły na prostokącie z betonu.
Hymn pionu.
Przez rogatkę z dachów światło się przemyca,
złodziejom dnia — kara.
Tramwaj, paw z blachy, ... gl-gl ... próżność swą rozgęgla.
Słońce = tylko benzyna lub para.
Człowiek = ptak z węgla.

The poem is typically schematic—a string of metaphors, with the literal equivalent of each given first, followed by its poetic vehicle. The poem's schematism is intensified by the use of equation marks in the last two lines, a common procedure in Peiper's early poetry; in addition to being purely descriptive, the poem is static.

To avoid being static, Peiper resorted to rhetorical figures as models of construction. Many of his poems use such stylistic devices as repetitions, contrasts, and parallels as well as the direct form of address—the speech, proclamation, and order—typical of the oratorical style. "Workers' Chorale" ("Chorał robotników"), one of the few socially committed poems in Peiper's early volumes, is based on several rhetorical figures and devices:

Shadow,
black bird,
the black bird of our sighs
sucks the golden udder, sucks the sun,
a black bird.

Ah, we want to have it.
We badly want to have it.
To have it!
To have it!
We want to have the golden udder.

For us your song,
for us your golden song,

for us—black—your golden song,
your song sculptures the world for us,
the world for us,
the world.

We look. We look? We steal with our eyes!
We steal, steal, steal
with our eyes.
Smoke has a knife,
the smoke of our sighs has a knife,
a knife,
it cuts the sun into pennies and distributes the pennies.
The smoke has a knife
and cuts.

Cień,
czarny ptak,
czarny ptak naszych westchnień
ssie złote wymię, ssie słońce,
czarny ptak.

Aaa, my chcemy je mieć.
My bardzo chcemy je mieć.
Mieć!
Mieć!
Złote wymię chcemy mieć.

Nam twój śpiew,
nam złoty twój śpiew,
nam czarnym złoty twój śpiew,
twój śpiew rzeźbi nam świat,
nam świat
świat.

Patrzymy. Patrzymy? Kradniemy oczyma!
Kradniemy, kradniemy, kradniemy
oczyma.
Dym ma nóż,
ma nóż dym naszych westchnień,
ma nóż,
kraje słońce na grosze i grosze rozdaje.
Dym ma nóż
i kraje.

The entire poem is built upon repetitions and contrasts: contrasts between black
and gold, shadow and sun, smoke and the knife, and repetitions of metaphorical
images within each stanza that are carried, in a modified form, from stanza to

stanza. Within each one the composition follows the musical movement of a song that starts in a low, subdued tone, then rises to a crescendo and finally dies out. In each stanza there is also a culmination point, in the first three it comes at the fourth line, in the last and longest stanza it occurs in the seventh. With the exception of the second stanza, the rising musical movement is accompanied by the development of metaphor—the lines repeat the initial image or statement, but with each repetition it becomes more developed, specific, and precise. In the first stanza the vague shadow in the first line assumes the specific shape of the black bird in the second line, and this in turn is associated with the emotion of dissatisfaction ("sighs") in the third line and is related to the speaking voice ("our"). The line then leads directly to the action of the fourth line. The second stanza, not based on a metaphor, but on an exclamation, is the exception to this pattern. The movement of a rising crescendo and the building up of images not only characterizes the individual stanzas but gives structure to the whole poem. The general movement is toward larger and larger units, and toward expansion of the initial situation—the number of lines in successive stanzas increases (5,5,6,9). The last stanza is the summation of all the previous motifs—the black bird becomes smoke with a knife, the golden song is concretized as money (the "pennies"), while the desire for possession and welfare turns into stealing, the imposition of economic equity (distributing the "pennies"), and the violent revolutionary act of cutting. The vocal, rhythmic structure reflects the spontaneous manner in which the poem was written. Peiper recounted that just before going to sleep, in a state of great emotional intensity, the poem imposed itself upon him primarily as a rhythm, which soon became transformed into syllables and words. "These words appeared as images, and nearly all the muscles of the mouth and throat that took part in their enunciation were moving; only the vocal cords did not sound and the lips did not open."[12] Peiper's confession is remarkable in the context of his attitudes toward the creative process and is totally inconsistent with his theories of willful artistic creation. Although Peiper was probably unaware of it, his account has a striking similarity to André Breton's description of the hypnagogic origin of automatic writing that was included in the first surrealist manifesto. It is symptomatic that Peiper did not publish this text until 1936, when his attitude toward poetry had changed and he was no longer writing poetry.

The writing of the "Workers' Chorale" marked the implementation of the concept of the "blossoming poem" that was introduced in *Nowe usta*; Peiper's third volume of poetry, *Once,* realized a second phase of this concept. The rhetorical structure of his early poetry opened the way for the "blossoming system," which emphasized structure based on repetitions. The "Workers' Chorale" had used repetition in a manner similar to that of the poems in *Once,* that is, repetitions that build up an image or event by expansion into wider and wider circles. Although Peiper's "blossoming system" does not use the forms of direct address that were frequent in his earlier rhetorical poems, their structure based upon an exposition followed by a fuller development of particular parts shows the same concern about clarity of speech. This trait was characteristic of his oratorical style. The poem that opens the volume *Once* is a good example of the blossoming system, and, in addition, represents Peiper's happy identification with the city, its flora, and life.

Flower of the Street

Silver. Street. Rally of colors. Sidewalks.
Women. Straw sheafs of fragrances. Dresses of looking glasses.
Sun on rainbowlike threads of an invisible stem.
A shop window. A car. I who do not ride in it.

The skin of the street envelops the car's dress coat in silver;
The sidewalks—dreaming—lie on women's dresses.
A shop window fertilized with saliva of light
throws on my back the proclamations of the sun.

Silver, skin of the street, spatters on the sides of a car
carrying happiness fat as a wheel.
Women's dresses, under straw sheafs of fragrance, looking glasses
of dreams of bottles and a liquid world
reflect the sidewalks on themselves, which gaily
the noon hour has sowed with colors.
The sun has put itself out for sale
in the shop window and pours golden salt
onto my back, greedy holder of warmth.

I tear off that sun from the shop window,
I think it into the straw sheafs of women's fragrance,
I wrap it in sidewalks torn off from women's dresses,
I pour it into the silver, then with the car into my own head
and, taking home this unnamed flower of the street
I paste it in the herbarium of smiles on the first page.

Kwiat ulicy

Srebro. Jezdnia. Wiec barw. Chodniki.
Kobiety. Chochoły z woni. Suknie ze zwierciadeł.
Słońce na tęczujących nitkach niewidzialnej łodygi.
Okno sklepowe. Auto. Ja, który nim nie jadę.

Skóra jezdni osnuwa srebrem frak auta.
Chodniki marząc leżą na sukniach kobiecych.
Wystawa sklepowa zapłodniona śliną światła
odezwy słońca rzuca mi na plecy.

Srebro, skóra jezdni, pryska w boki auta,
wiozącego radość tłustą jak koło.
Suknie kobiet, pod chochołami z woni zwierciadła
butelkowych snów i ciekłego świata,
odbijają w sobie chodniki, które wesoło
południowa godzina barwami obsiała.
Słońce na sprzedaż się wystawia
w oknie sklepowym i złotą solą
sypie w moje plecy, chciwe ciepła imadła.

Zrywam to słońce z wystawy sklepowej,
wmyślam je w chochoły z woni kobiecej,
owijam w chodniki z kobiecych sukien zdarte,
wlewam w srebro, potem z autem w własną głowę
i, wziąwszy do domu ten nienazwany kwiat ulicy,
w zielniku uśmiechów wlepiam go na pierwszą kartę.

The poem has four stanzas of four, four, nine, and six lines, respectively. The first stanza, in a rapid, telegraphic style, evokes a busy city street in the summer. With one exception, only nouns or elliptical sentences are used. The only verb, in the last line, introduces the speaker in an ironic and ambiguous manner. He is both part of the described scene—for a brief moment the possibility is held out that he might be in a car, not on the sidewalk—and at the same time removed from the scene because the verb is negated. The second stanza is built of three sentences and four verbal forms that connect the separate elements in the first stanza—the street and silver are associated with the car, the sidewalks with women's dresses, and the sun with the shop windows and the narrator. The disconnected objects take concrete form in three images, and the position of the narrator-observer is more specific. The third stanza is more dynamic than the first two, the three images are fully developed, and they acquire more speed and active movement (the silver spatters, the car carries, the women's dresses reflect, the noon sows, and the sun pours golden salt). In addition to these external, concrete, visual images the third stanza introduces a psychological dimension. The passenger in the car, referred to as "happiness fat as a wheel," evokes feelings of wealth and smugness; the social sensitivity of the poet is also hinted at. The women's dresses like "looking glasses of dreams of bottles and a liquid world" provide a Freudian image of sexual desire. The narrator's back, a "greedy holder of warmth," is a more direct confession of the speaker's curiosity, his happiness, his desire to catch the warmth and the particular quality of this noon hour on a busy street. This last image gives the impulse to the autothematic fourth stanza that brings all the elements back together, but this time as material for the future poem. The distance between the poet and the speaker of the poem disappears. All the verbs are now in the first person singular, and metaphorically they describe the successive stages of the poetic process: experience (tearing off the sun), imagination (thinking it into the straw sheaves), metaphorization (pouring it into the silver), memorization and composition (pouring it . . . into my own head), and at last the writing itself (pasting). Like the flower of the title, the poem has developed from a bud into a full blossom that now can be put into the herbarium of poetry.

The gradual development and complication of the images is in direct correlation to the greater and greater enlargement of syntactic units: from nouns and elliptical sentences in the first stanza, through simple sentences in the second, to compound and intricate sentences in the third, and—finally—to the single complex sentence of the fourth stanza, a sentence composed of one subordinate and six coordinate clauses. As in Peiper's earlier poetry the sentence is the fundamental structural unit of the poem. In all the blossoming poems the complexity of the imagery is dependent on the complexity of the sentence, and it follows all the

intricacies of their contours. The structure of the blossoming poems requires in-
cremental repetitions as the larger units are gradually built up, and the effect is
that of a villanelle. A rhyme scheme is used, and although it does not exactly fit the
villanelle pattern, the cumulative effect of the repetitions is similar. Often the structure of the blossoming poems, the gradual unfolding of an image or vision, requires
considerable length: "Flower of the Street" is the shortest, others vary from 42 to
148 lines. The length of individual parts in each poem as well as its compositional
pattern differ—characteristically, the initial image or event is gradually developed
and then these developments and the poem as a whole display a new dynamic
quality. The poems in *Once* are less static than those of the first two volumes, and
more often they are centered around an event rather than an object or concept. In
this respect "Flower of the Street" is an exception, unless we agree that its subject
is not the noon hour and the street but rather the creative process itself.

In the final phase of Peiper's poetry—the first episode of which is the blossoming poems—the poems are longer and they almost always have a plot. Thematically
they are similar to the earlier poems. Aside from the absence of programmatic
poems, the main subjects remain poetic craft, sexual love, and especially social
issues—the plight of workers, unemployment, inflation, political persecution—which
now became more prominent in his poetry. In his earlier poetry social themes were
never associated with the speaker or lyrical subject of the poems; in the late poetry
social themes frequently include a personal problem, that of the poet's role and
involvement in the social struggle. In one of his later poems, "A Sunday Journey"
("Wyjazd niedzielny"), Peiper referred to his social commitment by saying, "This
is the wordman's second second the second half." The line indirectly suggests a certain split between the two commitments, to art and to social causes. In the same
poem an encounter with the unemployed leaves the poet with a feeling of guilt,
because aside from his poetry ("words") he does nothing to help them. A similar
internal conflict is the subject of Peiper's last, long narrative poem, *For Example,*
whose young protagonist is torn between his artistic inclinations, his sexual boister-
ousness, and his sympathy for the workers' cause. His recurring question, which
also ends the poem, is "What to do?" His indecision, justified in the poem by his
youth, probably echoed Peiper's own conflict. Characteristically the poem is psychological and alternates between third person narrative and internal monologue.
If the social orientation of Peiper's later poems reflected a general tendency of
Polish poetry in the 1930s, it also curiously coincided with the internal line of
development of Peiper's own poetic style, of the evolution of his poetry away
"from diffuse metaphoricalness . . . toward a distinct situationality." [13] The general
tendency of Peiper's later poetry toward a more realistic, even documentary poetry
went hand in hand with its growing social orientation; it would be difficult to
separate the two in terms of cause and effect.

Peiper considered his poem *For Example* a departure from all his previous
poetry. He attributed this to the subject matter of the poem and to its timeliness,
which he believed predetermined the straightforward realism of the poem and its
structure, which is based on chronology of events and the psychology of the protagonist. This statement is true when considered from the point of view of Peiper's
earlier attitude toward experience and reality in poetry. And yet, rather than a

departure, the poem could be considered a consequence, if only one of several possible consequences, of the evolution of Peiper's poetry over a span of fourteen years. Peiper's poetry was the fullest realization of his poetics, and with the exception of his very last poems there is no discrepancy between them. He protested when he was considered exclusively as a theoretician at the expense of his poetry, and he denied that his theoretical writings were prescriptions on how to write poetry. Yet it is impossible to avoid the overwhelming impression that his poetic practice was to a large extent determined by his theories, and that the theories are the basis of both the virtues and shortcomings of his poetry. The evolution of Peiper's poetry can be seen as the result of an internal contradiction in his poetic tenets. The contradictory requirement of rigid structure with a simultaneous total freedom in the juxtaposition of metaphorized sentences led, as we have seen, to the idea of structural supports and the use of rhetorical figures. These were the direct antecedents for the concept of the blossoming system, which in turn, because of its structural properties, veered toward a more narrative plotlike poetry that by its very nature was more realistic. By asserting that his last poem was a departure from his earlier poetry, Peiper tried to ignore this contradiction in his poetics and its consequences in his own poetry.

The narrative form and realistic style of Peiper's late poems can be explained by the internal dynamics of his poetics, but they might also have a deeper psychological cause. Peiper's general approach to poetry, both in theory and practice, it seems to me, had its deepest motivation in his own personality. It was Peiper the man who was behind Peiper-the-poet and Peiper-the-theoretician. This might appear paradoxical for a writer who more than any other fought against the concept of poetry as the expression of feelings, and who maintained that it is not the living self—or identity—that matters, but the writing self. A writer, also, who rejected all demands for sincerity in poetry, and for whom the only truth important in poetry was the truth of poetic craft. It is difficult to find another Polish poet so adamant in dissociating personal experience from the act of writing poetry. And yet, paradoxically, one of the most illuminating commentaries is his autobiographical novel, *He Is 22 Years Old.* Peiper wrote the novel after his last poem, *For Example,* had been published in January 1931, and it is telling that he turned to the novel when he had stopped writing poetry or, most probably, could not write poetry any longer. His novel was a thinly disguised autobiography. Why the poet whose greatest effort for many years had been to build a thick wall of obscure metaphors around his own person turned to intimate autobiography is best explained by the psychological notion of self-repression.

The young protagonist of Peiper's novel, Ewski, is tortured by the constant suppression of his own feelings and his inability to manifest them. The personality trait leads him to adopt secretiveness as a conscious, willful manner of behavior and an attitude toward life: "One has to bury what is dear in life deeply inside oneself. Not to show it, not to speak of it. . . . You will be quiet, you will be silent. You will hardly be, citizen Zeron." Peiper the theoretician wrote of "pudor poetae," of the "shyness of feelings" and the need to disguise them behind pseudonyms. Self-repression on the psychological plane was willfully translated into an aesthetic theory of self-repression. However, the need for self-expression that was so severely repressed in his poetry reasserted itself and returned with all its force in the novel. The same kind of self-revelation in his poetry was impossible for Peiper, since this would mean disloyalty to his own ideal of poetry. To avoid violating his integrity and to remain faithful to his principles the poet needed another form of expression, and the novel best suited these needs. In his poetry there were already indications of this future evolution. In comparison with the early poetry of *A* and *Living Lines,* the blossoming poems of *Once* not only made use of a realistic narrative mode but also willingly adopted the first person singular pronoun. And the poetic speaker is much more prominent in these poems than before. The last poem, *For Example,* is to a considerable extent a reflection of the author's dilemma. Peiper's silence as a poet after 1931 can be seen as the final, tragic consequence of a conflict that from the very beginning was close to the source of his creativity. This conflict was best described by Karol Irzykowski, a contemporary of Peiper and also the most astute critic of his poetry. In a passage referring to the whole of Polish Avantgarde poetry he wrote, "The poetry by the young poets is self-conscious to a much higher degree than older poetry, hence the internal inhibitions, self-criticism. . . . Inside, for someone who knows how to read between the lines, there takes place the silent creative-noncreative tragedy of the young generation." [14] The organic link that united Peiper's theory and poetry resulted in a deadlock for his own creativity.

With Peiper the theory of construction had been pushed to and beyond its limits. By stressing the antirealism of the poem's frame of reference, by affirming it need have no basis or analogy in the recognizable world, and by pushing it beyond the boundaries of human psychology, he cut the theory off at its roots. He was an extremist, perhaps a fanatic, but it was his own poetry that suffered most of all. The theories remained, coherent, full of interest, Peiper's main achievement. Others were able to make fruitful use of them, and the best poetry was written by other members of the group.

JULIAN PRZYBOŚ

Karol Irzykowski's words described the creative tragedy of Tadeusz Peiper, but they could not be applied to the Avantgarde's prominent poet, Julian Przyboś. Przyboś wrote poetry from 1919, when he was nineteen years old, until his death in 1971. One reason why Przyboś's creative sources never diminished was his protean ability to change and renew his poetic style throughout his life. He was able to adapt to new experiences, new realities, and new poetic models without denying his own poetic temperament. The changes in Przyboś's poetic style were not contradictions or betrayals of his earlier style, but a natural expression of his new poetic ego. Very likely Przyboś's weakness in theory provided him with a freedom that Peiper did not have—the freedom of not having to be loyal to and consistent with his own theories. And there was another reason for Przyboś's poetic prolificacy, a never-quenched desire to write the perfect work. This desire was somewhat reminiscent of Mallarmé's desperate pursuit of "l'Oeuvre," despite the differences in their poetic temperament and style. The idea of the perfect work and the simultaneous realization of its impossibility—of its purely hypothetical nature—appears and reappears in all of Przyboś's writings. In the preface to the first volume of his collected essays he confessed, "I would give all this book of prose for one poetic work, not yet written, which would satisfy me fully." [15] At the same time he realized that the fulfillment of this desire was contradictory to his nature as poet, "since having written [a perfect poem] I would stop to live by poetry, that is, by the thirst and hunger for the final, perfect poem." [16]

Unlike Peiper or Brzękowski, Przyboś was not a theoretician. His essays were often reactions to the work of other poets, writers, and artists, but most of all they were notes on the margin of his own poetry, and the direct outcome of his poetic experience. "I wrote them on the side of my poems, on the margin, on the second or further plane of poetry, which I have always considered to be my first thing." [17] Przyboś's theoretical writings do not propose an original poetic program but reflect on the various stages of his own poetic development. In his long career Przyboś changed his ideas on poetry as well as his poetic alliances several times. Initially he was a faithful adept of Peiper, but a couple of years after the closure of the *Switch* in 1927 he turned against the master in an almost adolescent rebellion, moving close to the associationism of French surrealism. Przyboś's views on poetry oscillated between two poles. On the one hand were the ideas of rigor, discipline, and structure inherited from Peiper; on the other hand was the acceptance of associationism and the need for visualization, what might be called the decerebralization of Peiper's metaphor. The duality of these poetics was best rendered by the title of Przyboś's collection of essays, *Line and Murmur (Linia i gwar,* 1959); the rigid, structural geometry of the line was opposed to the unstructured chaos of the sound of murmuring, or humming. Przyboś found his own poetic formula in a happy balance between the rigor of Peiper's poetics and the freedom of surrealism. Out of this balance grew some of his best poetry, and especially the volume characteristically entitled *Equation of the Heart (Równanie serca,* 1938). In his earliest articles published in the *Switch,* Przyboś was entirely under the spell of Peiper, and like Peiper, stressed the importance of rigor and economy in poetry and rejected both emotionality and the idea of poetic inspiration. Przyboś spoke of pure poetry and lyricism that, like pure painting and sculpture, relied on relationships between various elements and was not a conglomeration of personal confessions. Poetry was not description but a purposeful organization of poetic vision. This poetry was the expression of a new despiritualized attitude toward the world, and it reduced the essence of the world to mechanical events. Where Peiper spoke of the "shyness of feelings," Przyboś referred to the discipline and masculine dignity of laconism. Sneering at the "poetic infantilism" of contemporary Polish poetry, Przyboś called for a new poetry of things: "Be men. Be ashamed of the childish unruliness of feelings in poetry. Don't cry. Don't be buffoons. The age of reinforced concrete stretches out its hands for your poems. Be worthy of the active will of the period, which shapes the man who is fortified by the awareness of his greatness." [18]

The first two volumes of Przyboś's poetry, *Screws (Śruby,* 1925), and *With Both Hands (Oburącz,* 1926), grew out of this despiritualized and materialistic outlook. The prevailing themes are the city, technology, and physical labor, which are presented not as static realities but as a clash of forces, an enormous explosion of energy. Przyboś's early poetry is tense and dramatic; reality is presented as a dynamic interplay of geometrical figures set into rapid, often frantic and violent,

The cover of Julian Przyboś's *With Both Hands*

motion. Nothing is quiet, the poems are full of noise and movement. The sense of hearing and sight are assaulted by verbs, participles, adjectives, and nouns, almost all active and violent and following rapidly one after the other. Blocks, tubes, cones, cylinders, spheres, rectangles, triangles, squares, and circles all tremble, hit, drill, push, break, gallop, roll, honk, or peal in a vertiginous tempo. As the title of one of his early poems indicates, it is a *perpetuum mobile.*

The most striking feature of Przyboś's early poetry is its pathos in tone, vocabulary, and imagery. The tone is elevated and often similar to a hymn or ode in praise of labor, technology, and progress. In his metaphors Przyboś tended toward hyperbole, heroics, and glorification. His workers are titanic, technology is exaggeratedly powerful. Much of the effect of the early poetry comes from the vocabulary, from words that are strong and loud both semantically and phonetically. To give his words even more resonance Przyboś relied on the forceful beating rhythm of a hexameter and regular rhymes usually in couplets. A good example of Przyboś's early poetry, both in subject matter and in style, is the poem "Roofs" in which the modern city grows into mythic dimensions:

Roofs

Higher!

Intricate surfaces, pyramids of floors,
whirling surfaces, rising surfaces,
image-forming.
Turning
of massive space,
cramps
of cities being born.

In the living pathos of construction, in a geometrical dimension
the cubic soul of the capitals climbs, growing.
It growls with elevators of momentum, hangs on a jack,
it will jump! On radio towers it will liberate thought from matter.

From under the convulsive network of cables it spreads,
bursts with a fury of lines, the perpendicularity of the plummet,
with the triumph of height it stretches the vault's arch,
like delight it tickles boundlessness with a lightning rod's needle.

It hangs tops in clouds like enormous pendulums,
it sways—stops—settles in the forms of the angle-rafters.
Higher! With the bars of my arms I will push aside the throats of the streets,
set the tension with fingers like the brace of a rheostat.

The huge colossus of the city will flash like electricity,
will jump like a wall into the air and swell with space,
blow up all the squares, burst the structure of mass,
thrust out the circle of infinity like a cast-iron span.

Into the foundation,
the ferroconcrete of berths
topple
with the thrusts of the vortex!

Already
the speed
of the toothed cogs
of wheels
bores into the belly of factories.
It tears
down
along the grooves
of shafts.

With the whistle of vibrating drills,
the biting tooth of a pickaxe,
a spark,
with a mechanical head,
pressure: a million atmospheres,
strike
in the globe's central
nerve!

And again
with the simplicity of set forms
rise to the clouds, rhythmic apparatus.
Above the red workshops of foundries, above the undulating sheet-iron,
with the reverberation of six o'clock sirens of factories
flow into the steely dusk of the sky and the distances of stars brought nearer:
into the roofs.

Dachy

Wyżej!

Płaszczyzny kręte, piramidy pięter,
płaszczyzny wirujące, płaszczyzny wznoszące,
figurotwórcze.
Masywnej przestrzeni
skręt,
rodzących się miast
kurcze.

W żywym patosie konstrukcji, w geometrycznym wymiarze
wspina się, urastając, sześcienna dusza stolic.
Warczy windami rozmachu, zawisa na lewarze,
wskoczy! Na wieżach radia z materii myśl wyzwoli.

Spod konwulsyjnej sieci drutów się rozprzestrzenia,
bucha wściekłością linij, prostopadłością pionu,
triumfem wyniosłości rozpręża łuk sklepienia,
jak rozkosz łechce bezmiar igłą piorunochronu.

W chmurach zawiesza wierzchołki jak gigantyczne wahadła,
kołysze się — przystaje — osiada w formach narożnic.
Wyżej! Sztabami ramion roztrącę ulic gardła,
prężność rozkręcę palcami jako korbami opornic.

Jak elektryczność błyśnie, podskoczy murem w górę,
przestworem napęcznieje olbrzymi miasta kolos;
rozniesie wszystkie place, rozsadzi mas strukturę,
wypnie, jak lane przęsło, nieskończoności koło.

W fundament,
w żelazobeton posad
ruń
sztychami wiru!

Już
pęd
zębatych trybów
kół
wwierca się w fabryk brzuch.
W dół
rwie
rowami
szybów.

Świstem drgających świdrów,
oskardów ciętym kłem,
skrą,
mechanicznym łbem,
ciśnieniem: milion atmosfer,
uderz
w globu centralny
nerw!

I znów
prostotą zakrzepłych form
wydźwignij się do chmur, miarowy aparacie.
Nad hut czerwone hale, nad falujące blachy,
kiedy godzinę 6-tą syreny fabryk odhuczą,
płyń w zmierzch stalowy nieba i gwiazd zbliżone dale:
w dachy.

Przyboś's city is a technological marvel, a fantastic generator of energy. The poet's exalted attitude toward the city betrays the outsider: only someone born and raised in the countryside, for whom the city was a total novelty, could react to it in this way. For Peiper the city was his natural environment, for Przyboś the city was a mythical colossus, a pyramid whose surfaces rise vertiginously, whose towers and lightning rods reach into the sky. In Przyboś's attitude there is much of the adolescent's enthusiasm for everything new and powerful, his youthful ambition is expressed in the wish to raise upward: the word "higher" is repeated twice in the poem as an order. Every element in the city strives upward—it rises, climbs, jumps, and hangs in the clouds. The city is a living organism with a soul, belly, and nerves. The anthropomorphization of the city and objects does not represent their functionality, rather it places them in a context that is purely aesthetic. When Przyboś writes that an elevator "growls" or a lightning rod "tickles," he is contemplating technology from an artistic, nonfunctional point of view. Man himself sets the colossus of the city into motion—his control of electricity, the source of energy, and his power burst the old structures of tradition and break God's circle of infinity.

In the early poetry of Przyboś, objects such as batteries, tramways, or cities are described as living creatures, while man is most often represented in terms of a machine. The poet's dehumanized concept of man is related to the dehumanization of emotions and is in keeping with the Avantgarde demand for masculine brevity in poetry. Conventional emotions such as joy or sadness are extremely rare in Przyboś's poetry, even more rare is their direct expression. Most often the current of emotion is transferred to inanimate objects and nature; in the poem "Roofs" it was the dynamics of a modern city, its streets and buildings. Another typical feature of Przyboś's style, a correlative of this despiritualization of man, is the expression of emotion through gestures and external activities. In "Roofs" the power of the poet-demiurge is expressed by comparing his arms and fingers to bars and a crank, by his effort to push streets aside and establish a level of pressure. In another poem woodcutters become like the wood on which they work:

> The clumsy squares of the hand
> stiffen in the knotty clamp,
> dense wrists clatter,
> the furious trunks wriggle.

> ["The Woodcutters"]

> Prężą się w zworze sękatej
> niezdarne dłoni kwadraty,
> klekocą zwarte przeguby,
> wiercą się wściekłe kadłuby.

> ["Cieśle"]

To project the feeling of boredom, Przyboś describes external gestures: "On the stairs, floors, along the walls of corridors / I loiter and knock, and boredom grinds me / in the wall and in lime" ("Po schodach, piętrach, wzdłuż ścian korytarzy / szwendam się i obijam, i nuda mnie miele / w murze i wapnie") ("Each Day" ["Co dzień"]).

One of the key images in the early poetry of Przyboś is the circle and wheel, symbol of constant movement and one of man's most important technological inventions. In Polish, both the circle and wheel are designated by a single noun and in many poems there is a playful ambiguity of the two that disappears in English translation:

> In rushing speed in pushing speed
> Turns of the circle rims of wheels
> Constant and well-made sliders
> Turning wheels
> Turning wheels
>
> Long-range distances
> Of the circle.

["Perpetuum Mobile"]

> W rwącej szybkości prącej szybkości
> Obroty koła obręcze kół
> Suwaki ustawiczne i składne
> Obracające się koła
> Obracające się koła
>
> Dystanse dalekonośne
> Koła

["Perpetuum mobile"]

If the wheel is a distant reflection of the circle, there is nevertheless a tension and opposition between the two. The circle belongs to the order of tradition and religion, symbolizing God's perfection, while the wheel is a symbol of man, his inventiveness and labor. In the modern technological world of Przyboś God is replaced by man, the turning of the circle is replaced by the rims of the wheel. The rushing wheels of machines represent Promethean rebellion, and the dominant movement is upward, toward the sky, the sun, the Circle:

> On winged wheels set in powerful motion,
> toward distance spread out by the attack of sky-high roads
> pushing in ceaseless labor, hard and constant
> we go, moved by mechanical breathing.

["On Winged Wheels"]

> Na uskrzydlonych kołach w pęd wprawieni potężny,
> ku rozpostartej dali szturmem dróg niebosiężnych
> prąc w niewstrzymanym trudzie, twardzi i ustawiczni
> jedziemy, poruszani oddechem mechanicznym.

["Na uskrzydlonych kołach"]

The early poems show a desire to transcend the human condition, to raise man to the status of God. The new hero is as mythical and colossal as the new technological world in which he lives and his power resides in reason, will, and self-discipline. He is both Sisyphus and Prometheus rising to the sky in defiance of the gods.

The Avantgarde nature of Przyboś's first two volumes consisted primarily in their subject matter and choice of themes. The next three volumes—*From Above (Sponad,* 1930), *In the Depth a Forest (W głąb las,* 1936), and *Equation of the Heart (Równanie serca,* 1938)—realized a specific concept of poetic language that was a variant of the more general poetics of the Cracow Avantgarde. Like Peiper, Przyboś considered the ability to create metaphors the essential trait of poetry; but although he made it the basis for his poetics, his concept of metaphor differed considerably from that of the author of *Nowe usta.* Przyboś criticized Peiper's metaphors for being a game of concepts, a juxtaposition of abstractions without appeal to the visual imagination. He preferred visual metaphors more immediate in their effect than the very literary metaphors of Peiper that required a preliminary intellectual understanding to be appreciated. And yet a great number of Przyboś's metaphors are, like Peiper's, nonvisual and intellectual. In his excellent book on the Cracow Avantgarde, Janusz Sławiński[19] explained Przyboś's criticism of the "unimaginability" of Peiper's metaphors as an objection primarily against the arbitrariness with which Peiper treated the established semantic possibilities of words. Behind Przyboś's criticism was the conviction that metaphor should have its motivation in language, that its play of meanings should be self-explanatory in the context of linguistic meanings common to both poet and reader.

Many of Przyboś's metaphors contain a violation of existing linguistic norms and their effect comes from a clash between the expected and the unexpected use of words but, unlike the metaphors of Peiper, "the moment of surprise is here introduced not only by the 'arbitrary' departure from semantic custom, but by the possibility of bringing this 'arbitrariness' back into custom."[20] In the metaphor, "The wind opened the hills in astonishment" ("Wiatr wzgórza z podziwu otworzył"), the reader expects the phrase "to open the eyes in astonishment," and the substitution of "hills" for "eyes" is the source of the metaphor. In the passage, "Return from your journey! / You have wandered enough in express horizons" ("Wróć z podróży! / Dość już tłukłeś się w pośpiesznych widnokręgach"), the reader expects the word *trains* but finds instead *horizons,* which not only creates a metaphor but also gives the poem much broader scope. A similar substitution is even more visible, though more complex in its implications, in the comparison, "Like a year the table flowed by over the chair" ("Jak rok stół nad krzesłem upłynął"), where the use of *like* explicitly points to the poetic procedure being used. The verb *to flow by* (upłynąć) is commonly used in expressions referring to the passage of time, such as "a year flowed by" or more commonly "time flowed by." In Przyboś's metaphor, however, the word has been unexpectedly applied to a concrete object without any temporal dimension, a table—specifically the writer's table. As the poem is about writing and memory, the association of time with the table—activated by the verb *flowed by*—is also motivated by the context of the poem.

One of the most common devices used by Przyboś in his poetry is the restoration of literal meaning to a hackneyed metaphor. The most frequently quoted

The cover of Julian Przyboś's *From Above*

example is "The streets of Warsaw, / paved with good intentions, left me" ("Odeszły mię ulice Warszawy / dobrymi chęciami brukowane") where the more general word *road* is replaced by the specific *Warsaw streets*, which in turn restores the literalness of *paved* without excluding its figurative meaning. Przyboś's procedure is paradoxical and his metaphor is the result of a "demetaphorization" of a metaphor already embedded in language and accepted by common usage. While in a "normal" metaphor the literal meaning provides a background against which there is a play of new secondary meanings activated by the context, in Przyboś's metaphors a reverse process occurs: the figurative meaning recedes into the background, while the very literalness of expressions becomes the source of the metaphor. The same method is employed when the poet uses a recognizable syntactic pattern but fills it with words not usually used within the pattern. To be understood the new construct requires the infringement of syntactic rules. In the sentence, "The air under my breath was not moved into a bird" ("powietrze pod mym tchnieniem nie wzruszyło się w ptaka"), the verb *to be moved* is used in an unusual syntactic situation that imposes a new meaning on the verb, "to change into," "to be transformed into." This is facilitated by the etymology of the expression "to be moved (emotionally)" from the verb "to move"; the verb denoting emotion contains the notion of movement, of stirring and change, in its own etymology. Przyboś's metaphor violates the syntactic order of this verb (by putting the unexpected preposition "into" after it) and brings out its concealed possibilities.

It should be emphasized, however, that the new meanings Przyboś gives to established expressions—whether by metaphorizing a word, or literalizing a metaphor—do not entirely supersede the old meaning. Much of the effect of his metaphors consists in the continual interplay between the established, accepted meaning of the word and its new poetic meaning. The new context is effective because of the conventional subcontext with which it establishes a relationship, not in spite of it. In his theoretical writings Przyboś repeatedly stressed the importance of juxtaposition or what he called "the between-words" ("międzysłowie"). "From words one makes . . . poems, literature, declamation, but not poetry. Poetry comes from what is between and among words." [21] No word is exact or poetic in itself since meaning and exactness result from juxtaposition and from the clash of words with one another. Przyboś spoke of the "sphere of high tension" between words, "so that the poetic spark shoots from one word to another . . . so that between sentences nonstriking thunder continually circles." [22] A unique feature of his poetry is that this juxtaposition occurs not only synchronically within the poem—that is, between words and sentences next to each other—but it also takes place diachronically, between a word used in the metaphor of the poem and the same word as it is used in everyday language. The high tension between words that Przyboś alluded to occurs along two separate axes, one depending on the immediate context of the word and the second depending on the word's semantic ballast confirmed by social usage and rooted in tradition.

Sometimes Przyboś obtains analogous effects by relying on the sound similarities of words rather than on semantic substitution. In *From Above* a whole cycle of poems contains plays on words akin to puns. Yet this play with sounds is used by Przyboś with considerable restraint. Much more frequent is a very subtle use of sound similarities that occurs in the majority of his poems and performs a function like metaphor by establishing relationships between words semantically distant. Rejecting the mechanicalness of traditional rhyme, Przyboś denied its function as a necessary criterion for poetry. With Peiper, he no longer thought the distinction between poetry and prose was based upon versification but shifted this distinction and moved it into the very nature of poetic language itself. Przyboś went even further in this respect than Peiper, who for structural reasons retained regular rhymes but spaced them further apart than normal practice. Instead of rhymes Przyboś relied mostly on sound similarities distributed throughout the text of the poem without any regular pattern of versification. Each of Przyboś's poems and especially those written in the thirties presented a crisscrossing web of sounds, establishing complex relationships that grew directly out of the content of the poem.

In the measure that I was approaching in my practice the *uniform* formation of poetic vision, I abandoned the mechanical application of sound similarities; I looked for harmonies which would come from the very tissue of the poem. I struggled to connect rhymes and assonances with the content of the poem. With sound similarities I united sentences which in some way corresponded to each other: through similarity, or through the opposition of image and emotional tone. Thus, not directed by the mechanical sequence of rhymed verses, I used sound similarities to tie together phrases which were sometimes very distant or very close.[23]

As an example I would like to quote in Polish "Chwila" ("A Moment"):

> Leżę opryskany jaskrami na trawie.
> Jak jętki drgają nad stawem rojne iskry upału.
>
> Spoglądnę, ze wzroku rozwinę
> kwiat: dmuchawiec
> w błękit się wzbija.
>
> W powiewie zapachu
> ginę
> i jednodniowy mijam.

> I lie down sprinkled with buttercups on the grass.
> Swarming sparks of heat quiver over the pond like May flies.
>
> I will glance, from sight I will develop
> a flower; a dandelion puff-ball
> shoots up into the blue.
>
> In the breeze of the fragrance
> I perish
> and lasting a day pass by.

In this short poem about summer, creativity, and transitoriness there are at least six separate families of sounds. The first and the most obvious is based on the sounds *r, s,* and *k: opryskany, jaskry, iskry.* These are onomatopoeic, imitating the sound of sparks. The words *drgają, trawie,* and *wzroku* are partly related to this group. The second group of sounds contains three verbs in the first person singular form: spoglą*dnę,* rozwi*nę,* and gi*nę.* The common sound is the first person verbal ending; the first two verbs emphasize creative, demiurgic actions of the speaker of the poem while the last one, united to them by the same ending, ironically undercuts this demiurgic quality and the creator perishes together with his creation. Semantically related to this group is a third group composed of the two verbs wz*biją* and *mija*m. The two are in opposition if their meaning is considered out of the context of the poem, yet within the poem they both denote the ephemeralness of natural phenomena, of the flower and of man. The fourth group of words, composed of *jętki* and *błękit,* is in sharpest opposition despite the greatest similarity of sounds: the smallness, the mobility, and the short life of the May flies is contrasted with the vastness, immobility, and immutability of the blue sky. The fifth group, based on the sound *-wie,* connects words denoting nature· *trawie, dmuchawiec, powiew, kwiat.* Finally the last group, based on the sounds *-ch* and *-u,* associates the words dm*uch*awiec and zapa*chu,* both of which suggest the lightness of breathing, blowing, and smelling, and through this the momentariness of life. On the other hand the sound *-u* connects these two words with *upału,* an additional relation being that all three words are last words in a line. Semantically *upał* (heat) also could suggest the difficulty of breathing. The sound *ch* unites these words with the title, "*ch*wila," making this suggestion more sustainable and rounding out the message of the poem that life is but a moment.

The general tendency of contemporary Polish critics is to emphasize the nonvisuality of Julian Przyboś's Avantgarde poetry and the purely linguistic character of his metaphors. In their impressive analyses of Przyboś's poetry, both Jan Prokop and Janusz Sławiński assumed that the effectiveness of the poet's metaphors is not "in their visually dazzling imagery, but in their semantics."[24] Although Przyboś's masterly manipulation of language justifies such an approach, the treatment of his poetry exclusively within the boundaries of semantics unnecessarily limits their breadth. A different reading of this poetry reveals that one of the most striking and also most appealing qualities of Przyboś's metaphors is their strong visual basis. The result is a distinct and original poetic vision.

Przyboś's many statements about the need for the visual confirms the possibility of a different interpretation of his metaphors. In his poetry a surprisingly large number of expressions refer directly to vision and seeing: "I look, in eyes bordered by shadows / the trees gave a start: they grow visibly" (from the poem "Stars"); "I will glance, from sight I will develop / a flower" ("Moment"); "In the eyes the road light as a line / Foresees us first as a distance" ("Windows"). Eyes are one of the key images in his poetry, and the verb "to see" is one of those most frequently encountered. Aside from words and expressions denoting vision, a large number of words and images connote vision, such as windows, mirrors, curtains, and lights.

The emphasis on the activity and process of seeing is one aspect of the importance that Przyboś ascribed to experience in poetry. Experience—both sensory and emotional—occupies a prominent place in Przyboś's writings. All of his poems are "situated" in both time and space: "I did not want to write a poem that wouldn't be attached like a plant to a seen landscape, or that, like a plant, would not grow out (but suddenly, visibly) of a designated place on Earth. . . . I already know that I wouldn't be able to write a poem if I couldn't locate it on the map of places on the Earth that I had experienced with my senses." [25] Although the poet put aesthetic and life experiences on different planes, the complete divorce of experience from the creative act—so characteristic of Peiper's poetry—is absent in the poetry of Przyboś. Visual experience was one of the ways in which the poet remained close to his object, and it also guaranteed the authenticity, the verifiability of his metaphors. According to Przyboś, Peiper's poetic word, which expressed only itself, led to the negation of the very nature of the word, that is its subordination to a feeling subject. It is characteristic that where Peiper spoke of the antirealism of metaphor, Przyboś preferred to point out its mythic role. Not unlike the French surrealists, he saw in metaphor a means by which poetry can transpose the world of facts into the surreal world of legend, and for him the power of metaphoric vision depended on the power and depth of the poet's emotion.

The visuality of Przyboś's metaphors is of a special kind. Although their justification is in visual experience, their effect is unrealistic and borders on the fantastic. Przyboś relies on what might be called "optical illusion," largely because he never perceives objects as standing still, but in movement, frequently in rapid movement. This is especially true in Przyboś's earliest poetry, which reflects the poet's dynamic concept of the world in continual motion and change and is a source of the fantastic element in his imagery: "The windows jumped out of the walls / into stretched-out pairs of hands" ("Okna wyskoczyły z murów / w wyciągnięte ramiona par") ("Demonstration" ["Pochód"]). "The city square will crash down like a felled oak tree" ("Plac miejski padnie w objęcia jak powalony dąb") ("The Impression" ["Wrażenie"]). Often sound combines with a visual impression to form a "synaesthetic" optical illusion: "The breeze broadened the branches with whispered leaves" ("Powiew gałęzie liśćmi szeptanymi szerzył") ("Drzewiej"—"Tree-er," a neologism). Or: "The clatter rapidly nails the poles together into a dense fence" ("stukot zbija szybko słupy w gęsty parkan") ("King Huta—Vistula" ["Król-Huta—Wisła]). The optical illusion can also be an effect of light: "The lamps like big dandelion puffballs separated from the poles by light" ("lampy jak wielkie dmuchawce odłączyły się od słupów światłem") ("Eiffel").

In Przyboś's poetry this illusion is closely connected to his extensive use of metonymy, which Karol Irzykowski considered to be the source of his poetic vision. The critic defined metonymy as a substitution of one object for another not because of their similarity—as with metaphor—but because of the proximity of their relationship. He described the characteristic feature of Przyboś's metonymy as "the reversal of relationships between phenomena, a rolling over in the cosmos." [26] Examples of this figure are abundant in Przyboś's poetry: "The road, repeated by hooves, strides over the height, / it can be seen as it rides in the harness of chestnuts, through which / it threads two horse's heads, lengthened from speed" ("Droga, powtarzana kopytami, okracza wzniesienie, / widać ją, jak jedzie w uprzęży z kasztanów, przez które / przewleka dwa łby końskie, wzdłużone od pędu") ("Landscape" ["Krajobraz"]). "The village scuffs along with hundreds of clogs" ("wieś znowu człapie setkami chodaków") ("The Huts" ["Chaty"]).

The effect of optical illusion and metonymy in Przyboś's poetry is accomplished by transgression of natural laws governing phenomena. Endowing inanimate objects with movement and depriving them of their physical properties is a function of the particular vision of the speaker of the poem. Przyboś's images always presuppose a subject directly involved in an experience that is almost always associated with rapid movement. A good example is the following poem:

Lights at the Station

The wheels wind up the rails,
the stoker exchanged one arm for another.
The engineer wheezes full speed ahead,
hands flaming with ten fingers
he drags over the piston,
working,
until he unravels from the night a signal: the light,
he will string the road on its ray.

The train, reeled in to the skein of the station, died out,
the glass spheres burst with light,
the crowd, scattered, sparkled from transparency!
From the outspread fires
someone with his glances lights up for us—ourselves:

With a pole the poor fellow from the gasworks
raises his eyes.

Światła na stacji

Koła zwijają szyny,
palacz zamienił jedno ramię na drugie ramię.
Maszynista pełną parą sapie,
ręce płonące dziesięcioma palcami
nasuwa na tłok,
czynny,
aż wysnuje z nocy sygnał: światło,
drogę na promieniu napnie.

Pociąg, w kłąb stacji namotany, zgasł,
szklane kule zaniosły się światłem,
tłum, rozwiany, wybłysnął z przeźroczy!
Z rozniesionych ogni
ktoś rozjaśnia spojrzeniami nam — nas:

Człowieczyna z gazowni
podnosi wraz z drągiem oczy.

The metonymy that opens the poem, "The wheels wind up the rails," can be apprehended only if we adopt the same vantage point as the "persona" of the poem, the train engineer looking down upon the rails from the height of a rapidly moving locomotive. The engineer of Przyboś's train is active: he creates the motion of the train, he marks out its direction ("he unravels," "he will string the road"), but at the same time his perception of reality is dictated by the very situation he has created. This dual interrelationship of subject and object, active and passive, is already contained in the first lines of the poem and is further accentuated by the division of the poem into two parts. The train engineer passes from an active force in the first part, a creator of energy, to become the object of this energy in the second part. In the second stanza he dies out like the train; the light he created and directed to lead the train now turns upon himself: "From the outspread fires / someone with his glances lights up for us—ourselves." The active and creative force of the second stanza is light itself as well as the eyes of an anonymous "someone," while the persona of the poem becomes identified with both the poet and the reader, and the collective "us" becomes in turn the object of a play of lights and glances. The double action of being illuminated and looked upon is the source of self-revelation in the poem. Two semantic families of words are opposed to each other—the first implies obscurity, the closing of the self and introverted motion: "the wheels wind up the rails," "the train, reeled in to the skein of the station," "the night," and the train "dying out." The second group of meanings implies opening up, light and the exposure of the self: "he unravels . . . the light," "the glass spheres burst with light," "the crowd . . . sparkled," "someone . . . lights up," "glances," and "eyes." Typically for Przyboś—who as a poet is always directed outward—it is this second motion of extroversion and opening out that prevails.

If Przyboś uses metaphors of movement and light so extensively, it is because they are the most "natural" agents of optical distortions and, even more important, because they allow the poet to change relationships between objects and alter reality in accord with his individual poetic vision. The narrator or persona of Przyboś's poems is rarely if ever a detached observer but is usually immersed in the experience he undergoes and actively creates at the same time. He is both subject and object of the events of the poem. One could speak of the dual dynamics in Przyboś's poetry whereby the poet or speaker becomes the object of his own actions. Similarly, objects are never seen in their own natural state but only through the lens of a poetic vision, a lens that the critic Kazimierz Wyka called Przyboś's "Cyclopean eye." [27] They are not so much presented as created. Another critic has described this as Przyboś's "creationist attitude": "The most intricate images of Przyboś become clear if we admit that he treats the world as a projection of human individuality, most often his own, and therefore looks at objects as if he was creating them." [28] A result of Przyboś's creationist attitude is that the presence of the poet can be strongly felt. In many poems the poet introduces himself directly ("I see," "I look," "I listen"); many of these verbs in first person singular imply an active attitude or designate a specific action, as in the poem "Stars" ("Gwiazdy"):

Bard of the hands, worker of pride, I elevate myself with sight
up to the stars, the pressure of stars grooves my right shoulder,
the sky hangs with a helmet, I snatch the sky on the temple
and I lift on myself the night raised from the stars.

Wieszcz rąk, robotnik dumy, wywyższam się spojrzeniem
pod gwiazdy, ucisk gwiazd prawe ramię mi żłobi,
niebo nawisło hełmem, niebo porywam na ciemię
i noc, wzniesioną z gwiazd, podnoszę na sobie.

Sometimes the poet's presence is suggested in a more oblique manner as in "Lights at the Station," or by addressing a second person, "you" ("look," "you leave").

The image of himself that Przyboś presents in his poems is rarely his everyday documentary personality but an imaginative, creative construct that varies from poem to poem. The poet identifies with the construct, but the construct is never just the poet. It is often a perceptive vehicle of the poem whose senses—primarily the eyes—the poet follows in the course of the poem, and who provides the basic point of view. There are profound emotions connected with these perceptions that surely come from Przyboś himself as well as from this imaginary perceptive vehicle. The vehicle is sometimes a persona who has a considerable distance from the poet himself, such as the engineer in "Lights at the Station," but sometimes the distinction between the perceptive vehicle and the poet is hard to establish. Przyboś's "creationist attitude" thus acts not only on external reality but on himself as well. Kazimierz Wyka recalled the poet in a eulogy: "It was a figure elaborated according to a model for himself which he carried in himself.... It appears as if Julian Przyboś carried in himself, carried morally and existentially, the self-portrait. It looks, further, as if he was formed according to this self-portrait by the effort of his own will, a faithfulness to his most primary feelings and experiences. He remained faithful to them in a severe and demanding way."[29] This self-creationism acted backward as well as forward, toward the present and toward the past. For Przyboś, recalling the past was also the moment of its creation. In his autobiographical poems ("Gods," "Chopping the Sycamore"), the image of his childhood and boyhood accords with the image the adult poet wanted to see. These poems "are rooted, but at the same time, how strongly they are wanted. The child in these cycles is a construction on the model of the future poet's self-portrait."[30]

Przyboś's creationist attitude is the result of an exercise of will and mind, but at the same time it is connected with the domain of vision. In Przyboś's poetry there is an implicit theory of vision akin to the theory of vision of the Polish constructivist painter, Władysław Strzemiński. This theory, which Strzemiński called *unism*, was based on a manner of seeing best described as synthetic. Przyboś was fascinated by unism and became one of its main interpreters, writing about it extensively. He explained the nature of unistic vision in the following manner:

To facilitate the understanding of this way of seeing, imagine you are looking from the window of a train going through a region that every now and then changes its form; you catch in the retina of your eye a thousand diverse landscapes, and then you desire to see them *all* suddenly in an instant, arrested in one window frame. If you have an eye that knows how to unite the images, how to associate one with the others, exchange colors and lines, shuffle them endlessly—you will in the end receive an image that is cleared of specific, individual lines and colors, you will receive an image not so much composed of all the others previously seen but which results, is verified and reduced to almost *one single* color, almost *one single* form.[31]

Przyboś's description of unistic vision in many respects describes the nature of the vision behind many of his own metaphors, and most of all the overlapping of different images. I am referring to the particular kind of image used by Przyboś that could be called "double" or "multiple" and is related to the imagery relying on optical illusion discussed earlier, but at the same time constitutes a fairly distinct group in itself. The term *double image* comes from the visual arts; the technique of the double image was extensively used in medieval as well as in surrealistic painting.[32] My use of this painterly term is not accidental as Przyboś was not only a great connoisseur of modern painting, but on many occasions proved to be one of its most astute and enthusiastic critics. While the images that give an effect of optical illusion are closely connected to the metonymic figure, double images are closer to metaphor and bring similarities of objects into relief: "Evening, coachman of shadows, drives the hills / like horses, stopping the view in front of a closed city, / afterwards at a stream he waters the sun which is hanging low" ("Wieczór, woźnica cienia, wzgórzami jak końmi / powozi, zatrzymując widok przed miastem zamkniętym, / po czym słońce, zwieszone nisko, u strumienia poi") ("Landscape" ["Krajobraz"]). The metaphor develops along two axes that overlap; the first refers to the evening and the landscape, the second uses the metaphoric vehicle of the coachman and horses. Another example: "From that split distance the passed roof starts to move between my fingers like a fin of air. I unfurl it over you, baldachin in the procession of the dream" ("Z tej rozpłatanej oddali miniony dach ruchomieje między moimi palcami jak płetwa powietrzna. Rozwijam go nad tobą, baldachim w procesji snu") ("Feather of Fire: Do You Hear" ["Pióro z ognia: Czy słyszysz"]). Three images overlap here, the roof, the fin of air, and the baldachin, forming a multiple image. The overlapping is associated with movement ("starts to move," "I unfurl it," "the procession") as well as with distance, both spatial ("distance") and temporal ("passed"). But above all the passage is the result of dreaming—dreaming about the distant past in which various elements, as in a dream, overlap each other. The use of dream as a basis for poetic vision is not accidental since the phenomenon of the double image is most common in dreams.[33] Similar in their underlying principles are the two following passages: "From inside the sleeve of the dream you let out a lark it fluttered at the height of a low bow —and it sowed itself into the furrow, bird-grain" ("Z zanadrza snu wypuściłeś skowronka, zatrzepotał na wysokości ukłonu—i wsiał się w bruzdę, ziarno-ptak") ("Feather of Fire: Eagle" ["Pióro z ognia: Orzeł"]) and: "a spine of a blackthorn pierced my heart, opened into a bird's beak and a nightingale fluttered under the arm of my wife" ("cierń tarniny zakłuty w moje serce rozwarł się w dziobek ptaszęcy i słowik zatrzepotał pod pachą mej żony") ("Feather of Fire: 21 Shots" ["Pióro z ognia: Ofiaruj linię"]). The double image is really triple: path-bouquet-explicit by the hyphenated word "bird-grain," in the second passage it is the spine-bird's beak-nightingale. In each case movement ("fluttered") is involved, and in the first example the underlying cause of the double image is dream. The next passage is somewhat different: "From under the violin bow, having skimmed along sight the path sneaked away and spiraled in the orchard into a bouquet and a moustache" ("Spod smyczka, ześliznąwszy się wzdłuż spojrzenia, wymykała się ścieżka i w sadzie zawijała się w bukiet i w wąs") ("Feather of Fire: Offer a Line" ["Pióro z ognia: Ofiaruj linię"]). The double image is really triple: path-bouquet-moustache. What is interesting about this image is that it not only associates sight with movement ("skimmed," "sneaked," "spiraled"), but with hearing as well (the violin bow). The image is a combination of the visual and aural similar to the synaesthetic effects mentioned earlier with respect to images based on optical illusion. A curious double aural metaphor can be found in the same series of poems: "21 shots reverberated the frontier of the new homeland, measured by the breadth of the echoes, subsiding for so long that the twentieth shot was a whisper of stones, and the twenty-first a silenced fallen leaf, and the twenty-second . . . " ("21 wystrz- ałów rozlegało granicę nowej ojczyzny, mierzonej na szerokość ech, cichnąc tak długo, że dwudziesty wystrzał był szeptem kamieni, a dwudziesty pierwszy zamilkłym liściem opadłym, a dwudziesty drugi . . .") ("Feather of Fire: 21 Shots" ["Pióro z ognia: 21 wystrzałów"]). The overlapping "echoing" aural sensations are shots, a whisper of stones, a silenced fallen leaf.

The examples just quoted present the double image as it occurs within a single sentence or a single metaphor. Very often, however, two images coexist and overlap not only within a single metaphor but within a whole poem. Not infrequently a poem is built upon a dialectical tension between two or more overlapping visions.

The Violinist, the Movement of His Hands

And the dusk girl was passing,
darkening her brows, paused in the rain,
opens,
a sound and . . .
(While he muffled the vibrating chords
in a strange city, a singing bass,
he swished with the bow, caught a ring . . .)
. . . from her purse the black mirror of a puddle fell out.
He picked it up, to look at his own sadness.

But between the movement of the hand
and
the time
evening fell,
an empty case.

Skrzypek, ruch jego ręki

I mijała przedwieczorna panna,
czerniąc brwi, przystanęła na deszczu,
otwiera,
dźwięk i...
(A on struny wibrujące głuszył
w obcym mieście, śpiewającym basie,
śmignął smyczkiem, złowił pierścień...)
...z torebki wypadło jej czarne lusterko kałuży.
Podniósł je, by się przyjrzeć własnemu smutkowi.

Ale między ruchem ręki
a
między czasem
zapadł wieczór,
pusty futerał.

This half-playful poem that catches the sensation of the short moment between dusk and evening relies on the juxtaposition of two developed images or contexts, the image of the street violinist, and the metaphoric image of dusk as a girl passing by. It would be more precise to speak not of juxtaposition but of the overlapping of images; the poet's intention shows through the composition of the poem, and the sentence developing the first image—the dusk girl—is interrupted in the fourth line by the parenthetical three-line sentence, which develops the second image—the violinist—and is picked up in the eighth line exactly at the point where it was dropped. The ninth line refers again to the violinist. The overlapping technique is further emphasized by the punctuation and typography of the poem: the suspension points at the end of the first part and again before the continuation of the sentence about the girl, the parenthesis enclosing the sentence about the violinist, and the suspension points at the end of that sentence. The punctuation stresses the simultaneity of the events because the poem is describing a single moment, and the simultaneity is emphasized by the conjunction "while." Also there is overlapping of sounds: the "sound" of the falling mirror overlaps "vibrating chords" and the "singing bass."

It is characteristic of Przyboś that the realistic image of the violinist, based on perception, is treated in the poem with the same amount of verisimilitude as the metaphoric image of the dusk girl, which is based on poetic vision. The effect of the balancing of these two qualitatively different images is playful. However, in other poems by Przyboś the same device acquires a much broader scope and is used to express the poet's attitude toward reality and experience. This is the case with the poem entitled "Four Quarters." It describes Przyboś's impressions of Paris and at the same time communicates his emotional attitude toward the city, which he treats as a symbol of Western civilization:

1

My shadow flashed by passing me on a double avenue.
I go,
with the top of my head I feel the flickering touch
of leaves, pure lightness,
not here, where I am, but there, to where I see.
The bottom of the distance is filled after sunset by a windstorm,
red rose of the winds outspread on a stem;
the factory chimney wanders far away with me.

From there the cars endlessly spin out the perspective, perspective,
which
breaks suddenly at the knees.

From the anthill of wingless cars pure speed will fly away:
    an airplane.

2

Traffic swarmed with cars, iron and the wall ground glass on the curves,
the sparking material spattered me from close by.
It is here.
The last man disappeared devoured by the crowd,
only a policeman remained like a marmot whistling on a molehill.

Touched by his wand the square spurted out with a fountain.

M'sieur! Plant the pit jumping in your whistle!
Only a nail sprouted on the roadway . . .
Smoke, the sprout of gasoline, withered before it unfolded,
battered down in a hail of buildings.

It is here the golden current spends the triumphant night.

I watch for when the poem will change into a skyrocket.

3

From the packed hall, with the symphony falling toward the door like a bullet,
winged by the music I struggle along the boulevards.
I hear the houses like ruins after a bombardment.

Below a plank fence a street musician, blinded angel
sheds
one wing of his hat
feather after feather,
slowly . . .

he stretches and shrinks floors with the steps on the bellows of his accordion.

Nike
in a victorious flight beats against the pavement with an invisible head,
with a pink vacuum,
the light.
On the Seine dawn moves the flood held by chords.

Vincent van Gogh with a branch of blossoming almond
restored my sight of the world.

4

A shadow staggered at the muzzles of the streets.
A volley of cars pierced it through,
aiming
at the jumping dot.

The policeman froze in the whirling sphere.

And again he waved with his arms, rewrapped,
bandaged the wounded place—

The traffic overgrew
the pavement with rubber wheels.
The heart of the tree beat in the raised wand.

The audible aspen, entirely made of the trembling of motors
began to tremble,
and, transparent with the air, with distance and spreading,
sank into the depth of the forest out of sight,
no one's—

Ney from the monument raised his sword, ordering his own death.

Cztery strony

1

Mój cień podwójną aleją mijając mnie przemknął.
Idę,
czubem głowy odczuwam dotknięcie ruchliwe
liści, czystą lekkość,
nie tu, gdzie jestem, lecz tam, dokąd widzę.
Dno oddalenia wypełnia po zachodzie wichura,
czerwona róża wiatrów rozwinięta na łodydze;
czynny komin fabryczny wędruje daleko wraz ze mną.

Stamtąd samochody rozsnuwają bezustannie perspektywę, perspektywę,
która
rwie się nagle u kolan.

Z mrowiska bezskrzydłych aut wyfrunie ich czysty pęd: aeroplan.

2

Ruch mrowił się od aut, żelazo i mur mełły na zakrętach szkło,
iskrzasta materia obryzgała mnie z bliska.
To tu.
Ostatni człowiek znikł pożarty przez tłum,
został tylko policjant jak świstak na kretowisku.

Tknięty jego pałeczką plac wytrysnął fontanną.

M'sieur! Zasadź pestkę skaczącą w świstawce!
Tylko gwóźdź wykiełkował na jezdni...

Dym, pęd z benzyny, nim rozwinął się, zwiądł,
obtłuczony gradem kamienic.

To tu złoty prąd pędzi noc triumfalną.

Patrzę, kiedy wiersz przemieni się w racę.

3

Z nabitej sali, symfonią spadającej ku bramie jak pocisk,
szamocę się bulwarami, oskrzydlony przez muzykę.

Słyszę domy jak gruzy po bombardowaniu.

Pod płotem z desek grajek, oślepiony anioł,
roni
jedno skrzydło kapelusza
pióro po piórze,
pomału...

piętra schodami rozciąga i kurczy na miechu harmonii.

Nike
w locie zwycięskim bije o bruk niewidomą głową,
różową próżnią,
światłem.
Świt wzrusza nad Sekwaną zatrzymaną akordami powódź.

Vincent van Gogh gałązką kwitnącego migdału
przywrócił mi wzrok nad światem.

4

Cień się słaniał u wylotów ulic.
Salwy aut przeszywały go na wskroś,
mierząc
w skaczący punkt.

Policjant zastygł w wirującej kuli.

I znów machał ramionami, przewijał,
bandażował zranione miejsce —

Ruch zarósł
gumowymi kołami po bruk.
Serce drzewa zabiło w podniesionej pałeczce.

Dosłyszalna osika, cała z drżenia motorów,
zaczynała drżeć,
i, przejrzysta powietrzem, odległością i szerzą,
zapadała w głąb boru zaoczna,
niczyja —

Ney z pomnika wzniósł szablę, rozkazując swoją śmierć.

The whole poem is an example of a developed double image in which two different orders and two visions are constantly juxtaposed: that of the city and civilization, and that of nature; that of the place where the poet is—Paris—and of the place he remembers—his native countryside; of presence, and of absence. One vision or what might be called visual setting is associated with the present moment and the streets of Paris, while the second is composed of memories of the absent Polish homeland. Even the speaker of the poem is double, split between the one here and the one there, between the physical speaker who uses the pronoun "I" and his shadow. The relationship between these two speakers in the poem is paradoxical, since it is the shadow that is connected with the city ("a shadow staggered at the muzzle of the streets"), while the pronoun "I" is reserved for the faraway land ("not here, where I am, but there, to where I see"). However—and it is typical of Przyboś's double image—this distinction is blurred, and when the poet says "I go" it refers both to the present moment and place, and to the past and the faraway place. The principle of double image penetrates most of the metaphors of the poem: the streets of Paris and the anthill, the policeman and the marmot, the policeman's stand in the middle of the street and the molehill, the pit and the nail, the smoke and the sprout, the hail and the buildings, the street musician and the angel, the policeman's wand and the aspen. The technique of the double image allows Przyboś to introduce tension into the very tissue of his poems. The reliance of metaphors on double images is not only the source of a dramatic confrontation between two realities, but it is also a means of interpretation of the reality that the poet perceives and describes by undermining its versimilitude. The relationship of the two visions is paradoxical because memories are endowed with the concreteness and realism of perceptions, while images that describe what the poet actually sees and what surrounds him in the most concrete and physical sense have the quality of phantasmagoria. All the objects around him are touched by a magic wand, and indeed the wand appears twice in the poem in the hand of the policeman. On the other hand the images from memory are faithful to reality, and they have the concreteness of physical objects, the immediacy of sensory experience. It is significant that when describing his past experience of nature the poet uses what is perhaps the least deceptive of the senses, the sense of touch ("I feel the ... touch of leaves"), while descriptions of the city rely exclusively on visual experience and the use of optical illusion, the agent of which is the movement and speed of cars. Curiously, optical illusion does not operate in memory but is only a characteristic of direct perception; images in memory are fixed, and only what we actually see can undergo transformation through the deceptiveness of vision.

In the poem there is a tension and play between images originating in the stability of memory, and those resulting from the deceptiveness of the eye. The originality of Przyboś's poetry is that these images overlap each other within a single metaphor, that they are simultaneous rather than existing side by side.

The whole poem "Four Quarters" is built on the paradoxical opposition of perceptual vision and mnemonic vision that translate the opposition between the solidity of the "native realm," of "roots" and the "past," versus the deceptiveness of the present, of the foreign city and "not belonging." This opposition and juxtaposition of the two visions expresses the complexity of Przyboś's attitude toward the modern city and civilization, a tremendous attraction—as in his early stage—but at the same time an increasing attachment to his peasant origins. The last striking image in "Four Quarters" summarizes the negativism of Przyboś's attitude toward Western European civilization, which is inflicting its "own death"—the poem was written in 1937. The military imagery, especially prominent in the third and fourth sections, leads to this final image, as well as the imagery showing nature's inability to survive in the urban environment ("The last man disappeared devoured by the crowd," "only a nail sprouted on the roadway," "Smoke, the sprout of gasoline, withered before it unfolded").

At the end of the third section of the poem there is a sentence about the poet recovering his sight, "Vincent van Gogh with a branch of blossoming almond / restored my sight of the world." The lines acknowledge the importance of the faculty of sight for Przyboś but, even more important, they point to the source of his poetic vision. Przyboś's perception of reality incorporates two perspectives. On the one hand, the perspective of nature, "the branch of blossoming almond," which is also a part of his childhood memories, the "there" of the poem—the mnemonic images of the natural world provide depth to present reality, which by its nature is flat: "From there the cars endlessly spin out the perspective, perspective, / which breaks suddenly at the knees." On the other hand, Przyboś acknowledges his debt to art and more specifically to the visual art of painting in the formation of his view of reality. The third section of the poem leading to the sentence quoted above associates music and hearing with "blindness" or difficulty ("the street musician, a blinded angel," and the poet who "struggles" along the boulevards after listening to a symphony); to them Przyboś opposes painting as the source of vision.

Once again there is a striking similarity between Przyboś's double or multiple images and Władysław Strzemiński's concept of "after-sight." Strzemiński believed that a painter can paint only what he has seen, and that his final vision is the centralization of all the aspects of what he has seen. It is a synthesis of what Strzemiński called "after-sight," the imprint that the seeing of an object leaves on the retina of the onlooker. Similarly, Przyboś's metaphors are a complex sum of different images impressed upon the eye and originating in different experiences, places and times; the final vision is a "continual play of sights and after-sights."[34] In "Four Quarters" it is the immediate vision of a modern city and the mnemonic vision of nature; in "Lights at the Station" vision is directed outward toward the world with a reverse direction inward, toward the speaker of the poem; in "The Violinist, the Movement of His Hands" there is a realistic vision of the violinist and a metaphoric vision of the evening; in the poem "In the Whistle of an Oriole," which will be discussed later, there is the present adult vision of a bird and the dream vision of childhood. The double vision is not based simply on the overlapping of two different physical realities; frequently there is also an overlapping of two or three different temporal unities. Often the present, the past, and the future overlap. What is coexists with what was or will be. With Przyboś it is sometimes difficult to distinguish between the various periods to which he refers, because the distinction between present and past is blurred and they are not represented one next to the other but one over the other. Przyboś often uses various tenses within a single poem, occasionally within a single line, such as: "I walked—I will go—I go" ("Yesterday").

Przyboś's multiple images reflect still another observation about vision discussed by Strzemiński, that with the exception of the first objects seen after waking, we never see an object during the day without the after-sight of the objects seen previously. Thus purity and "singleness" of vision is not possible. Especially in the autobiographical cycles many of Przyboś's poems describe the moment of waking, and they are an attempt to capture this short moment of primordial purity of vision; they also show an almost instantaneous process of building images and confusion between dream and reality. In one of his poems about childhood the poet describes the moment of waking:

> The eyelids, grazed with fingers, from under the wings of the brows
> flew away exposing lightness up to the ceiling,
> the nimbus of the room, the straw cloud
> of the hut
>
> fled from the eyes
> gigantic
> —the crossing of consciousness into a white, unexpected strange land.
>
> ["Chopping the Sycamore: The
> Crossing of Consciousness"]

> Powieki, muśnięte palcami, spod skrzydełek brwi
> uleciały rozsłaniając jaśnienie po pułap,
> nimb izby, słomiana chmura
> chałupy
>
> uciekały od oczu
> olbrzymie
> — przelot jawy w białą, niespodzianą obczyznę.
>
> ["Ścięcie jaworu: Przelot jawy"]

Like birth, waking is the moment in which two realities meet: the reality of sleep and dream, and the reality of the palpable external world. It is the moment of transition in which the experience of birth is relived with daily regularity, the first encounter with light and the accompanying sensation of strangeness. The moment of waking is a point at which the selection and separation of dream and reality has not yet been accomplished but is being accomplished, therefore it is an ideal moment of

double vision of the external and the internal. In the poem it is the mother's voice—
in keeping with the underlying symbolism and imagery of birth—that pushes the
first reality away, causes the dream to disappear and the second reality to take on
its concrete shape:

> The world,
> hit by mother's voice, came close, cleaved,
> at the window on a branch, on a moment, it was hanging—
> and under the body of the boy like a nest it lay . . .
> It dawned its name:
>
> > "Morning."

> Świat,
> trafiony głosem matki, zbliżył się, rozłupał,
> u okna na gałęzi, na chwili, zawisnął –
> i pod ciało się chłopca jak gniazdo podłożył...
> Zaświtał swoje imię:
>
> > ,,Rano".
>
> > [Ibid.]

There is a connection between Przyboś's fascination with the moment of
waking and the double image, and the importance he attributed to the moment he
called "the between-words" in poetry. "Not the word but the *between-words* is
important. Poetry depends on these currents between one word and another, on the
sparks shooting from the creative juxtaposition of words and phrases."[35] The
moment at which two images meet and overlap is exactly the moment of "poetic
current" to which he referred in his theoretical writings. We have seen this can be a
juxtaposition of two or more meanings of a word as in the play with idiomatic expressions or it can be the juxtaposition of several visual images within a single metaphor or of several images within a single poem. A structural principle is involved in
all of these procedures: they all emphasize the moment at which two meanings of
an expression or two images in a metaphor are present—the moment of their interplay. This moment corresponds to the moment of waking, and in all three instances
there is an impression of blurring and ambiguity before the objects fall into focus.
It is the moment at which the identity of a word or image is evasive, at which it
both is and is not itself. In poetry it is the instant of possibility and ambiguity, of
illusion and at the same time of maximal allusiveness. In comparison with these
visual images the allusiveness of Peiper's "pseudonyms" and "verbal equivalents"
was very limited: "What is needed is not a pseudonym but a polyonym, a poetic
image or system of images in a poem that would move the imagination in such a
way that the 'maximum imaginary allusions in a minimum of words' could produce
an emotion never named, an expression of reality that was without name until
now."[36] By increasing the allusiveness of metaphor the technique of the double
image created a kind of poetry that was not identified with words but existed in
the space between words. It was a poetry of multiple perspectives.

The visuality of Przyboś's metaphors is also connected to the associationism
that is a structural principle of organization in his poems written in the 1930s. He

defended the visual quality of his metaphors as a means of facilitating the associational process of the reader, and he criticized Peiper's rhetorical sentences—also the purely intellectual and abstract quality of his metaphors—as obstacles to the immediacy of communication. Since Przyboś sought a more immediate and preintellectual communication with the reader, the visual image rightly seemed more easily apprehended by the imagination than the conceptual metaphor of the older poet. Peiper's complex sentences, in which distant concepts were united by rhetorical devices, precluded a free course of associations in the reader because in his effort to encompass the totality of the sentence, the reader's imagination remained passive. This is why Przyboś did not look for structural supports in rhetorical figures but instead based the structure and cohesiveness of his poems on the associational quality of his metaphors. This associationism is particularly prominent in the poetry Przyboś wrote in the late 1930s, the cycles *Chopping the Sycamore (Ścięcie jaworu)* and *Feather of Fire (Pióro z ognia),* where dream and memory play important roles. The following poem, which opens the autobiographical cycle *Chopping the Sycamore,* makes extensive use of the technique of associationism:

In the Whistle of an Oriole

In a moment, in the whistle of an oriole, when
the shadow
                    of a falling lash
weighed the line of its flight,
my father's sickle left near the gate recalled by a dream
lashed the dark blue of the sky into the first star
and blazed up from the retina
one
hundred, thousand, resounding million times.

Leś did not count
                    up to the last
sounds silvering ever more quietly
because a horse at the trough stamped into them
and whirling it kicked up from under its hoof
a sphere of darkness:

Thus two beams rumbled out a shadow from their oak tree.

The shadow, blown into by a breath, was dug out inside,
foamed over
including both:
the bay harnessed into the fog: tomorrow's journey,
a boy dreaming fortunes from circlings and instants—
the shadow bulged
and spurted up with the horizon
the highest
on the thin straw of a dream.
It sank into the high night.

Toward night the cock's beak bent into a half-moon
turned red
and on the dawning chords
with a broken rainbow
crowed.

The dawn grew silent.

W gwiździe wilgi

W chwili, gwizdnięciu wilgi, kiedy
linię jej lotu zważył
              opadającej rzęsy
cień,
sierp ojca porzucony na uwrociu przypomniany przez sen,
zaciąwszy granat nieba w pierwszą gwiazdę,
rozbłysnął od źrenicy
jeden
sto, tysiąc, dźwięczące milion razy.

Leś ostatnich
             srebrniejących coraz ciszej brzmień
nie doliczył,
bo w nie tupnął koń u żłobu
i skłębiwszy spod kopyta kulę zmroku
wzbił:

Tak dwa dyle wydudniły cień ze swego dębu.

Cień, nadmuchany westchnieniem, wewnątrz się wygłębił,
wyszumiał,
ogarniając ich obu:
gniadosza wprzężonego w mgłę: jutrzejszą jazdę,
chłopca śniącego wróżby z kołowań i chwil —
cień pęczniał
i podrywał się nieboskłonem
najwyżej
na cienkiej słomce marzenia.
W wysoką noc zapadł.

Nad nocą dziób koguci skrzywiony w półksiężyc
szczerwieniał
i po świtających strunach
rozłamaną tęczą
zapiał.

Świt ucichł.

The poem presents a flash of memories from childhood in a moment as short as the whistling of the oriole, which the poet is watching with half-closed eyes. Memories pass in a chain of associations reminiscent of the dream mentioned in the poem, because it has elicited the first of those memories, the image of his father's sickle. Other memories include a horse, a journey in the horse cart, and his childhood dreams. The crowing of the rooster at dawn ends the dreams of both childhood and adulthood as well as the poem itself. The associations are both visual and auditory, most often they bring both sound and vision together (the "resounding . . . blaze," "silvering sounds," "dawning strings," the cock crowing "with a broken rainbow," "the dawn grew silent"). Typical for Przyboś, the poem develops in time from night to morning. Associationism often implies spontaneity and randomness, or lack of rigorous structure, yet Przyboś's poem creates the impression of extreme cohesiveness and order. Its highly metaphoric language and intricate system of associations betray the absolute control of an author who is conscious of the effect of his art.

It is interesting to compare the associationism of Przyboś with the associational techniques used by the French surrealists, especially because these were probably the source of inspiration for the Polish poet. Despite vituperative denunciations of surrealism as a "utopia," a "sophisticated bluff," and "mystification," Przyboś revealed, by his frequent references to surrealism in his writings, that he was fascinated by the movement. Although its philosophical tenets were unacceptable to Przyboś, it provided a counterbalance to the strong rhetorical tendencies of Peiper. Przyboś found two poetic ideas in surrealism, the visuality of the poetic image and associationism, which were lacking and even excluded from Peiper's poetic system. And yet Przyboś used both of these techniques in a manner entirely different from that of the surrealists. For them, the play of associations as well as the technique of the double image were valuable because they revealed the artist's subconscious. Their purpose was not so much artistic as psychological—they were a means for expressing as truthfully as possible the artist's individuality, his self. The attitude of Przyboś, however, was in keeping with Polish Avantgarde theories and contrary to that of the surrealists; he considered poetic vision to be the result of intellect, of a "perspicacious labor of thought,"[37] a matter of intense conscious effort, not of an irrational and subconscious illumination. The path to the new poetic vision was by way of elaboration of a new style, "just as through mechanical religious practices one can achieve faith."[38] Form, rigor, and discipline were the conditions of the artistic work, and the poet defined form as the "line" of metaphorization that "cannot be overdrawn."[39] Przyboś's associations and metaphors were controlled and manipulated for the specific effect he wanted to achieve. Faithful to the principles of the *Switch,* he saw the poem as a structure and an organization, and not as a means of direct expression. The play of associations was intended to impose a particular vision. Przyboś spoke of poetry as an organizer of the reader's emotions, "The very manner of connecting words and sentences, the very arrangement of poetic vision is supposed to evoke in the reader a specific 'lyrical' emotion, an emotion which by its very nature is incommensurable with the (corresponding) life emotion, and yet is related to it in some deeper way."[40]

Przyboś saw the principal evolution of modern sensibility in the shifting of the creative effort from the subject to the object. In this his position was just the opposite of that taken by the French surrealists, for his favorite moment of the day was just before waking, theirs was just before falling asleep. In the hypnagogic state described by André Breton in the first surrealist manifesto, attention is directed inward toward sleep and dream, drifting further and further away from perceptive reality. It is the moment of closing off the outward world, of the descent inside the personality. In the moment of waking on the contrary the entire will is strained toward outer reality, it is the moment of opening toward the world. Przyboś's world view is synoptic and the movement of his poems is outward, from night to day, from darkness into light, and from oneself into the world. It is not directed toward the personality of the speaker of the poem but toward a new perception of external reality; it is directed away from the self, the "I," toward the "non-I." Przyboś's poetry offers a new vision of reality, and even if this vision is highly personal and individual, its object is a reality that, once recognized behind its metaphoric distortion, is common and familiar.

JAN BRZĘKOWSKI

Julian Przyboś always considered Jan Brzękowski to be a very special "poetic" friend. He based this friendship on certain common experiences such as participation in the *Switch,* an almost simultaneous poetic debut, and common youthful enthusiasms as well as on their divergences, which united rather than separated them. "Almost everything divides us: he industrious and practical in everyday life, in poetry a dreamer and brilliant juggler—I a dreamer in day to day life, and an 'iron' rigorist in art. Thanks to the contradictions I consider this friendship fruitful in my life."[41] Przyboś's characterization of the two poets is wonderfully accurate. In comparison with the highly elaborated poetry of Przyboś in which every line, every metaphor is carefully worked out, Brzękowski's poetry gives the impression of casualness and facility, of leaving much more up to chance. While there is lightness and playfulness in Brzękowski's poems, the verbal texture in Przyboś's poems is so thick that the reader has to struggle through it as through a thicket. Przyboś's characterization of Brzękowski is pertinent not only in its opposition of the two poets, but it also points to a certain duality in Brzękowski; generally and somewhat superficially Brzękowski could be identified as a romantic and a realist. This duality between romantic and realist is particularly manifest in the very first volume of his poetry, *The Pulse (Tętno,* 1925) but it is also present in his later poetry and in his poetics.

The Pulse is thematically similar to the early poetry of Peiper and Przyboś, written in praise of the present moment, of technology, physical labor, and the new man. We find the same subjects as in the other two poets—trains, airplanes, engineers, workers, speed and movement, as well as the same elevated tone. But here the similarity ends. The personality of Brzękowski shows through the style and imagery of the poems. Unlike the early poetry of Przyboś, in which imagery, vocabulary, and rhythm match the subject matter, in *The Pulse* there is a clash between its programmatic subject matter and its style, which is still very much under the spell of symbolist poetics. Brzękowski's trains and airplanes are closer to romantic sailboats than to the technologically sophisticated machines of his day:

> The train like a tape flows into the station,
> the pain of the breath of distant countries trembles in it,

the whistle of the locomotive pulses with nostalgia,
which grows in the darkness like a symbol.

["Rushing Film"]

Pociąg jak taśma na dworzec przypływa,
odległych krain oddechu w nim drży ból,
tęsknotą tętni gwizd lokomotywy,
która w ciemności wyrasta jak symbol.

["Pędzący film"]

As the key image in Przyboś's early poetry was the wheel, symbol of speed and movement, the key image in the early poetry of Brzękowski is the boat—a majestic ocean liner, a romantic sailboat, a pirate ship, or an armored battleship. Brzękowski's imagination returns time after time to this favorite symbol of nineteenth-century poetry, used by both the romantics and the symbolists, from Lermontov's "Sail" and Wordsworth's "Goodly Vessel" to Rimbaud's "Bateau ivre" and Valéry's "Cimetière marin." Brzękowski's preference for the boat reveals that he was steeped in romantic and symbolist tradition, but it also proves that when writing *The Pulse* Brzękowski did not yet have a style at his disposal that could match the subject matter he had chosen—that there was a disparity between the traditional diction of his poems and his newly adopted world view. Most important, however, Brzękowski's predilection for boats reveals the basically romantic sensibility that did not disappear in his mature years but became more integrated with his poetics. In his later poetry the romantic penchant often found outlets in sensational, erotic, and dream themes, but it was then accompanied by another feature that is romantic par excellence—irony.

In 1925 Brzękowski was poetically too immature to resolve the duality between his romanticism and realism, and many of the poems in his first volume seem to be written in two different styles that coexist within a single poem without harmoniously merging:

Dull morning coolness favors the circles of dreams,
The sharp coldness of the frost teases with the needle of touch,
How good it is when one is thinking
To hear the whirling propeller of an airplane!

["On Joseph Bereta, Mechanic"]

Matowy chłód ranny sprzyja kręgom marzeń,
Ostre zimno mrozu drażni dotknięć igła,
Jak dobrze jest wtedy gdy się myśli waży
Słyszeć samolotu kręcące się śmigło!

["O Józefie Berecie mechaniku"]

The stanza is divided into two parts, each belonging to a different emotional and stylistic convention. The first two lines are descriptive and their diction, their subjectivity or "moodiness," belong stylistically to the poetry of Young Poland (so violently disliked by the Avantgarde), while the last two lines are futuristically programmatic. To counterbalance the symbolist style in his earliest poetry Brzę-kowski reverted to a straightforward prose style that was propagandistic in tone and reserved for the message of the poems. Similarly programmatic are the titles of Brzękowski's poems ("The Engineer Peter Roll," "On Joseph Bereta, Mechanic," "Miners"). The two poetic styles and two opposed sensibilities collide when presented simultaneously, and only occasionally is there a happy marriage—rather atypical of Brzękowski's early poetry—as in the following poem:

The Interrupted Song

Wooden beams dozed like dried stalks
Thrown in a heap on the high road's sheet metal,
The world whitened with the sailing dust
And the smell of wood dazed like mint.

The sun shone like a wooden ring
Nailed high up on the boiler of the sky.
As he lifted the beams the woodcutter always sang,
When suddenly stopping he stabbed silence with silence.

Przerwany śpiew

Drzemały belki jak zeschłe badyle
Rzucone kupą na blachę gościńca,
Świat się wybielił żeglującym pyłem,
A zapach drzewa odurzał jak mięta.

Słońce świeciło jakby krążek z drzewa
Przybity w górze na nieba baniaku.
Podnosząc belki cieśla ciągle śpiewał,
Gdy nagle milknąc ciszę ciszą zakłuł.

Because the poem is not openly programmatic the symbolist atmosphere, especially of the first stanza, and the choice of metaphors do not jar. It is interesting to compare this poem with a contemporary poem by Przyboś, "The Woodcutters," because of the coincidence in the subject of the two poems and, even more striking, the difference in tone and imagery. Przyboś's poem is entirely concentrated on action and full of active verbs, geometrical figures, noise, and a rapid tempo. The atmosphere of Brzękowski's poem on the contrary is of heat, dozing, slowness, and silence, betraying a personality that is not compatible with slogans such as "city, the mass, the machine" and "the embrace of the present," as well as with the postulates of rigor and indirectness in the expression of feelings. Przyboś had a need to oppose Peiper's "classical" rhetorical side, but Brzękowski felt this need even more. He carried the opposition further, almost to the very negation of the basic Avantgarde postulates.

More than Przyboś, Brzękowski's poetic temperament was constrained and stifled by the formalism of orthodox Avantgarde poetics. Although he considered the classicism of the Polish Avantgarde to be a historical necessity because of the specific situation of Polish literature, and an antidote to the exceptionally strong and enduring Polish romantic tradition, Brzękowski nevertheless deplored the "classical inhibitions" of Avantgarde attitudes. In an autobiographical poem written in 1933, Brzękowski spoke of these inhibitions in his own poetry:

> I was not able to shout
> I was ashamed of strong words like a woman of her belly
> I was ashamed of ordinary feelings of ordinary transposition
> words soul heart and spirit
> I could not introduce myself in a simple way
> I am
>
> ["Autobiography"]

> nie potrafiłem krzyczeć
> wstydziłem się słów mocnych jak kobieta swego brzucha
> wstydziłem się uczuć zwyczajnych zwykłej transpozycji
> słów dusza serce i ducha
> nie mogłem przedstawić się w sposób prosty
> jestem
>
> ["Autobiografia"]

Indirectness of emotion and rigorous constructivism appeared to him as classical in their ideal of equilibrium, moderation, and the preponderance of reason over feeling. To him they also seemed to contradict the revolutionary character of the formal Avantgarde innovations: "In this way the literary movement which by its own spirit should be romantic—proclaimed in fact classicist postulates."[42] The paradox of this situation must have been strongly felt by a poet who by his nature belonged to a poetic tradition that he himself described as one of directness, fantasy, and expressiveness, traits often sacrificed in the interest of proportion and harmony. Thus, a little more than a decade after Peiper's complete and programmatic denunciation of romanticism in *Nowe usta*, an Avantgarde poet called for the rehabilitation of romantic attitudes in which he saw "the creation of a new vision of the poetic world and of a new imagination."[43]

In three of the volumes of poetry written by Brzękowski in the late twenties and early thirties—*In the Cathode (Na katodzie*, 1928), *In the Second Person (W drugiej osobie*, 1933), and *Around the Compressed Mouth (Dookoła zaciśnietych ust*, 1936)—his romanticism took on different forms and hues from that of his early poems. It showed through in his fondness for the exotic and the sensational, in his strong sensualism, and above all in his fascination with dreams, all of which brought him close to French surrealism. By 1938 Brzękowski himself acknowledged this connection: "Today, when I look at these facts from a perspective of several years, it seems strange to me that no critic called Ważyk, Kurek or me a surrealist."[44]

In Brzękowski's poetry dream is important as subject but even more important as a source of metaphor and compositional principle. The words *dream* and *sleep*

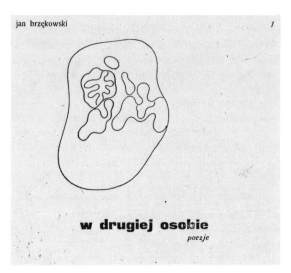

jan brzękowski

1

w drugiej osobie
poezje

The title page drawing by Jean Arp for Jan Brzękowski's *In the Second Person*

(and their derivatives) and the whole landscape of dreams are present in an overwhelming number of poems, all saturated with eroticism and, like the surrealists, with frequent Freudian symbolism. The romantic dreamer is accompanied by the sensualist, whose wealth of color, touch, smell, and taste speak of a "gourmandise of the senses."

unripe smile

the ostracism of dreams painted in red color, the color of greatness
and thought provident and sweet like a banana
but the eyes are the color of sky, sky built of oysters
which the sun adorns, great chicken egg of transformations

it is impossible to be too greedy—this plate of joy
testifies perhaps to physical health—but it isn't that—since
through hurry one has to simplify spring in the mouth
and pour May like a green smile into purple glasses

niedojrzały uśmiech

ostracyzm snów pomalowanych na kolor czerwony, kolor wielkości
i myśl zabiegliwa i słodka jak banan
ależ oczy są koloru nieba, nieba zbudowanego z ostryg
które przystraja słońce, wielkie kurze jajo przemian

nie można być zbyt łakomym — ten półmisek radości
świadczy może o fizycznym zdrowiu — ale to nie to — bowiem
należy wiosnę przez pośpiech w ustach uprościć
i maj jak uśmiech zielony nalać w kieliszki purpurowe

The characteristic Avantgarde association of the abstract with the concrete in a single metaphor ("plate of joy," "thought . . . sweet like a banana") seems to correspond with Brzękowski's special combination of intellectuality and sensuality, paralleling the split between the romantic and the realist. By resorting to dreams and eroticism, Brzękowski expressed his deepest self and also found an escape, a pretext for ignoring his realistic side:

> at night
> covered with stars and sleep
> we forget about the day
> the day knotty with events
> and accidents
> wrapped in a cover of everydayness.

> ["Tomorrow"]

> w noc
> gwiazdami okrytą i snem
> zapominamy o dniu
> dniu sękatym od wydarzeń
> i wypadków
> okrytych pokrowcem codzienności.

> ["Jutro"]

While the poet's duality was unresolved in his first volume, a new characteristic appears in his poetry beginning with *In the Cathode*—parody and irony, which act as mediators and as a solution to the pervasive dichotomy:

> And

> there is something unspeakably funny in it
> like distance, sorrow, waves . . .
> like the coquetry of sublime matters
> . . .
> it is sad like meeting in trains going in opposite directions
> and like ammonia
> and *amo*
> it wrings tears

> I

> jest w tym coś niewypowiedzianie śmiesznego
> jak dal, żal, fal . . .
> jak kokietowanie rzeczy wzniosłych
> . . .
> jest to smutne jak spotkanie w pociągach jadących w przeciwnych
> kierunkach
> i jak amoniak
> i amo
> wyciska łzy

In Polish, the irony is even more prominent because of the extensive play on sounds that can be only partly indicated in translation. In Brzękowski's poetry sound similarities often provide parody and ambiguity and even his use of traditional versification produces ambivalence and conflict with the untraditional content, the ambiguous associational imagery, and elliptical style. A critic has drawn a parallel between Brzękowski's poetry and surrealist painting: "The smooth forms of the regular verse in Brzękowski's poems played a role analogous to the technique of naturalistic description in the painting of the surrealists."[45] The same critic speaks of the "parodistic dreams" in Brzękowski's poetry, the automatism of its protagonists, the grotesque character of its eroticism, and the parodistic treatment of the motifs of crime, terror, sadism, and the macabre that frequently appear. The fantastic stories told in some of Brzękowski's poems are ambiguous: they imitate certain stereotypes, but at the same time they mock them: "The plots of sensational and melodramatic films perform here a peculiar function. They are treated parodistically, but at the same time in lyrical categories. Through them he expresses nostalgia for a naive and unequivocal world, an orderly world based on simple principles and moral criteria." Thus parody and irony in Brzękowski's poetry balance and check his basically romantic sensibility.

In many poems the romantic is treated in an ironic, derogatory manner, but in Brzękowski's mature poetry the poet makes a more serious attempt to accept and reconcile the duality. Many of these poems, especially in the volume characteristically entitled *In the Second Person,* are a dialogue with the self. The use of the second person singular pronoun "you" *(ty)* indicates a desire for distance, objectivity, and soberness, but not necessarily a rejection of his other identities. In "thought about permanent employment" such a dialogue takes place between the romantic dreamer—that part of Brzękowski that in *The Pulse* turned to symbolism, and in his later poetry to surrealism—and the realist—the poet of the *Switch* and the Cracow Avantgarde who controls and disciplines the unbridled imagination of the romantic dreamer by means of poetic form:

> you also felt the redness which the morning shouted
> when the sky grew into the sun a needless thistle
> you were a tower stinging the festering wound
> a rose in the hair.
>
> you
> were also the asphalt song broken at noon
> on your chest you caressed the dromedaries of sleep
> you wanted to populate
> the jungle of words
> and in December
> you hung on your neck the perspectives of July.
>
> you also
> kissed the evening with hot darkness
> you were love
> a big word and you charmed with the expression: like

you also
you
and he

I.

    myśl o stałym zajęciu

ty także czułeś czerwień którą krzyczał ranek
gdy niebo rosło w słońce niepotrzebny oset
byłeś wieżą bodącą rozjątrzoną ranę
różą we włosach.

ty
byłeś także asfaltową pieśnią rozbitą w południe
na piersiach pieściłeś dromadery snu
chciałeś zaludnić
dżunglę słów
i w grudniu
zawieszałeś na szyi perspektywy lipca.

ty także
wieczór całowałeś gorącą ciemnością
byłeś miłością
wielkim słowem i czarowałeś wyrazem: jak
ty także
ty
i on

ja.

While the form "you" translates the desire for distance and objectivity, the adverb
"also" that is repeated three times establishes a complicity between the two personae of the poet's personality. Brzękowski's awareness of his own duality is not
painful but is a source of additional perspectives and of a creative play of oppositions. The first two stanzas of the poem reveal the contradictions (sun / thistle,
tower / wound, July / December), and the last stanza brings their resolution; in
the poetic act as in the act of love, the "you" and the "I" merge.

Dream, important as a theme in Brzękowski's poetry, also defined the nature
of his metaphors. While Peiper's metaphors had a subjective motivation in an anecdote or story, and Przyboś's were semantically or visually motivated, the motivation of Brzękowski's metaphors—aside from aural and visual effects—is frequently
to be found in dreams. It is the world of the dream that is most often the source
for the boldness and the strangeness of unexpected "surrealist" combinations of
words, concepts, and images:

At night
hot like eyelashes like a bird
nestled into the blueness of foreign thoughts

you walk on the toothless streets, streets like
a pomegranate, like
a poppy field in a dream.

["Eyebrow"]

Nocą
gorącą jak rzęsy jak ptak
wtulony w niebieszcz obcych myśli
idziesz bezzębnymi ulicami, ulicami jak
granat, jak
makowe pola we śnie.

["Brew"]

The recognition of dreams is also a recognition of the imagination. In an essay written in 1938 under the ostensibly rebellious title "The Liberated Imagination," Brzękowski polemicized with Peiper for whom the creative process was a matter of craftsmanship and intellectual construction. Brzękowski rehabilitated imagination in the creative process and refused to see the essence of poetry in its formal aspect: "The fundamental element of poetry is not form, not beautiful metaphors or sentences, but images in *statu nascendi,* the forge of images or metaphors itself—*the imagination.* The poet is he who possesses poetic fantasy, who knows how to transpose it later into words. Without poetic imagination there can be no question of true poetry, although a good craftsman knows how to give quite similar pseudo-poetic products without it."[46] The last words in the passage refer to Peiper, whose metaphors, according to Brzękowski, were typical of purely formal poetic figures. In blatant disagreement with Avantgarde attitudes, Brzękowski considered the imagination to be the essence of poetry, the poetic act as the moment of liberation of the imagination. To produce poetic images of true value and not formalistic metaphors, the poet's imagination had to be entirely spontaneous. Brzękowski distinguished between image and metaphor; while a metaphor was a single image expressed in two words and was an element of form, the poetic image on the contrary was a developed metaphor, a chain of poetic thoughts expressed in words. He said in another essay,

> In this way the metaphor assumed an even more noble form, since it does not substitute the comparison of two verbal symbols between which the conjunction 'like' has been omitted, but it directly expresses emotional elements that are poetically organized. The metaphoric sentence expresses in a *poetic manner* some life or visual reality of a specific emotional hue that can be expressed only by that and not another system of words.[47]

In his distinction between metaphor and poetic image, Brzękowski introduced the concept of time. In distinction to the purely formal character of a simple metaphor, the poetic image—that is, a "metaphoric sentence"—was "a group of images united by the community of their vision in time."[48] Alone among the Avantgarde poets, Brzękowski turned his attention to the problem of time both in his theoretical writings and in his poetic practice. The opposition of metaphor to image implied an opposition of space versus time, and of two different concepts of poetry—poetry to be read and poetry to be recited and heard. Poetry existed both statically and kinetically, both on the printed page and as a word spoken in time. According to Brzękowski this gave rise to an unstable and constantly changing equilibrium between the two aspects. The way in which a poet approached poetry—to be read silently or spoken—determined its character and structure: spatial in the first case, and temporal in the second. Brzękowski opposed the Avantgarde concept of poetry as being solely to be read in print and found Avantgarde poetry individualistic, indirect, static, exclusively spatial, and three-dimensional. "The poetry of the Avantgarde had until now one deficiency above all: it rendered poetic reality, but it did not express its becoming in time."[49] Brzękowski pointed out the predilection of Avantgarde poets for descriptive "landscape" poetry, as well as the amazing disparity between twentieth-century poetry and prose, where time was one of the central preoccupations from Proust to Joyce. In introducing his new perspective into Avantgarde poetics he proposed to substitute "thinking in time" for "metaphoric thinking."

Brzękowski called for "the saturation" of poetry with time, and for a poetry that was "an organization of poetic reality in time."[50] As with the poetic image, poetic time was not a formal element for Brzękowski but a component of the imagination. It was independent of physical time and relied entirely on its suggestiveness, its ability to communicate to the reader the sense of duration, "the reciprocal temporal shifts and relations which exist in the imagination between elements of a certain system or between several different systems."[51] In poetic practice this meant stressing temporal sequences, successions, oppositions in time, emphasis on duration, becoming, lapse of time, passing from the detail to the whole, from the concrete to the abstract, and vice versa. In his attempt to introduce time into poetry Brzękowski rehabilitated the anecdote as *par excellence* temporal in nature. In his own poetry he used story freely, especially in his socially oriented poems and "fantastic" poems that are poetic transpositions of detective stories, sensational newspaper articles, and films. These poems also use cinematographic techniques: "The technique of feverish montage, the specific rhythm of narration based on the alternation of lyrical-dramatic formulations (accelerated) and epic (slow), the use of distant backgrounds and sudden close-ups, the passage from collectivity to the presentation of characteristic situations and the behavior of participants in a crowd, interruption of the sequence by the inclusion of graphic-symbolic shortcuts of a journalistic nature. . . ."[52] The following poem is one of the more successful examples of Brzękowski's use of these techniques:

Silk Shops

Boy
gaunt and pale, dreaming of the fragrance of the unknown woman,
    flogged every day with desire
next to your fourteen years—charred by fire
a new October happens and gives birth
to November in the year eighteen.

Strings of carts trailed along the road behind the grange, where
the blue loop of the high road bends to the west like a whip
and with a great racket they entered the marketplace, heated by
        the sun, russeted in the autumn
on which
noon rang with scrap iron against the silk shops
and looked into moldy vestibules.

at that time—
the chestnuts had already become bald frost crackled on mustaches
        bristling russetly
and it was falling on entrails steaming from vodka
the silk shops were muffling the tumult of the day, amid which
the rifles of volunteer guards were shining
and in the bayonets attached to the sun—frost
which they cut like daily bread. Women
felt faintness in their thighs, the shaking of the road and
        discomfort—
blue yards of silk hung from the shelves swollen with warmth
        and the tavern—
a swarm throbbing with humming smoked with steam.

it is not known who fired, it isn't known what for—
fear threw itself in the door mixed with the uproar of voices
and the stream of blood, which—made the bayonet pink.

("people, have control over yourselves"—said the doctor as
        he took the lancet in his hand)
lamentation
struck the sky and hung on the bells.

"the army is coming!"—someone suddenly shouted and right away—
a roar ran out from the taverns. already the peasants brandishing
        whips
were filling the town with the hurried creaking of carts—
in the northern part of the market
shining helmets of soldiers glistened in the sun.

the soldiers, splendid and ominous,
helplessly stood there—where the russet stain in front of
        the silk shop
coagulated in the sun into rusty autumn.

At night
in the tumult of dreams, among blood and bandages, smashing
        the bars of a cage
you sweetly raped unruly and fat women
white blood-stained rumps glistened in the sun like helmets

when on the marketplace—
firing
the new silk shop—was being stormed.

Bławatne sklepy

Chłopcze
wychudły i blady, śniący o woni kobiety nieznanej, żądzą smagany co
dzień
obok twoich lat czternastu — zwęglonych od żaru
nowy Październik dzieje się i rodzi
listopad w r. 18-ym.

Sznury wozów ciągnęły drogą za folwarkiem, kędy
sina pętla gościńca na zachód zakręca jak bicz
i wielkim jarmarkiem wjeżdżały na rynek, w słońcu wygrzany, wyrudziały
w jesień
na którym
południe żelastwem dzwoniło po sklepach bławatnych
i zaglądało do omszałych sieni.

o tej porze —
kasztany już wyłysiały mróz chrzęścił na wąsach nastroszonych rudo
i opadał na trzewia dymiące od wódki
bławatne sklepy tłumiły dnia tumult, wśród którego
błyszczały karabiny ochotniczej straży
i w bagnetach na słońcu zatkniętych — mróz
krajały jak chleb codzienny. W udach
kobiety czuły niemoc, drogi trzęsienie i niewczasy —
bławatne poły sukna z półek zwisały ciepłem wydęte a szynk —
parą dymił gwarem rozszumiały rój.

nie wiadomo kto strzelił, nie wiadomo po co —
lęk rzucił się w bramy zmieszany z głosów wrzawą
i krwi strumieniem, który — zaróżowił bagnet.

(„ludzie miejcież upamiętanie "— mówił pan doktor gdy ujmował w
rękę lancet)
lament
w niebo uderzył i zawisł na dzwonach.

„wojsko idzie! "— ktoś krzyknął nagle i już —
wrzask z szynków wybiegł, już chłopi wymachując batem
wozów pośpiesznym skrzypieniem napełniali miasto —
na północnej części rynku
błysnęły w słońcu lśniące hełmy żandarmów.

żandarmi, wspaniali i groźni,
bezradnie stanęli tam — gdzie ruda plama przed sklepem bławatnym
tężała w słońcu w rdzawą jesień.

Nocą
w tumulcie snów, wśród krwi i bandaży, rozbijając pręty klatki
słodko gwałciłeś kobiety krnąbrne i grube
błyszczały w słońcu jak hełmy białe pokrwawione zady

gdy na rynku —
strzelając
rozbijano — nowy sklep bławatny.

The poem both begins and ends with a personal recollection of adolescence and its story is like a flashback of memory. The incident in the village is presented within the framework of biography and the memory of the events is inseparable from the memory of the poet's own sexual fantasies at the age of fourteen. The two moments, subjective and objective, coincide when they both foreshadow the oncoming crisis: on the personal plane it is the passage from adolescence to maturity, and on the historical plane violence in a small provincial town signals the October revolution. Constant shifts of perspective take place not only between internal and external reality but also within the story itself, between a general overview of the scene and specific details or bits of conversation reminiscent of the cinematic close-up. The technique of the close-up, flashback, shifting perspective, and alternating planes of reference are all characteristic not only of film but also of the novel.

What attracted Brzękowski to the techniques of films and to a lesser degree the novel was the effect of accumulation and the simultaneity of facts, impressions, experiences, and emotions. They were not limited to a single fact or emotion typical of poetry. In an excellent study on Brzękowski the critic Janusz Sławiński points out the kinship between simultaneity in film, in poetry, and in dreams: "The simultaneity of many realities means, in film, the parallelism of several actions, and in poetry, ambiguity. Multiplication of meanings, and with it, multiplication of images. Movement in the sphere of semantics: mutual pushing and penetration of meanings, parallelism and simultaneity of different chains of associations."[53] All of these characteristics apply to dreams as well as to the type of poetry proposed and practiced by Brzękowski. The importance of dreams in his poetry, as subject and source for his metaphors, has been discussed earlier; we touch here upon another aspect of dreams, their structural properties. These were important formative elements in the structure of the poems of the author of the volume *In the Second Person*. Brzękowski wrote in an essay: "A poem is a poetic phenomenon organized independently from the laws of Aristotelian logic and the systems existing in nature. This is why the surrealists justly paid attention to the enormous importance of this a-practical factor that develops unlike everyday reality and which is the dream."[54] But rather than accept dreams in all their chaos and disorganization, like the surrealists, Brzękowski proposed to use in his poetry recollection, poetically organized, which had the advantage of rendering "the process of becoming, of change in time, and not only the system of poetic imagination."[55] Brzękowski connected the problem of time with the structural concept of the ellipsis, and called for an "elliptical style" that would include a temporal element and be an ellipsis developed in time. Both ellipsis and poetic time implied intensification and acceleration of imaginative experience for poetic reality is both faster, more intense, and therefore shorter than the time of ordinary reality.

In his ideas on poetic structure Brzękowski stands between the totally un-structured free-associationism of French surrealism and the postulates of rigor and order of the Cracow Avantgarde. Although he accepted associationism as a principle of poetic construction, he did so with reservations. For him writing was always a struggle between two factors: poetic consciousness, the necessity of discipline and construction, and the sense of external reality, which is disorderly, rich, always threatening order, and difficult to contain within a poetic structure. The spon-taneity of associations is controlled by conscious creative effort—here the Polish poet differed from the French surrealists—but unlike Peiper and Przyboś, Brzękow-ski gave imagination much greater license. He made a distinction between the con-struction and the structure of a poem: "Construction is something more than struc-ture. It is a structure according to a principle, each element is indispensable and connected with others by the aid of certain means unique in the given case. The core of the construction is the idea itself." [56] The poet illustrated his distinction with the example of a crystal, the edges of which give an indication of its structure and the angle under which the surfaces meet, but its construction can be known only after having studied its axis. According to Brzękowski the poem can be struc-tured consciously or unconsciously, but the construction can only be the result of a conscious effort with a certain principle in view. He admitted that the poems of Przyboś and Peiper are "constructed" because they are the product of a con-scious constructive effort, whereas in his own poetry a few poems are "constructed," the rest only "structured." Faithful to his poetic temperament, Brzękowski broke with Peiper's model of construction and engineering, with what he called "the legend of construction." [57]

The elliptical style and associationism that Brzękowski promoted together with Przyboś but in opposition to Peiper meant for him—but not for Przyboś—a certain loosening of structure, resulting in what he called a "free" structure in his poems. The concept of ellipsis signified an even distribution of tension in a poem, and to achieve it he eliminated elements that serve as links and transitions in the poem, that is, the elements of "low poetic intensity." The elliptical style was characterized by discontinuity and sudden jumps from word to word, from metaphor to metaphor. Janusz Sławiński has described Brzękowski's elliptical style in this way: "The image is developed as if by 'portions,' not in the rhythm of parts resulting from each other, but in the rhythm of a succession of parts in which 'the empty places' perform a function as signals of change of direction of associations. Where, therefore, the junction or node of the whole course did not really exist in fact—but where they were contained in the potentially loaded 'between-words.'" [58] Unlike Peiper, Brzękowski was not interested in connecting images and metaphors—a key idea of tight construction, but opted instead for associationism and ellipsis, which were constructive only insofar as they were the result of a selec-tion. The poem became a sum of "subimages," of smaller poetic images that formed a whole when taken together. In the poetry of Przyboś, ellipsis consisted only in the elimination of less important elements, and even his most associational poems had a rigorous structure. In Brzękowski's poetry ellipsis often explains the free-associational leaps; the associations are looser and do not always revolve around a single conceptual axis, as in the poem "The Women of My Dreams":

The weight, the color of words is known
and yet it is otherwise—

on corn manes
on gray and thirsty earth
they trod heavily like pregnant mares
swinging their hips with wind from the mountains
the women of my dreams

the sky the copper fire shouted—shouted with a wider and wider range
and below the sun grew, saltier—salty like blood
it entered the mouth, a trembling bird.

from above a tree
the horizon measured noon on the blue shield
it hung over the bay with a milky breast

the red sea was whitened by a gull
when—
chopping heads
the sun let a woman's head into the horizon
cut off
like a stump.

Kobiety moich snów

Znany jest ciężar, barwa słów
a jednak jest inaczej —

po grzywach zbóż
po ziemi siwej i spragnionej
kroczyły głucho jak ciężarne klacze
biodrami kołysząc z wiatrem gór
kobiety moich snów

niebo miedziany pożar krzyczał — krzyczał coraz szerzej
a w dole rosło słońce, słońsze — jak krew słone,
w usta wchodziło drżący ptak.

znad drzewa
horyzont południe na niebieskiej tarczy mierzył
nad zatoką zawisał mleczną piersią

czerwone morze przebieliła mewa
gdy —
słońce ścinając głowy
głowę kobiecą w widnokrąg wpuściło
odciętą
jak pniak.

The poem is primarily about desire and sexuality, which are associated with fertility (pregnant mares, the milky breast) but also with violence (the sun "salty like blood," the sun "chopping heads"). There is an interplay between masculine elements (corn, sun, bird, and tree) and feminine elements (earth, mares, women, sky, shield, breast, the sea). Each stanza develops a different image in which these two elements form a new pattern. Aside from this general principle there are no logical connections or development between individual images. The opening lines of the poem are an admission that the poet is not using words literally. This and similar poems by Brzękowski are best described in his own words, "The subject matter is somewhat hazy, but full of emotional content that is contained within it in a potential state, and has the ability to evoke images or emotions in the reader or listener." [59] Just as the source of Brzękowski's poetic images is neither logic nor syntax, the poet did not consider syntax to be a major constructive element and he disagreed with Peiper that the ambition of the Avantgarde was the creation of elaborated, sophisticated sentences. On the contrary, he saw the possibility of achieving interesting poetic effects by loosening syntax. In his own poetry Brzękowski stressed his use of contrast rather than homogeneity in connecting the various elements in the poem, a contrast "that endows the poetic images with full expressiveness by simultaneously bringing out aspects that are both positive and negative, elevated and humorous, great and petty, colorful and colorless, both contained in them and existing outside them. Only after having exhausted these possibilities resulting from opposition and contrast is an impression of fullness produced, of satiation, a certain emotional relaxation." [60]

In his theoretical writings Brzękowski called his concept of poetry *integral* and *metareal*, referring to two different aspects of his poetics. While the first identified him as a member of the Cracow Avantgarde, the second brought him close to surrealism and at the same time put him distinctly apart from it. The adjective "integral" referred to the homogeneity of poetry, that it "contains in itself a postulate of exclusivity toward elements that do not belong to the same system," [61] and this was the fundamental point of departure of Avantgarde poetics. "Integral" defined a poetry of maximal condensation, tension, and allusiveness, of cohesiveness of images and sustained metaphorization—a poetry standing in opposition to the poetry of mood or reflection. "Metareal" expressed an attitude toward poetry contradictory in many ways to that of the Avantgarde, without, however, negating any of these other definitions. It designated a poetry in which the imagination played an outstanding role. Metarealism naturally brings to mind "surrealism" with which it shares a common opposition to realism, but in contradistinction to surrealism, metarealism stressed the need for a poetry that was controlled and organized. Above all, metarealism stipulated the desubjectivization and objectification of the imagination, and consequently of poetry. In so doing, Brzękowski separated himself both from surrealism and from the poetics of the Avantgarde.

To the scholastic treatment of the essence of life, which in poetry is dogmatic, naïve realism, we oppose a new revival of what is human, a *new humanism* of our times saturated with greatness; we proclaim the poetic synthesis of the romantic way of seeing the world and of external reality, a poetry of the new man based on the imagination. A poetry that is neither realist, nor romantic, nor surreal. It goes far beyond these designations, it is metareal.[62]

Thus the conflict between the romantic and the realist that burst out in the youthful poetry of *The Pulse,* and persisted concealed behind irony and parody in the early 1930s, found by the time of *Around the Compressed Mouth* (1936) a solution in a poetic attitude that was a dialogue between Avantgardism and surrealism, and an acceptance of both the limitations and the freedom of the imagination.

JALU KUREK

The poetic debut of Jalu Kurek coincided with the debuts of his two future associates in the *Switch,* Julian Przyboś and Jan Brzękowski. Like *Screws* and *The Pulse,* Kurek's first volume of poetry, *Heat Waves (Upały),* was published in 1925. Unlike the two volumes of his friends, it was not published by the *Switch* but by a small publishing house in Warsaw called the Almanac of New Art whose editors were sympathetic to the new art of the times but were less exclusive and programmatic than the editor of the *Switch,* Tadeusz Peiper. In 1922 the young Kurek sent his poems to Peiper, who refused to publish them as foreign to the spirit of the *Switch,* but he did not exclude the possibility of future collaboration between the poet and the Avantgarde group—a collaboration that in fact developed during the second series of the *Switch* and continued with the appearance of *Linia,* of which Kurek became the chief editor. Despite his close formal association with the *Switch,* Kurek's poetic temperament, described by Brzękowski as "lyrically effusive," placed his poetry on the margin of the official Avantgarde program. Kurek himself admitted that from the beginning his poetry could not be contained within the limits of Avantgarde poetics. Brzękowski was puzzled, even, by the very association of Kurek with the *Switch,* whose concepts such as the "shamefulness of feelings" and indirectness in poetry were diametrically opposed to Kurek's poetry. And yet it seems as if Kurek himself did not feel estranged or out of place in the Avantgarde group. Judging by his later statements, even more than Brzękowski and Przyboś he remained loyal to the spirit and to most of the theories of the *Switch.* An attentive reading of Kurek's poetry reveals traits that made this association and loyalty both inevitable and understandable rather than puzzling.

Salient in Kurek's poems is the speaking voice and the presence of a "feeling" subject. The overwhelming majority of his poems is written either with the first person singular pronoun, or the first person plural pronoun. When the poet does not speak in his own name he identifies with the personae of his poems, whether they are rebellious workers, passengers on a sinking ship, or the American poet Walt Whitman. Although Kurek frequently reverts to this procedure, which a critic has labeled "the poetry of role," [63] the speaking voice or persona of the poems is not always consistent or easily identifiable. It is common that in the course of a single poem there is a passage from "I" to "we," while the relationship between them remains blurred. Frequently poems are addressed to a second person; this further enhances the presence and audibility of the speaking subject. The people addressed in Kurek's poems represent an even broader spectrum than his personae—they range from God, the Madonna, and Rimbaud, to the earth, clouds, and poetry.

If the identity of the speaking voice is sometimes blurred, this is even more true of those to whom the poems are directed; occasionally Kurek designates them in the most general terms such as "brother" or "friends." Kurek's use of the form of address indicates a need for dialogue and a need to speak out his emotions and the blurring of the identity of the persona and the addressee increases the subjectivity of the poems and raises their emotional temperature.

Kurek presents the world not so much through the prism of his vision—as was typical for Przyboś—but through the prism of his emotions. His world is basically egocentric, as in the following poem:

earth

mornings beat on the pavements with the iron hammer of steps
who imprisoned us in the green armor of your furious pupils

words are like roses we don't want roses stars smell like flowers
the swaying squares of cities will hum under my armpit

you hang the damp sheets of meadows in my irises
and I bury myself in you with the painful question mark of hands

someone like the ocean combs your wet hair in the mirror of the sky
the telegraph of the sun ticks out for me the last cables

night leaves you faint kicked by hobnails of heels
when you wake you are white and in your eyes you have the green of a forest

yesterday died today and tomorrow will wake day after tomorrow
someone will open the blue for me with a rusty key

ziemia

ranki biją po brukach żelaznym młotem kroków
kto nas w zielony pancerz twych wściekłych źrenic okuł

słowa są jak róże nie chcemy róż gwiazdy pachną jak kwiaty
pod pachą mi zaszumią rozkołysane miast kwadraty

rozwieszasz w mych tęczówkach wilgotne prześcieradła łąk
a ja się wpinam w ciebie bolesnym pytajnikiem rąk

ktoś ci jak ocean mokre włosy w lustrze nieba czesze
telegraf słońca mi wystukuje ostatnie depesze

noc cię zostawia omdlałą skopaną ćwiekami obcasów
a kiedy się budzisz jesteś biała i w oczach masz zieleń lasu

wczoraj umarło dzisiaj a jutro się zbudzi pojutrze
ktoś mi otworzy błękit zardzewiałym kluczem

Both thematically and formally the poem is representative of Kurek's poetry, especially his early poetry. The speaking voice moves back and forth between the first

The cover of Jalu Kurek's
Songs about the Republic

person singular and first person plural pronoun, reflecting Kurek's contradictory desire for poetry to be both intimately personal and an expression of more collective attitudes. Similarly, the emotion expressed by the poem is not simple and unequivocal, but conflicting and contradictory. The conflict between the poet's love of nature and his programmatically futuristic sympathy for civilization and the city is a central theme in his poems.

In Kurek's poetry there is a strong social and civic current. Three of the five volumes published between 1925 and 1939 could be described as "committed" poetry—these are *Songs about the Republic (Śpiewy o Rzeczypospolitej,* 1930), *II Songs about the Republic (II Śpiewy o Rzeczypospolitej,* 1932), and the long poem *Mouth for Help (Usta na pomoc,* 1933). The poems in these volumes are exhortations for work and the construction of the new independent Poland. Many were written on the occasion of a public event such as the inauguration of the radio station in Cracow, the death of the explorer Amundsen, or the return to Poland of the mortal remains of famous Polish writers. Programmatic in tone and content and formally simplistic, these poems are the least interesting part of Kurek's poetic output. The long poem *Mouth for Help* unconvincingly combines a social theme with a personal theme of love. Kurek's sense of social commitment found its best outlet in the numerous novels he wrote throughout his career. The best known of these is *Influenza Rages in Naprawa (Grypa szaleje w Naprawie,* 1933), which was widely read in its time, translated into several languages, and won an award of the Polish Academy of Literature in 1935. Kurek treated his own social poetry with reservations. He wrote, "From the beginning my poetic output breaks into two branches: the first—the proper and main branch—is pure lyrical poetry of an innovative character; the second, with regard to its artistic expression, is a rather accessible and simple kind of poetry. This second type . . . does not constitute the full expression of the author's poetic convictions, but in his understanding it fulfills an important and useful task." [64]

Kurek rightly places his *Songs about the Republic* close to Peiper's narrative poem *For Example,* and situates both in the context of "applied poetry" that was part of Avantgarde practice in the 1930s in response to Poland's increasingly tense political and social situation. Formally the roots of this poetry can be found in the early programmatic poetry of the Avantgarde that celebrated the new modern civilization of the city, the masses, and the machine. Although other Avantgarde poets wrote in the same poetic convention, its specific form—which bordered on the manifesto and political proclamation—was curiously more congenial to poets like Kurek and Peiper, but for different and to a certain extent opposite reasons. With Peiper it corresponded to his rhetorical tendency while with Kurek it went hand in hand with his strong emotionality, and related to it, his need to be the mouthpiece of a collectivity. In poets like Peiper and Kurek these two opposite dispositions— the rhetorical and the emotional—found not only a common outlet, but were often almost indistinguishable from one another.

The last stanza of the poem "earth" contains a line that denies and confuses the natural sequence of time: "yesterday died today and tomorrow will wake day after tomorrow." The divisions between days become obliterated and particular units merge together into one eternal, everlasting, and infinite time, symbolized by the blue sky. This is a surprising ending to a poem that progresses according to a movement rhythmically measured by different times of day from morning to evening. Preoccupation with time, toward which Kurek had an adversary attitude, runs through much of his poetry. Calendar and clock time is the element that confines and limits the poet's freedom. In one of his poems, "Poetry," day is compared to a rustling clock, a minute to a "fist of unfulfilled dreams," and an hour is a shout from women on the shore delaying the desired journey—poetry. It is the monotonous, deadly time of train schedules: "The clatter of trains mutilates the nights, / nights drowned under the armpits of dreams, / since childhood I know this monotonous murder of hours" ("Stukot pociągów kaleczy noce, / noce utopione pod pachami snów, / od dziecka znam to monotonne mordowanie godzin") ("Mouth for Help" ["Usta na pomoc"]). Time measured by the clock and the sun is a threat to the poet and his integrity: "Each day breaks me who is straight in your smooth mirrors" ("Dzień każdy łamie mnie prostego w twych gładziutkich lustrach") ("Time" ["Czas"]). The poet tries to escape: "Save me from your stinging symbols, scorching stars" ("Od twych symbolów kłujących, parzących gwiazd mnie ratuj") (ibid.). Opposed to measured time is the limitless time of infinity, which is also the time of mystical unity: "I alone slowly enter the studded chest: into infinity. / . . . . . . / Belted by your sight, by the ribbon of mystical sanctifications / I sink into your all-powerful hands drenched with light ("Tylko ja z wolna wchodzę w okutą skrzynię : w nieskończoność. / . . . . . . / Przepasany twym wzrokiem, wstęgą mistycznych uświęceń / wtapiam się w twoje wszechmocne, światłem ulewne ręce") (ibid.). The freedom that infinity brings is also, paradoxically, imprisonment ("the chest"), the moment of mystical communion is also the moment of self-annihilation ("I sink into your . . . hands").

The desire to wrench himself away from physical reality to become submerged in a mystic unity with nature can be seen in another recurrent motif of Kurek's poetry—the eyes. A poet of emotions and not of landscape—despite his strong attachment to nature—Kurek does not want to see: "Throw your eyes behind you. / . . . . . . / I leave without the eyes" ("Oczy za siebie rzuć / . . . . . . / Odchodzę bez oczu") ("Mouth for Help" ["Usta na pomoc"]). The eyes, like too precise a vision, hamper mystical experience. In Kurek's poetry the eyes are frequently associated with wounds and injury: "the dusk . . . swam across my one injured eye" ("Zmierzch . . . jedno oko skaleczone przepływał mi wpław"); and: "Nail your raptures soaked in wounds / in the freshest wound of the heart: the eyes" ("Wbij swe zachwyty ubroczone w ranach / w najswieższą ranę serca: w oczy"). The corollary to this is Kurek's preference for night over day, and it is not accidental that in the poem "The battle of day with night" night emerges victorious at the end of the poem.

Kurek's strong mystical current can also be felt in the tone of his numerous openly religious hymns, prayers, and litanies. One of his best known poems is addressed to the Virgin Mary:

to the Madonna

Not to pray in churches taut and straight as a sentence,
the saddest are winding streets not tired by waiting.

I saw you, standing in the rain, writing with your eyes in the heavens,
unfortunately I am a poet and would like to live in your hair.

Open gate of the sky, your eyes become wet,
you stand in the street in which wild windows have bitten.

Rain is the son of the sun, blessed music of clouds,
how many times the mansion of spring blossomed and hummed in your hair!

How many starry meditations I drown in you, tower of spirey dreams,
eternal signal flowing near our heads!

If I love you like the sun, then I love you like rain,
how much dearer to me is the one who is the dearest!

We have to wait for the sun only one night,
while for rain we must wait a month or two months.

Holy grass, not stepped upon in the cloud of green grazings,
you steam rain of love in which I wish to plunge.

You are the bell of terror which no one hears,
shepherdess tending deer on the cord of silence.

The fragrance of your damp meadows pours into my mouth,
I stand in the open church, the deer praying in the streets.

Praised be your eyes, washed in blossoming downpours,
in which I rinse my poems that are strong and hard like trees.

Blessed be your feet bleeding with the lips of mothers
from which I grow upwards toward you with a sharp shouting flower.

do Matki Boskiej

Nie modlić się w kościołach napiętych i prostych jak zdanie,
są najsmutniejsze ulice kręte i nie zmęczone czekaniem.

Widziałem Cię, stojącą na deszczu, oczyma piszącą w niebiosach,
jestem niestety poetą i chciałbym zamieszkać w Twych włosach.

W ulicy, w którą się wgryzły obce, dzikie okna,
stoisz, otwarta bramo nieba i oczy Ci mokną.

Deszcz jest synem słońca, błogosławioną muzyką chmur,
ileż to razy we włosach rozkwitał i szumiał Ci wiosenny dwór!

Ileż gwiezdnych rozmyślań w Tobie topię, wieżo strzelistych snów,
wieczny sygnale płynący obok naszych głów!

Jeżeli kocham Cię jak słońce, to kocham Cię jak deszcz,
ileż mi droższy ten, który najdroższy jest!

Jedną noc tylko czekać musimy na słońce,
na deszcz zaś trzeba czekać miesiąc albo dwa miesiące.

Nie wydeptana trawo święta w obłoku zielonych przeżuwań,
parujesz deszczem miłości, w którym się pragnę unurzać.

Jesteś dzwonem na trwogę, którego nikt nie słyszy,
pasterko pasąca łanie na postronku ciszy.

Woń Twoich polan wilgotnych w usta mi się leje,
w otwartym kościele stoję, modlący się w ulicach jeleń.

Pochwalone Twe oczy myte w rozkwitłych ulewach,
w których płuczę me wiersze mocne i twarde jak drzewa.

Błogosławione Twe stopy broczące ustami matek,
od których rosnę wzwyż ku Tobie ostrym, krzyczącym kwiatem.

Because it is in the form of a prayer, Kurek's poem has been compared to Blaise
Cendrars's "Easter in New York," but the similarities are external and formal rather
than spiritual. Cendrars's poem is profoundly humanistic; moved by the human
suffering which he witnessed, the poet addressed a Christ in whom he did not
believe. The tone of Kurek's poem is one of worship and its imagery is curiously
baroque, reminiscent of the well-known litany to the Madonna of Loreto in the

liturgy of the Polish Catholic church, to which there are numerous allusions. The spirit of mysticism permeating the poem is also akin to baroque religious poetry.

Like the poem "earth," "to the Madonna" is structured around a similar dichotomy. The world of nature—sun, rain, grass, clouds, damp meadows—is opposed to the world of man and civilization—the street, "taut churches," "wild windows." The Madonna is identified with the world of nature of which she is an integral part. Thus the contradiction between city and nature parallels another puzzling contradiction of Kurek's: his fundamentally religious and even somewhat mystical nature conflicts with the defiantly antitraditional, atheistic attitudes of the futurist and Avantgarde movements with which he was associated. Occasionally Kurek mentions his contradictory nature in his post-World War II writings: "In many cases I constitute a stream of contradictions." [65] However only one of his poems, significantly entitled "My Pain," seems to speak directly of the contradictions that must have been at least felt by the poet at the time if not consciously acknowledged. The poem is openly autobiographical:

The day reduces to the sum of lines: the horizon.
Unaware, the evening already falls and smells of the next morning.
Slowly I raise over the simple-minded confusion
a soul full of fright and inspiration.

Measure me, how far I am from simplicity!
I know. This is why I purposely chose madness.
What could someone else do with these twenty-six years,
not having anything inside him but impetuous blood?
. . . . . .

Friends, I do not conceal it, I am not ashamed, I suffer.
I suffer with the new world.

Rise, proud like pain, sculptured in straight lines,
cancelled by the day, cut by the sunset, submerged by the stain of dawn.
The moon which became cool in your eyes
stings me distinctly in the face like the title on a book.

The landscapes which were sweet but boring
tired me, therefore I hand you an organized lament,
a faultless speech of emotion.
How can I explain before you
that the face speaks not only with the mouth,
that I know songs which are like a man naked,
that the world is for bringing out the man?
This fire must be taken up again.
It waits for us.

Dzień upraszcza się sumą linii: horyzontem.
Już nieświadomie się zmierzcha i przyszłym rankiem pachnie.
Z wolna wynoszę nad prostolinijny zamęt
duszę pełną przerażeń i natchnień.

Zmierzcie mnie, jak daleko jest mi do prostoty!
Wiem. Dlatego ja umyślnie wybrałem szaleństwo.
Cóż mógłby ktoś inny zrobić z tych dwudziestu sześciu lat,
nie mając w sobie nic prócz gwałtownej krwi?
. . . . . .
Przyjaciele, nie kryję tego, nie wstydzę się, cierpię.
Cierpię na nowy świat.

Wstańcie wyniośli jak ból, rzeźbieni w liniach prostych,
dniem przekreśleni, ścięci zachodem, zalani plamą świtu.
Księżyc, który w oczach waszych ostygł,
kłuje mnie w twarz wyraźnie jak na książce tytuł.

Te krajobrazy słodziutkie, lecz nudne
znużyły mnie, więc podaję wam płacz zorganizowany,
mowę wzruszenia wzorową.
Jak mam tłumaczyć się przed wami,
że twarz nie tylko ustami przemawia,
że znam pieśni, które są jak człowiek nagi,
że świat jest na to, aby podkreślał człowieka?
Ten ogień trzeba podjąć na nowo.
On na nas czeka.

["mój ból"]

Far from being accidental and external, conflict and contradiction are an inherent part of Kurek's personality, whether conscious or subconscious. It is interesting that contradiction is also one of the most characteristic and perhaps most attractive traits in his metaphors—a trait that accounts for the baroque aura of his poetry. Contradictory statements and oxymoronic figures abound: "rain is the son of the sun" ("deszcz jest synem słońca"); "drops huge as a crowd" ("krople olbrzymie jak tłum"); "this day which looks into our tanned faces / is not a day" ("ten dzień, który patrzy w nasze opalone twarze, / nie jest dniem"); "sweet crucifixion" ("słodke ukrzyżowanie"); "flowing with words I smoked like fire" ("płynąc słowami dymiłem jak ogień"). It seems plausible that it was precisely this natural tendency of Kurek toward contradiction, with all its poetic implications, that drew him toward Avantgarde poetics. The poet was sincere when he admitted that "the contestatory current corresponded to my deepest inclinations, and it accurately fitted my model of the imagination."[66] In Peiper's poetics Kurek found theoretical confirmation of an important element in his own poetry, his use of metaphor. It is true that not everything in these poetics suited Kurek's poetic disposition, but he was not a person to be discouraged by conflict and contradiction. He adopted from the Avantgarde what was most congenial to his poetry, primarily Peiper's concept of metaphor, and he ignored what was alien to his temperament, in particular the theory of the necessary indirectness of poetry. Before the *Switch* Kurek had another ally, Italian futurism, toward which he had a similarly eclectic and unorthodox attitude. Kurek described his first contact with the poetic theories of the *Switch* as "a revelation and a shock."[67] These two emotions are the exact measure and reflection of the simultaneous closeness and distance that existed between his poetry and Avantgarde theory.

If the poems of *Heat Waves* and *Songs about the Republic* were still in many respects alien to the poetics of the *Switch*, the volume *Mohigangas*, published in 1934, is clearly under the spell of Peiper. Alone among the Avantgarde poets Kurek seems to have assimilated and admired not only Peiper the theoretician but also Peiper the poet. There is a community of tone between the two poets, a similar tendency toward rhetoric—a great predilection for the form of direct address—as well as a similar treatment of metaphor as a purely cerebral product of the poet's mind. Following Peiper, Kurek believed that metaphor had no correspondent in the real world because poets "operate in a distinct, autonomous reality, on a second level where what is experienceable is mixed with what is imaginable. Under these conditions one can treat metaphor simply as a stylistic figure in linguistic manipulations. The poet carries out these operations according to his own model of seeing, vision, and vocabulary."[68] Neither Przyboś nor Brzękowski followed Peiper's concept of metaphor this far, or in this direction. For Kurek, poetry was above all an act of the imagination and the poet the perfect "organizer" of this imagination. The imagination was both source and motor force of poetry, and was inseparably tied to language. Only in and through the word could the poetic imagination be released. In Kurek's concept of the poetic act, experience played no role. His metaphors created their own autonomous reality with no connection to the reality outside it. Reality and its "truth" was not the goal of poetry and often remained in blatant contradiction with its poetic expression:

> These stone cubes raised in labor
> I touch with sight and hail with the poem.
> With what difficulty the structures rise, how people suffer,
> how hard the lines press, whose supple movement I praise.

["Multilevel Composition: Once More the City"]

> Te kamienne sześciany wydźwignięte w trudzie
> dotykam spojrzeniem i wierszem je pozdrawiam.
> Jak ciężko wznoszą się gmachy, jak bardzo cierpią ludzie,
> jak mocno gniotą linie, których ruch wiotki wysławiam.

["Kompozycja wieloplanowa: Jeszcze raz miasto"]

For Kurek poetic reality is superior to objective reality, and the poet is free to ignore it or change it at will, even to the point of contradiction. This explains why—in total agreement with Peiper—Kurek was disinterested in the pictorial visuality of the metaphor, and even hostile to it: "In my opinion, the appeal that is made to the eye and not directly to the intellect impoverishes culture. The process of the displacement of the word by the image . . . causes a shallowness of intellectual level."[69] In his theoretical statements Kurek seems to repeat Peiper, but his poetic practice anticipated these theories. Kurek's metaphor, based on contradiction and described earlier, is the best example of conceptual, nonvisual metaphor, and it is also similar to Peiper's metaphors. Because of its total absence of visuality, because of its arbitrariness and unaccountability, his metaphors often appear whimsical and incomprehensible to the reader. Indeed, the charge of unintelligibility was frequently leveled against the poetry of both Peiper and Kurek.

There is still another characteristic shared by these two poets, the fragmentariness of their poetic vision. Kurek was well aware of their kinship: "In distinction to Przyboś I do not believe in the unity of vision, I recognize the efficacy of the fragmentary visions of Peiper." [70] Following Peiper, Kurek chose *vision* over *image* because it seemed to be closer to the creative process: "Nothing descriptive, the flash of vision alone, an imaginative flow full of fragmentary 'sights.'" [71] It was not a coincidence that Kurek, like Brzękowski, was attracted to the technique of films because for him a poem was like a film in being an arrangement of fractional images. Both in poetry and in film "the result of choice in the mental process expresses itself precisely in this fragmentary manner." [72] Peiper was concerned with similar fragmentariness in his poetry and in his search for structure he resorted to rhetoric; its culmination was the concept of the blossoming poem. Kurek did not share this concern with structure and considered the blossoming poem a mistake, the "least happy" of Peiper's ideas. Kurek's poems rarely develop a single vision or image but proceed by what could be described as separate flashes. They are built around a series of metaphors according to a principle of juxtaposition, sometimes without any thematic or logical connection between individual stanzas or lines. This fragmentariness can also be seen in Kurek's predilection for the distich: the two-line stanza is united by rhyme and syntactically separated from the preceding and succeeding stanza, thus forming a self-contained entity. Most often the unifying element is to be found in the title, which points to the subject of the poem and plays the role of musical theme or pretext for the most intricate metaphorical variations; Kurek referred to this type of composition as "multilevel."

At first Kurek seemed to be the most removed from Peiper's poetics, but of all the Avantgarde poets it was Kurek who followed Peiper's own poetic practice most closely and interpreted his theory of metaphor most literally, which appears now less surprising. Kurek's effusiveness, his "uncontrollable lyricism" that was criticized by Peiper's group and "treated almost as an apostasy and the washing away of the canon," [73] might have been, paradoxically, the very reason for his attraction to Peiper's concept of metaphor. Peiper's theory permitted an interiorization, a subjectivation of the poetic process that agreed best with Kurek's poetic nature. It allowed Kurek to continue his natural tendency toward effusiveness and to write poetry that combined emotional impulse with highly cerebral manipulation of language. Emotion and cerebralism—in the best spirit of contradiction—are the hallmarks of Jalu Kurek's poetry.

3

DIFFERENT SOLUTIONS

ADAM WAŻYK

In all fairness to their individualities, the two poets considered in this section, Adam Ważyk and Józef Czechowicz, could not be classified with any of the groups discussed earlier. Despite affinities with both the futurists and poets of the Cracow Avantgarde that led to coincidental collaboration in the same magazines, Ważyk and Czechowicz found their own solutions and created their own avant-garde poetic models. Their presence together in this section does not indicate that they have traits in common—their approaches to poetry as well as their temperaments differed almost to the point of contradiction. Ważyk wrote in the 1920s, Czechowicz in the thirties. Ważyk was an intellectual, Czechowicz a poet of intuition. Ważyk's poetry was urban, realistic, and antitranscendental, while Czechowicz's poetry was pastoral, symbolic, and metaphysical. What united them was the same general attitude that defined the entire avant-garde movement: antitraditionalism, and the search for new poetic expression.

Adam Ważyk published his early poems in the *Almanac of New Art,* a short-lived magazine whose four issues appeared in 1924 and 1925. These were the years between the first and second series of the *Switch,* and this intermediate position best defines the position of the *Almanac* in Polish avant-garde poetry. Publishing both the ex-futurists and poets of the Cracow Avantgarde as well as those unattached to any group, such as Stanisław Brucz, Mieczysław Braun, and Ważyk, the magazine provided a common platform for "new art," a term synonymous with "avant-garde" but preferred because it avoided the confining association with the Cracow Avantgarde. Despite its heterogeneity the *Almanac of New Art* followed a direction of its own, though hesitantly at the beginning. It was distinct both from futurism and from the poetics of the *Switch,* but shared certain common premises with both. The position of the magazine became clear in an essay on French art written by the editor, Stefan Gacki, and published in the third issue. In his essay Gacki tried to summarize the traits and tendencies of avant-garde poetry both in France and in Poland; some of these belonged to the program of the *Switch,* such as the cult of present reality, economy in artistic expression, and especially constructivism, which Gacki saw as the most important characteristic of Polish avant-garde art. But the editor of the *Almanac* also pointed out other characteristics of new poetry either ignored or openly opposed by the Cracow Avantgarde. These were the exploration of the subconscious, the influence of film techniques on poetry, and above all the technique of juxtaposition used as a new way of connecting sentences within a poem—all of these were excluded from the poetics of the *Switch.* Gacki's essay as well as the selection of French poetry published in the *Almanac*—translations of Apollinaire, Max Jacob, André Salmon, and Pierre Reverdy—announced a possible new direction for Polish avant-garde poetry. Picasso's portrait of Apollinaire on the cover of the issue that included Gacki's essay pointed emphatically to the patrons for new Polish art favored by the editors of the *Almanac.* However, this new direction was never followed up, although its traces can be found in the poetry of Anatol Stern and Jan Brzękowski, its only significant representative remains Adam Ważyk.

Ważyk wrote only two volumes of poetry before World War II: *Semaphores (Semafory,* 1924) and *Eyes and Lips (Oczy i usta,* 1926). His early poetry is important, like the short-lived *Almanac,* because it offered an original and different poetic model within the framework of Polish avant-garde poetry. Ważyk's poetry was the only representative of "poetic cubism" in Poland. The two most striking characteristics of his poetry, the images and the structure of his poems, bring him close to cubism while separating him from the poetics of the Cracow Avantgarde. Ważyk opposed Peiper's treatment of reality, his concept of poetry as an act of arbitrary renaming of objects, and his famous definition of poetry as the conferring of pseudonyms. Instead, Ważyk conceived of the poetic act as a sympathetic identification with objects, in which the frontier between the subject—the poet—and the object—reality—disappears: "My bread, my pen, my pipe, its smoke— / converge with me into one pulsing whole" ("Mój chleb, moje pióro, moja fajka, dym jej— / schodzą się ze mną w pulsujące jedno") ("Apologue" ["Apolog"]). In the same poem, which opened his second volume and served as a poetic credo, Ważyk separated himself from symbolism: "I do not want a key from an abyss, from any wells; / isn't a pearl the pearl hidden on the bottom of the seas" ("Nie chcę klucza od przepaści, od żadnych studzien, nie jest perłą perła na dnie mórz ukryta"). Instead of inventing symbols or pseudonyms, Ważyk wanted to strip the surfaces away from reality, to penetrate the essence of objects, their inner life.

> I strip things of their bark and I cut through rings
> with a diamond kilned by a wise machine,
> with a flint that has the name of man,
> with a ruby,
> the mythology of my days.

> Odzieram rzeczy z kory i rozcinam słoje
> diamentem wypalonym przez mądrą maszynę,
> krzemieniem, który ma imię człowieka,
> rubinem,
> mitologią dni moich.

The final lines present a realization that the poet's knowledge of reality is subjective, and that the image of reality he offers is the expression of his own particular "mythology." This mythology derives not only from certain historically determined cultural habits that influence our concept of reality, but it is above all the result of individual experience—a conclusion substantiated in all of Ważyk's poetry. From a much later perspective, Ważyk saw in this attitude the essence of the avant-garde approach to poetry: "The traditional cultural relationships between people and objects receded into the background, giving way to what is unrepeatable in a given situation, in a given man, in a given thing."[1]

Ważyk's antisymbolism and his reliance on individual experience led him to an aesthetic attitude that concurred with the premises of cubism: realistic but not illusionistic, faithful to experience but not to the reality of vision, trying to reproduce the essence but not the appearance of objects. Ważyk's approach to reality and poetry explains the nature of his images—neither arbitrary nor symbolic, they are tied to the particular experience from which they arise and outside of which they have no raison d'être. Insofar as the particular experience was based on visual perception they are visually plausible, but often they appear visually arbitrary. Their justification is psychological as well as intellectual; they imply both visual and conceptual knowledge of the reality described, and the relation between that reality and the narrator of the poem:

> I saw a milk goat and I see it today,
> motionless and flat like a village in the imagination.
> I see a tower. The village from the tower looks like a dish
> filled with dill, cream, and sour apples.
>
> ["August 1925"]

> Widziałem kozę mleczną i widzę ją dzisiaj,
> nieruchomą i płaską jak wieś w wyobraźni.
> Widzę basztę. Wieś z baszty wygląda jak półmisek
> pełen kopru, śmietany oraz jabłek kwaśnych.
>
> ["Sierpień 1925"]

The comparison of a village to a dish with dill, cream, and sour apples is based on a conceptual image, the result of perceptions both past and present ("I saw," "I see") as well as experience that is outside visual perception (cream, the taste of apples). The image implies the passage of time and memory because it synthesizes both present perception and past experience. In the first two lines of the passage quoted, the poet himself suggests that his image is based on imagination and not vision, and he implies that objects seen in the imagination differ from those observed directly, for they are flat and immobile. Further, his knowledge of the village influences his perception of it and the image is a blend of these two factors. Like the cubist painters, Ważyk breaks with illusionism; his poetry is a presentation and not a representation of reality. The stanza assumes a relation to the visible world, but above all it is an autonomous structure, more concerned with the relation between the poet and the objects he evokes than with the relations between the objects themselves.

Ważyk's "subjective realism" explains his attitude toward time and space, which he treated with the same freedom and subjectivity with which he treated reality:

> I saw too many of you, too many,
> to tear the rose of years away petal by petal—
> centuries, blossoming with only a single rose:
> the defeat of Japan, or the fire of the first pine chips.

> ["Journey in Time"]

> Za dużo was widziałem, za dużo,
> abym płat po płacie zdzierał różę lat, —
> stulecia, kwitnące tylko jedną różą:
> klęską Japonji, lub ogniem pierwszych sosnowych szczap.

> ["Podróż w czasie"]

Ważyk's rejection of the divisions in time and space influenced the structure of his poems. It implied rejection both of static one-point perspective and chronological sequence. It led him to adopt the technique of juxtaposition explored by such poets as Apollinaire and Blaise Cendrars, whom he had read, admired, and translated. A successful example of this technique is the poem "Tramway":

> A spark struck on the lyre of the tramway
> star imprisoned in the delicate heart of telescopes
> This man run over O a dark haired young man
> A kiosk with newspapers casts a palm tree's shadow
> Let us look listen and smoke
> How much for the daily beauty of the kiosk?
> I read it aloud and hear your voice
> In this kiosk a crowd of eyes and foreheads watches out
> A spark flashes on the lyre of the tramway A stop
> In this kiosk among hungry mistresses
> I could not find the one I would take by the waist

> In the blood of the sunset women's knees!

> The tramway carried me away and extinguished me

Tramwaj

Iskra zaświeciła na lirze tramwaju
gwiazda uwięziona w czułym sercu lunet
Ten człowiek przejechany ach ten młody brunet
Kiosk z gazetami rzuca cień palmy
Patrzmy słuchajmy i palmy
Ile za dziennik ten piękna z kiosku?
Czytam go na głos i słyszę głos twój
W tym kiosku czuwa tłum oczu i czół
Iskra świeci na lirze tramwaju Przystanek
W tym kiosku znaleźć wśród głodnych kochanek
nie mogłem tej którą objąłbym wpół

We krwi zachodu kolana kobiet!

Tramwaj mnie uniósł i zgasił

The juxtaposition of several seemingly unrelated sentences in the poem disguises a narrative that follows a chronological sequence. The events can be briefly summarized: the narrator waits for a streetcar, while he is waiting he buys a newspaper and overhears a street conversation about an accident. As the trolley car approaches the stop, the narrator sees a spark flash; as he enters he catches a glimpse of women's knees; the trolley car departs. After an attentive reading it is possible to reconstruct the plot, but the poem creates the impression that all the events are simultaneous because it lacks any indication of temporal sequence. This impression is enhanced by the manner in which references to the plot are juxtaposed against references to the narrator's thoughts as they flash through his mind (observations about the kiosk, the tramway, his desires), as well as against direct quotations of the narrator (the sixth line) or of others (the third line). These are not indicated by punctuation or explanatory phrases, nor is there any distinction made in the presentation of external and internal, psychological events. Ważyk compared the structure of his early poems to film techniques such as montage, the close-up, and shifts of planes. He referred to Roman Jakobson's well-known distinction between contiguity and metonymy on the one hand, and similarity and metaphor on the other, pointing out that his poetry was based on the first of these principles. Combined with an elimination of punctuation, these techniques implied a reading that was "fluid" and sanctioned mental leaps.[2]

The technique of juxtaposition, which made sentences seemingly overlap one another, also brings to mind cubist painting and the technique known as *passage,* based on the running together of planes otherwise separated in space.[3] The result produced by this technique—both in cubist painting and in Ważyk's poetry—is an impression of fragmentation and ambiguity. Like the cubist painters, Ważyk does not describe reality but presents his unique perception of reality, showing certain details caught by the eye (women's knees) and the ear (news of the young man who was killed). These details are arranged in an artistic structure that attempts to be faithful to the fragmentariness of perception, at the expense of completeness and comprehensibility. The lack of connections reproduces the very act of experience, which is similarly haphazard and fragmentary. Ważyk 's technique makes reading difficult and requires an effort of reconstruction—similar to the viewing of a cubist painting, it creates a tension between the intellectual appeal of an internally consistent artistic structure, and the difficulty of interpreting this structure in terms of reality as we logically comprehend it. Ważyk's poetry presupposes a subjective viewpoint, and therefore its images and associations appear arbitrary. They give the impression of spontaneity and of being seized in their *statu nascendi*. The images of the tramway and the spark, aside from their realistic justification, appropriately correspond to the nature of human perception itself. Like a spark, compared to a "star imprisoned in the delicate heart of telescopes," the narrator's perception of reality is short, fleeting, and fragmentary. The human psyche, like a trolley in motion, perceives only certain elements of reality and not its entirety. Not only is vision of reality bounded by experience, outside of which nothing exists—the tramway's departure is the moment of extinction, both of the poem and the experiences that generated it—but to an even greater degree it is influenced by an internal factor, the state of mind that determines and colors perception. The comparison of the kiosk's shadow to a palm tree, of the sunset to blood, and of a telescope to the heart, all have a psychological motivation. They are caused either by a chain of associations (leading from the run-over young man to the blood of the sunset), or they are the expression of the narrator's desire, his hope of encountering the woman that would bring fulfillment to this desire. Speaking of avant-garde poetry in general, Ważyk has best described this particular aspect of his own poetry:

> The reduction of habitual relationships resulted in a world broken into fragments, into fractions connected in a mosaiclike manner. A world of loosened relationships opened the possibility of seeping in fragments of memories, dreams, and subconscious images. The subject did not express feelings or emotional states, but colored them with his vision. He could suddenly appear or disappear, he was an analytical subject dispersed into the vision and a very reduced human figure. He appeared not in order to be sad or happy, to love or suffer, he fulfilled far more immediate tasks, he became the element or a situation in the evoked universe.[4]

The majority of Ważyk's early poems are based on the active relationship between the subject and the reality he experiences. Usually a first-person speaker or lyrical "I" is prominent, either the poet himself or a persona. For example, the long narrative poem "Christopher's Wedding" ("Ślub Krzysztofa") is written from the point of view of its young protagonist, but it uses the third person singular form of narration, as in the following passage:

> Catherine danced there in a helmet of copper hair,
> like Achilles, a god among beasts and applause.
> Her blood was debased by the painting on her face,
> a spotlight that stripped her body bare,
> threw on her shoulders a triangle of perspective,
> with a hoarse voice spread out the harmony of her lips,
> fed members full of a man's vigor,
> with the power of angels struggling in an attic among bed linen.

Katarzyna tam tańczyła w miedzianych włosów kasku,
jak Achilles, bóg wśród bestyj i oklasków.
Krew jej poniżały malowidła na twarzy,
reflektor, który ciało jej obnażył,
trójkąt perspektywy narzucił na barki,
ochrypłym głosem rozwinął harmonię warg jej,
nakarmił członki pełne tężyzną mężczyzny,
siłą aniołów walczących na strychu wśród bielizny.

On the surface this passage is a description of a dancer in a night club, but it is highly stylized and has a more consistent relation to the state of mind of the viewer than to the objective reality being described. The passage, and the entire poem, is in fact a curious psychological portrait in which the thoughts and desires of the protagonist are not stated directly but communicated through subjectively distorted images of external phenomena. The isolation of parts of the dancer's body (hair, lips, and shoulders) is motivated both artistically and psychologically. The image of the dancer is infused with the sexuality of the viewer, not of the object but of the subject. It is in passages like this that cubism and surrealism meet in Ważyk's poetry. The cubist technique is used by the poet to translate the subconscious, and the distorted perception of reality finds its ultimate justification in desire. And yet Ważyk, unlike the surrealists, never gave full reign to the subconscious. Although references to night, dreams, and sexual desire are frequent in his first volume, Ważyk was too intellectual a poet to follow the path of the surrealists to its end and to abandon his art to the dictates of desire. His dreams and passions are contained within an intellectual construction, his language is sober and controlled. Ważyk was above all an artist who never overstepped the rules of artistic construction in favor of reproducing life, whether conscious or subconscious. In this he remained faithful to the spirit of the Polish avant-garde.

The uniqueness of Ważyk's poetry in the context of the avant-garde is more evident today, from the perspective of fifty years, than it was to his contemporaries. Recognized as an avant-garde poet, Ważyk was seen as an ally both by the poets of the *Switch,* where he published his second volume of poems, and by the poets of the younger generation who moved away from the *Switch.* Probably because of his youth—he wrote his early poetry between nineteen and twenty-one—Ważyk never declared his poetic stand in a theoretical form at the time, and the partisans of the Cracow Avantgarde as well as its opponents interpreted his poetry in a manner that suited their own attitudes. Although this spared Ważyk criticism, it also obliterated the real value of his poetry, its original contribution to the breadth of the avant-garde experiment. It accounts also for the isolation of Ważyk's poetry, and its lack of followers. Ważyk himself did not develop the concepts and techniques of his early poems any further; after the publication of his two volumes in 1924 and 1926, he wrote no more poetry until after World War II. By 1945, when he returned from the Soviet Union—where he had spent the war—to Poland as an officer in the Polish Communist army, his attitudes toward poetry and art had radically changed. A supporter of the Communist regime, Ważyk became one of the most outspoken and feared theoreticians of socialist realism. Although he wrote

very little, in 1955 he published "A Poem for Adults," a bitter and biting denunciation of the Stalinist period that cost Ważyk his party membership but brought him
fame and recognition among the writers of the entire Eastern bloc. Since then
Ważyk has been writing poetry, and his latest poems reveal a curious return to the
early poems. He has also become one of the most important critics of the avant-garde.
The anthology of French surrealist poetry that he prefaced as well as his *Strange
History of the Avant-garde* (1976)[5] are among the most perceptive critical appraisals
of Polish avant-garde poetry.

JÓZEF CZECHOWICZ

Józef Czechowicz once expressed the opinion that each writer has essentially one
thing to communicate, his attitude toward his own "metaphysics," refracted through
his individuality.[6] The thematic consistency of Czechowicz's poetry not only confirms this opinion, but permits a quick identification of the poet's metaphysics.
The author of some of the most pastoral poems in Polish poetry, Czechowicz distinguished between three spheres—that of life, of beauty, and of death—but his
own cosmogony was almost entirely contained within the last sphere:

> my destiny is the dead
> to play for you with steps of fire
> to summon the shadows on the sod of graves
> with the music of words to chase them toward you
>
>   ["my all souls'"]

> przeznaczenie to moje umarli
> wam krokami pożarów grać
> cienie wzywać na grobów darni
> słów muzyką ku wam je gnać
>
>   ["moje zaduszki"]

It is true that beauty is prominent in his poetry. The landscapes and townscapes,
especially frequent in his early volumes, are exceptionally beautiful and bucolic;
many of these poems capture the charm of a specific moment of the day, of dawn,
sunset, or night. The word *peacefulness* reappears in a number of them and tints
all his descriptions, creating the atmosphere of a pastorale:

> Prelude
>
> 1
>
> at dawn birds exploded from the brass soil
> a slender woman brought lightness
>
> 2
>
> unquenched bells musical cradles
> to remember to remember to forget

3

pink breeze like the face of a child
a flicker cutting the low grass
I will nod with a dark poppy
a motionless fragrance will hit me and I will die

4

a deer stands at the spring the stream whispers *ave*

Preludium

1

o świcie wybuchły ptaki z mosiężnych ról
smukła kobieta jasność przyniosła na głowie

2

dzwony nienasycone kołyski muzyczne
wspominać wspominać zapominać

3

powiewie różowy jak twarz dziecka
płomyku podcinający niewysoką trawę
ciemnym kwiatem makowym skinę
nieruchomy zapach uderzy mnie i zginę

4

jeleń stoi u źródła struga szepce ave

Czechowicz's belief that beauty resided only in physical reality explains his predilection for landscapes, and yet the beauty in his poetry is always precarious, filled with hints that peace and happiness are not going to last. Despite his strong attachment to the beauty of this world, his poetry expresses a desire to reach beyond physical reality, which, though omnipresent, is confining and incomplete: "everything everything is on the earth / so many / everything / so little" ("wszystko wszystko jest na ziemi / tak wiele / wszystko / tak mało") ("prison ["więzienie"]).

This explains why the "spiritual country" from where Czechowicz wrote his mature poetry of death and destruction did not have innocent landscapes and cities of antiquated charm—although these remained the settings of the majority of his poems. Instead it was a country on the "other side" of life, one to which he referred for the first time in his volume entitled *the ballad from beyond (ballada z tamtej strony,* 1932):

hoarse primeval shouts
crash over the glimmer of music
and the downpour of sounds flows off through ravines
these poems from mythical countries
unwilling to sing

["without a score"]

chrapliwe pierwotne krzyki
trzaskają nad światełkiem muzyki
i wąwozami popłynęła szumu ulewa
te wiersze z mitycznego kraju
nie chcące śpiewać

["bez nut"]

Beneath the pastoral tranquillity of many of his poems lies terror:

dark torso of a bridge over silence
all around redness
flames hanging
in the turbid stream of seconds
menace
with the flood of centuries
more terrifying than night
more terrifying than storm
than sleep

["alone"]

ciemny tors mostu nad ciszą
wszędzie czerwienie kołem
płomienie wisząc
w mętnym strumieniu sekund
grożą
powodzią wieków
straszniej niż noc
straszniej niż burza
niż sen

["sam"]

Czechowicz created a private world of symbols in his poetry, with recurring images of night, wind, storm, lightning, and fire. Wind and lightning are precursors of a catastrophe always represented as a storm, flood, or fire. His choice of symbols indicates that for him death was an unnatural event associated with violence or a cataclysm. Symptomatically, a number of Czechowicz's poems are dedicated to those who have died unnatural deaths—a suicide, a man drowned at sea, a soldier killed by a bullet.

Czechowicz's obsession with death bordered on fascination and reveals the emergence of a new sensibility in Polish literature during this period. Except for the poetry of Bolesław Leśmian—who belonged to an entirely different poetic generation—the theme of death was absent in the poetry of the 1920s, whether it was the poetry of Skamander with its stress on everyday life, that of the Cracow Avantgarde, programmatically antimetaphysical and optimistic, or the poetry of political propaganda and social commitment. Czechowicz's poetry broke the seal and reintroduced the forbidden subject into Polish poetry. It is important to stress that Czechowicz's preoccupation with death was not just a matter of a literary theme (if it was, it could be traced back to Young Poland). It stemmed from Czechowicz's personal vision of the world, from his strong premonition turning with the years into a certainty that a catastrophe, both personal and universal, was approaching. The poems written a few years later in a similar apocalytic vein by the young members of the group *Żagary* show that Czechowicz's obsession with death was a sign of a new sensibility that developed, to a great extent, as a response to the ominous atmosphere surrounding the political situation. In 1932 Czechowicz wrote: "When we go to sleep and when we wake up we are frightened by the ominous hissing of the unknown. The catastrophist feeling of the world stops to be a verbal symbol—it has become flesh." [7] As the future loomed more and more threateningly over the present, moments of happiness became increasingly precarious in Czechowicz's poetry. The serene tone of the first volumes *stone (kamień,* 1928) and *a day like every day (dzień jak codzień,* 1930) gave way in *the ballad from beyond* and *from lightning (z błyskawicy,* 1934) to a tone of anxiety and desolation.

The terror permeating Czechowicz's poetry was connected above all with the slow but irreversible passage of time. For Czechowicz, time was hostile, whether it was the ordinary time of the clock moving slowly by small bits ("the stream of seconds") or the rushing destructive time of the apocalypse ("the flood of centuries"). Time measured by the clock was hateful because it moved in only one direction, the direction of death, but the confusion of time was even more terrifying because it meant final apocalypse, a whirlpool in which everything would perish:

night midnight dawn and evening arose simultaneously
road stream willows seethe whirl thunder
and as the horses grow crushing the autumn with their huge size
in the funnel of terrible clouds you disappear and they and everything

["daybreak"]

zawrzały jednocześnie noc północ świt i wieczór
droga strumień wierzbiny burzą się wirują grzmią
a konie jak urastają gniotąc ogromem jesień
w potwornych obłoków leju znikasz i ty i oni i wszystko

["przedświt"]

Annihilation of time meant the annihilation of all dimensions, an end to the objects and beings whose identity depends on clear lines and divisions, whether spatial or temporal. The time of storm was one of destructive synthesis, engulfing everything and leaving only a great space, "a dark pit filled with echoes." Czechowicz was a poet of the present and future, not of the past. His rare evocations of the past served only as possible indications of what would happen in the future. In his early poetry the future was unknown and a source of anxiety, in his mature poetry it was tragic and apocalyptic, the source of despair. The only time of happiness was the present: "today's day has returned / returned like a prodigal son / let us kiss its temples" ("dzień dzisiejszy powrócił / powrócił jak syn marnotrawny / ucałujmy jego skronie") ("the ravines of time" ["wąwozy czasu"]). The present meant peace, and immersion in the beauty of surrounding reality.

As the pressure of time became unbearable a new theme appeared in Czecho-wicz's poetry, the desire to escape from time into the world of dreams. The happiest moment of the day was the evening: it brought the promise of a happy night, of sleep, peace, timelessness, and forgetfulness. It was the "fragrant arch" announcing "the mating song of the night." Sleep was an escape from reality, dreams were a liberation from the inexorable progress of time. In dreams, time is immediate and simultaneous: both past and future are telescoped into one everlasting present. Terrified by the inevitability of death and discouraged by the sense of his own powerlessness, Czechowicz turned to dreams as the only refuge and consolation. *The ballad from beyond* ends with three elegies whose titles translate his feeling of despair and discouragement, "elegy of impotence" ("elegia niemocy"), "elegy of sorrow" ("elegia żalu"), and "elegy of sleep" ("elegia uśpienia"). They speak of the uselessness of poetry in a time of apocalypse: "to go where to go / with a poem useless as smoke" ("iść dokąd iść / z wierszem jak dym niepotrzebnym"). The feeling of powerlessness was magnified by the awareness that his own poetic voice, comparable to a rustling of dry leaves, was inadequate to counteract the enormity of events. His "humming" poetry was out of tune with the thunderous times. The only escape was into sleep, away from the deadly grayness of life into the illusory colorfulness of dreams: "sleep enclosed life / relief sleep heavy but weightless / beautiful somnolent specters circle / in the bloody darkness of the skull" ("sen życie ujął / osłoda sen ciężki a nieważki / piękne zjawy sennie kołują / w krwawych ciemnościach czaszki").

The poet realized that the escape was illusory, that dreams were as deceptive as magic, a charm, or intoxication. The desire to abandon himself to sleep struggled with the will to stay awake, to work, and to fight time. In one poem ("Eros") the poet desperately struggles against the temptation to abandon himself to the timeless forgetfulness of the night, of Psyche. The internal battle between the two principles of male and female, day and night, Eros and Psyche, life and death, per-meates all of Czechowicz's poetry.

A similar duality characterizes his style. On the one hand there are the pastoral settings, its melody and flowing rhythm expressing the poet's natural penchant toward reverie, sleep, the abandonment of will, and death, while on the other the surprising artfulness and craft of his poetry are revealed in the metaphors, com-plex sound patterns, and careful composition, all betraying a will and determina-tion to work and resist the "deadly penchant." The poem entitled "melody on bells" is an excellent example of the dual nature of Czechowicz's poetry and sophisticated artistry. The English translation gives only an approximate idea of the complex sound patterns in the original:

> gypsy bell of the skirt
> bell gypsy olive wrist
> dusky
> blossom of southern shores

the bells of fir trees along the rails
beat against the train like a pulse
I look out in the wide stretch of fields
for goldenfaced evening

fragrant hills hills like bells
fond of wandering on the horizons
they stop here and there with a bow
lying down with a treble clef

bell why are your gray eyes
faded in the moon
why does the painful flame
shed blood
on the Indian summer's wool of the sheep

o bells bells monotonous bell
everywhere you are the bell of things of sentences
inspired by the dissonance of shadow
stop

because the gypsy bell of the skirt in fir trees
because hills dusky with evening the gray pond of the eyes
are remembered by a dream in the city
but truly it is time now to get up
to swim on waves labors hours
across

Nuta na dzwony

cyganka dzwon spódnicy
dzwon cyganka smagły przegub
śniadolicy
rozkwit południowych brzegów

choinek dzwony wzdłuż toru
o wagon biją jak puls
złotolicego wieczoru
wyglądam na rozłogach pól

pagórki wonne pagórki dzwonne
po widnokręgach lubią się włóczyć
przystają tu i tam pokłonem
leżącym wiolinowym kluczem

dlaczego dzwonem są te siwe oczy
w księżycu wypełzłe
dlaczego broczy
płomień bolesny
na baranków babioletnią wełnę

o dzwony dzwony dzwon monotonny
wszędzie jesteś dzwonie rzeczy zdań
dysonansem cienia natchniony
stań

bo cygankę dzwon spódnicy w choinach
bo pagórki wieczorem śniade oczu siwy staw
sen w mieście przypomina
ale naprawdę czas już wstać
płynąć po falach pracach godzinach
wpław

The poem is about time, which permeates all nature. Invisible, it is inscribed in every object and being, "everywhere you are the bell of things of sentences." The appearance of nature is deceitful because it disguises the "shadow" of time. The image of the bell as symbol of time is central, although neither appears literally in the poem. Its shape is suggested by the skirt of a gypsy, fir trees, hills, eyes. The elusiveness of time, its unnoticeable presence and monotonous flow—like the measured movement of bells, and their monotonous melody—are dangerous because they lull our consciousness and dissolve our will. The wish to stop time is futile, but the ending of the poem suggests that resistance to its passage is possible: in the will to remain awake, and in work. Only by working can we dominate rather than submit to time. The relative simplicity of this message is counterbalanced by the extreme artistry with which it is expressed—to use Czechowicz's own term, the poem is a "polyphonic song" where sounds, images, rhythms, and words interplay in such a way that form and content become inseparable.

Compared with the poetry of the Cracow Avantgarde, the most striking quality of this poem, and of all Czechowicz's poetry, is its rhythm and musicality and its lack of punctuation. These three elements are closely related to one another, reflecting the poet's desire to eliminate time and create the illusion of continual flow. Czechowicz was the first avant-garde poet to eliminate punctuation completely, and thus to weaken syntax by blurring the syntactical divisions between words. The effect is one of great fluidity and ambiguity: the images flow into one another as in dreams. Although Czechowicz's elimination of punctuation was motivated by his philosophical attitudes, it had far-reaching consequences in the structure of his poems as well—"the forms subjugate themselves to rhythms." The rhythmic structures are highly original because they do not create a sing-song effect, despite their exceptional melodiousness. Kazimierz Wyka explained Czechowicz's unusual "unmelodious musicality" as deriving from the images, which are not subordinate to rhythm, like traditional rhythmic structures. "For such is the rhythmic radiation, such is the internal instrumentation of Czechowicz's poetry, that its dominating element is the rhythm of images. Images are the main instrument, and only then is the rhythm communicated to the neighboring layers."[8] Wyka's observation helps to explain certain peculiarities of Czechowicz's rhythm, among them that it can change within a poem depending on the image that dominates a given passage. In this way a songlike uniformity is avoided. In the poem "melody on bells," for example, the rhythm of each stanza is different and subordinate to a particular image developed in the stanza: the bells, a train, wandering hills, a pond. And yet Wyka does not explain the complexity of Czechowicz's rhythmic structure.

In Czechowicz's poetry the rhythm results from an interplay of several different elements. First, there is the rhythm of the sentence; underneath the seemingly uninterrupted flow of words it is still possible to reconstruct syntactical units in most of his poems. In addition there is a rhythm of lyrical emotion particular to each poem and stanza. These two rhythms could be called, respectively, syntactical and musical. And there is still another element in Czechowicz's poetry that he referred to in his writings as "poetic" rhythm opposed to musical rhythm. Each of these rhythms interplays with the others but they do not coincide. While the syntactical rhythm follows the conceptual development of the poem and the musical rhythm is subordinate to the metaphoric, visual element, it is the poetic rhythm that produces the inner tension of Czechowicz's poetry, creating unexpected stops, new associations, the possibilities of new meanings or connections within the poem. The rhythm of the first stanza of "melody on bells" imitates the swinging motion of the bells. The absence of punctuation makes individual words *(cyganka dzwon spódnicy)* or clusters of words *(południowych brzegów)* act as independent musical notations, and become rhythmically autonomous units. Without obliterating the musical effect, the underlying syntactical units are similar to words in a song. Thus the stanza can be read either as a sequence of individual words that have equal value and form three measures of three beats each *(cyganka dzwon spódnicy / dzwon cyganka smagły przegub / śniadolicy rozkwit południowych brzegów)*, or, instead, according to syntactic units *(cyganka - dzwon spódnicy - dzwon - cyganka - smagły przegub / śniadolicy rozkwit południowych brzegów)*. In addition, it is possible to read the poem by following the line divisions and discover a different system of measures, pauses, and accents. In this reading, the third line consisting of the single word *śniadolicy* creates a rhythmic variation and breaks the three-beat imitation of monotonous bells. The isolation of *śniadolicy* is echoed later in the poem, in the fifth and sixth stanzas, with the words *stań* ("stop") and *wpław* ("across"). The coexistence of two rhythms in the poem—musical and poetic—corresponds on the thematic level to the poet's ambivalence about time: a powerful urge to let himself be carried away by its flow, to immerse himself in sleep and dream, and an equally powerful determination to resist it. More generally, one rhythm introduces harmony and the other disharmony, their interplay reflecting Czechowicz's inner split between a pastoral and apocalyptic vision of the world. Czesław Miłosz has likened Czechowicz's poetry to "chamber music made poignant by the counterpoint of dark philosophical and metaphysical problems."[9]

The musicality of Czechowicz's poetry is enhanced by an extremely intricate sound texture. In "melody on bells" the word choice not only approximates the sound of bells (the sounds *c, dz, g, n*) but it also creates a complex pattern of interdependences between words. While the lack of punctuation resulted in separations between words, sound similarities—like syntax—act in the opposite way by establishing connections between words. These connections are not syntactical but musical; each word in the poem has multiple sound associations with other words.

Different sounds and sound families attract each other, overlap, and echo one another. In the first stanza alone the words can be grouped in different ways according to different sounds. The fricatives *c, s,* and *dz* are present in eight out of eleven words. The consonants *n, ń* are in seven words, *g* and *k* in six. Aside from the repetition of single consonants, there are several sound clusters echoing each other: *dni (spódnicy, śniadolicy, południowych), cy (cyganka, spódnicy, śniadolicy), wi / wy (rozkwit, południowych).* Finally, the two rhyming words *przegub* and *brzegów* repeat almost identical sounds. The unusual sonority of Czechowicz's poetry results from the insistent repetition of certain sounds in a stanza. Each stanza, like a musical phrase, has its own tonality and its own particular combination of sounds, repeated in different variations. Aside from musical effects, the exploration of sound similarities between words can be a source of suggestive neologisms or new unexpected associations, as in the line *pagórki wonne pagórki dzwonne,* where the similarity of *wonne* and *dzwonne* implies a conceptual link between them. A similar, frequent procedure is the combination of words with a common etymology but that have become dissociated in everyday usage, such as *kamienie, kamienice* (stones, buildings), *żywica, życie* (sap, life), and *cierpko, cierpiąco* (sourly, sufferingly). Czechowicz's use of sounds did not rely on such conventional devices as onomatopoeia or rhymes. By interspersing regular rhyme with irregular rhyme and assonance, and above all by integrating rhymes in the general sound pattern of a stanza, he avoided the stereotyped harmony of traditional poetry. Despite their ubiquity his sound effects are subtle and result in a truly Baudelairean "suggestive magic."

Czechowicz's sensitivity to sounds and musical effects is seen even in his metaphors. Generally speaking his poetry continues the type of metaphorization characteristic of Avantgarde poetry, and like all the Avantgarde poets Czechowicz favored combinations of the concrete and the abstract: "anxiety smokes" *(niepokój dymi),* "terror beat toward me with a wing" (*ku mnie skrzydłem uderzyła trwoga),* or "weeks trample over the beds" *(depcą tygodnie po łóżkach).* It is also possible to find in Czechowicz's poetry metaphors based on optical illusion, similar to those of Przyboś: "the supple whip of the runners bent at the finish" *(gibki bicz biegnących u mety się zagiął),* or "the windmills rock the horizon" *(wiatraki kołyszą horyzont).* However, the most original of Czechowicz's metaphors make use of sounds. They are based either on what might be called auditory illusion—for example, "an echo stitches together the empty space with steps" *(echo krokami pustkę zszywa)—*or they transform a visual effect into an auditive effect, sometimes vice versa: "a whisper dripped through my hands" *(szept ściekał mi przez ręce),* "the sun rings over the river" *(słońce dzwoni w rzekę),* "shadow pours" *(cień leje się),* "the noon pours dry and rough" *(południe przesypuje się suche i szorstkie).*

In the poems of Czechowicz a musical rhythm together with extremely sophisticated sound patterns produce a complex system of echoes and unusual stresses. Rhythm and sound put into relief elements in the poem not necessarily indicated by the syntax. In this way he created an "open structure" as opposed to the closed structure of Peiper, who had demanded that poetic emotion be subjugated to the sentence, and that the rhythm of the poem be that of its sentences. Czechowicz turned the order of importance around and made the sentence subordinate to the internal melody of the poem. The structure of his poems had a more *organic* tie with the poet, as the rhythm on which it depended translated the internal, personal rhythm of the poet's emotion, and was not a result of a syntactic rhythm subordinate to impersonal grammatical rules. By stressing melodiousness in poetry, Czechowicz broke away from the poetics of the Cracow Avantgarde. When he described his own creative process he emphasized the importance of the "musical moment" without which his poems could not have been written. Although his poems were intellectually conceived, the actual writing could not begin without what he called a "musical swinging" that was the moment of lyrical outburst, the moment a poem acquired its particular rhythm and melody. He observed that both the source and the "axis" of his poems were musical: "the birth of a poem is in the musical order of things."[10] Czechowicz recognized the importance of craftsmanship, in agreement with Avantgarde poetics, but he saw it only as the last stage of writing poetry, a stage preceded by two other stages: one conceptual, and the other musical. Like the associationism of Przyboś and Brzękowski, the musicality of Czechowicz's poetry both altered and broadened Avantgarde poetics. In 1938 a critic quoted a particularly melodious stanza of Czechowicz and observed that nothing like it had ever before been written in Polish poetry. In the context of the Polish avant-garde Czechowicz created a new poetic model, and although no other Polish poet recreated his captivating rhythms and sonorities, many of his innovations (such as the elimination of punctuation) were eagerly adopted by poets of the next postwar generation.

By 1936 Czechowicz's anxiety had turned into desolation. The poems of the volume *nothing more (nic więcej,* 1936) are devoid of any pastoral atmosphere. Dark visions of destruction have taken the place of descriptions of nature. The central images are of fire, flames, and ominous glow ("sulphurous gleam," "flaming pillars," "glowing earth," "anxiety from fire"). The tone has also changed, it is now that of an urgent warning addressed to everyone, not just himself. The "I" has become part of the entire community destined for death: "we are all enveloped by the same spell." There is no longer a desire to escape into dreams. On the contrary, it is now important for the poet to meet death "eye to eye" and not to be struck by it unaware, while lost in dreaming.

> dispel visions swim out from this yarn
> watch out a shot a flight overhead a grenade strikes nearby
> and has rolled into the ground and suddenly earth spurts upward
> flames clap in the air with vertical planks of roses
>
> and now nothing more
>
> ["in the battle"]

> spłosz wizje wypłyń z tej przędzy
> uważaj odstrzał przelot granat uderza tuż
> i oddudniło w gruncie i ziemia nagle w górę
> płomienie klaszczą w powietrzu pionowymi deskami z róż
>
> i już nic więcej
>
> ["w boju"]

The determination to be alert is accompanied by an exasperation because others refuse to see or ignore the signs of the catastrophe. People are so immersed in petty, everyday reality that they neither hear nor understand the warning of the poet:

> because when the cat the sycamores silence of streets and panes
> strangle with an embrace of odors
> the broken mirror of sand
> with the sun's madness shouts
> why do you trouble yourself
> but this is my shout
> for the storm
> against the blind

["from day to the bottom"]

> bo kiedy kotek jawory cisza ulic i szyb
> duszą uściskiem zapachów
> lusterko rozbite z piachu
> szaleństwem słonecznym krzyczy
> po co się tak trudzisz
> a to jest mój krzyk
> za burzą
> przeciw ślepym

["od dnia do dna"]

The change in tone coincides with a change in style, which is no longer flowing and melodious, but harsh. The syntax has become more complicated. Sentences are broken by numerous appositions and parenthetical clauses. The lines correspond less frequently with syntactical units that require an effort to be reconstructed. Instead of providing fluidity the absence of punctuation creates an additional complication. The growing sense of approaching catastrophe is accompanied by a greater complexity of style, as if language were no longer capable of expressing the ominous unknown.

In this volume the tone, style, images, and title all translate his exasperation and hopelessness. The premonition has become a certainty, anxiety has become despair, and the desire to escape has changed into a heroic determination to accept fate. The title poem of the volume "nothing more" ("nic więcej") illustrates this new stage very well:

> anxiety of fire
> whitish-gray waterfall
> mother's streaming hair
> as she combs it in half
> sadness flies in through the windows
> to dream out to sleep to the end
> reach the cathedrals with the last
> turn of wheels

chapped like the background of a mosaic
a hand on the shaft of a spade
the crime can be mine
and the good gift
johnny joanna anna
an autumnal stalk whispers
from where in the damp eyes
is the reddish glow

thus the signum marked me
drowning I see in a whirling vortex
I see who hews my days
of pain and numbers

they will decide nothing
the flaming columns lie down
in a row
here is the sickle
there will be a storm

    nic więcej

niepokój z ognia
siwobiały wodospad
rozwiane włosy matki
gdy je czesze rozcięły na pół
smutek wlatuje przez okna
dośnić dospać
dosięgnąć katedr ostatnim
obrotem kół

jak tło mozaiki spękana
ręka na trzonie łopaty
moja może być zbrodnia
i dobry dar
janku joanno anna
szepcze jesienny badyl
skądże to w oczach wilgotnych
rudy żar

tak naznaczyło mnie signum
tonąc widzę w odmęcie
widzę kto dni me ciosa
z bólu i cyfr

niczego nie rozstrzygną
słupy płomienne w rzędzie
kładą się
jest kosa
będzie wichr

The poem presents a spiritual autobiography: it begins with memories from child-hood, and ends with an image of the poet's death. Youthful feelings of sadness and anxiety change to resignation and a realization that throughout his life he has car-ried a stigma of pain and death. The desire to sleep and dream, and the hope of achieving poetic fame ("to reach the cathedrals"), give way to doubt about the value of poetry that can be a crime as well as a good gift (the similarity of sounds in "zbrodnia" and "dobry dar" indicates their perplexing proximity). The poem ends with a presentiment that the universal catastrophe is on its way, and the poet's own death is only a preliminary. Stylistically the poem is stark. Stripped of meta-phors and sparse in sound effects, with hardly a single audible melody, it contains only symbols of death and destruction.

In *nothing more* Czechowicz reached an emotional limit from which there were only two possible ways out. He could either stop writing altogether or change and turn from depressing hopelessness to something else. Czechowicz did both. His very last volume, *a human note (nuta człowiecza,* 1939), differs from his pre-vious volumes in subject matter, tone, and style—then he stopped writing. A num-ber of these poems continue to explore the theme of death, but the poet's attitude has changed once more, this time from despair to detachment and reconciliation. The poems written by Czechowicz in 1938 and 1939, just a few months before his sudden, almost accidental, death from a German bomb, already come from the perspective of "beyond." Czechowicz's exceptional ability to project himself into the future and to the moment of his own death led him to experience the future with the same immediacy as the present. In *nothing more* this tendency had reached its culmination and the present had almost disappeared from his poetry. In the earlier volumes there was a constant struggle between the future and the present, death and life, evil and beauty. In *nothing more* the future engulfed the present and the only feeling remaining was hopelessness. The poems in *a human note* unexpectedly reveal a new attitude, more detached and intellectual; they bring a realization that the future is in fact already contained in the present, that death is with us while we are still alive, consequently there is no need to anticipate it: "tomorrow lies in wait in everything / before clocks reach it" ("jutro czyha we wszystkim / nim do niego zegary dotrą") ("pious rhymes" ["rymy pobożne"]). This new realization accounts for the relative absence of anxiety, awe, or exas-peration in *a human note.* Because the apocalypse is taking place now the poet has already emotionally undergone the experience of his own death and is more peaceful.

A poem with the revealing title "apple of life" ("jabłko życia") attempts to come to terms with the reality of death, but is above all an appraisal of his own life and poetry:

> more than a single year passes from the palms that write
> to chase away the thick fluffy throng of visions
> giving eyes to the night and one's heart to the narcissus
> and I too go away flight isn't easy
>
> smoke will blossom one day over the evil chasms of time
> an old man I will calmly enter the light of eternal fires
> for I lived by the double force of waiting and loving
> and I won't flee with a palm I will seize life like an apple

niejeden rok uchodzi od dłoni które piszą
aby odgonić wizyj puszysty zwarty natłok
oddając oczy nocom a serce swe narcyzom
uchodzę i ja także ucieczka nie jest łatwa

zakwitną kiedyś dymy na czasu złych otchłaniach
spokojnie wejdę starzec w odwiecznych ognisk światło
bom żył dwojaką siłą czekania i kochania
i nie ucieknę dłonią żywot ujmę jak jabłko

Compared to his earlier poems, "apple of life" is written from an entirely new temporal perspective. Death is no longer projected into the future and is seen as a continuous process ("more than a single year passes from the palms that write") whose terminal point coincides with the present ("I too go away"). The opposition between poetry and reality, and the realization that while the poet is immersed in his visions time flees, continues the development of the earlier theme of dream and sleep. What is new is that the dual nature of his poetry, split between love of beauty ("giving . . . one's heart to the narcissus") and the premonition of death ("giving eyes to the night")—between day and night, present and future—is no longer felt as a conflict but as a force. In fact this duality "of waiting and loving" assures the poet his future place in the pantheon of art: "an old man I will calmly enter the light of eternal fires." The perspective has shifted, and while death has moved into the present, the future is now associated with values resistant to the destruction of time. In "apple of life" Czechowicz's projection into the future goes beyond the time of his death, or even the time of the general catastrophe, into a time when he will continue to live as a poet in the memory of others. His own poetry has become a guarantee of survival, and the poem ends on a strong reaffirmation of his recovered control over fate.

While poems like "apple of life" brought a resolution to the problem of death that pervaded all of Czechowicz's poetry, a large number of poems in *a human note* depart sharply from previous volumes in subject matter and in style. The new subjects of hunger, poverty, and deprivation as well as the tone of compassion place this volume in a new context, and many poems come close to socially committed poetry. Czechowicz admitted that *a human note* expressed his sense of community with people, and that its very title defined his position as that of a humanist, not an aesthete. The poems show greater simplicity; many have regular stanzas and rhymes, straightforward syntax, and less intricate metaphors. Both stylistically and thematically *a human note* is another step further away from the Avantgarde position. The volume also shows that Czechowicz was searching for a new mode of expression, that his poetry had reached the end of a cycle. He believed he should never repeat himself, but should always invent. To continue to write creatively, Czechowicz needed a new inspiration and a new style. Several of the poems in *a human note* imitate the language, diction, and rhythm of folk songs, but it seems doubtful that folk poetry could have provided Czechowicz with a lasting poetic model. Since he did not write any more poetry before his death the question remains open, but it is significant that when he was asked in 1939 about his poetic projects, Czechowicz seemed uncertain. It may be justifiable to suppose that

Czechowicz's poetic destiny had been fulfilled by 1939, despite its brevity. Only twelve years separated his first from his last volume, but within that time he wrote seven volumes of poetry, each one reflecting a different emotional and poetic stage. It is as if the poet's strong premonition of his early death had accelerated his creativity.

The importance of Czechowicz in the evolution of Polish poetry has been repeatedly affirmed by both poets and critics, and yet critics hesitate to assign him an exact position on the spectrum of Polish poetry in the period between the two wars. Czechowicz himself associated his poetry with that of the avant-garde, but he understood the avant-garde as a general trend of contemporary poetry, not the specific poetics of the *Switch*. Overlooking particular schools and movements, Czechowicz spoke of an "avant-garde attitude" and identified it with a constant search for new and better expression, "constant creativity, constant becoming and elaboration." [11] In opposition to a classicism based on the acceptance of established canons, he defined this attitude of creative instability as essentially romantic. The importance of Czechowicz—and the very reason for the difficulty in finding a classification or compartment for him—is that he served as a link between the Avantgarde and post-Avantgarde poetry. His poetry both belonged to and overstepped the poetics of the Cracow Avantgarde. Czechowicz shared with the Cracow poets their respect for poetic craft, and he subscribed to their dogmas of indirectness, rigor, and tight construction. He wrote: "Poetry is an indirect art because it translates the artist's emotion into a system of words, sentences, and concepts that constitute an autonomous whole in relation to the impulse that created them." [12] He agreed with Peiper and Przyboś that poetic emotion had no value in itself and was worth only as much as its artistic expression was worth. But Czechowicz was far from reducing poetry to poetic craft or expression; he conceived it as a metaphysical quest. For him, the value of poetry, like that of science, was related to its cognitive power: "The only social value of art consists in the fact that through an aesthetic experience, it brings both the artist and the recipient of the work closer to this metaphysical knot of the world, and by the same token it deepens us and makes us better, more elevated." [13]

Czechowicz's conviction that poetry is a metaphysical quest entailed an ethical attitude. His concept of "pure poetry" was an ethical rather than aesthetic concept; it implied an attitude on the part of the poet toward his own writing. Considering poetry to be a mission, Czechowicz demanded that it present a vision of the world rather than an expression of the poet's ego. Above all poetry was to be the expression of the poet's cosmogony; aside from being an artist, the poet should be a "cosmocrator" and a "theocrator." Czechowicz spoke of the mythical role of poetry; poets were to be spritual guides, hence "the source of art must be pure." [14] Poets were bound by certain ethical duties, especially by the duty of emotional, intellectual, and artistic discipline. Since the *Weltanschauung* of a poet depended on his individuality, Czechowicz extolled spiritual greatness, powerful individuality, and heroism. And he invoked the individual moral responsibility of the poet. Because poetry had a cognitive nature similar to that of philosophy, it must be subject to the same severe discipline and ethics. The high intrinsic value of his art and his bridging of the avant-garde period and the poetry of the thirties make

Czechowicz the focal point of twentieth-century Polish poetry. He promoted a concept of poetry totally foreign to the spirit of the twenties by identifying poetry with a metaphysical quest. For the poets of the twenties metaphysics was a forbidden word, largely because of its associations with the mysticism of the Young Poland movement. It was probably the only point on which both the futurists, the poets of Skamander, and those of the *Switch* all agreed. Czechowicz's conviction that the true source of poetry was metaphysics can be seen as a reaction against the materialism and empiricism of both Skamander and the Cracow Avantgarde. His stress on the metaphysical and ethical aspects of poetry places him closer to the next generation of Polish poets, especially the poets of *Żagary* with whom he shared a catastrophist view of the world. The poetry of Czechowicz was the first sign Polish poetry was entering a new stage that was philosophical rather than aesthetic.

4

THE NEW
VOICES IN POLISH POETRY

BEYOND THE AVANT-GARDE

From the Twenties to the Thirties

In the history of Polish poetry the period between the two world wars had the attributes of a true renaissance—and this is true of the other arts as well. It brought a total re-evaluation of traditions together with entirely new poetic propositions. This twenty-year period could be roughly divided into two stages, and the breaking point between them would fall around 1927, at the end of the second series of the *Switch.* The first stage, during the 1920s, was the time of the most creative ferment: three poetic and artistic movements followed on the heels of one another, formism, futurism, and the Cracow Avantgarde. They all "happened" within merely five years, between November 1917 (the opening of the first exhibition of the formists) and May 1922 (the publication of the first issue of the *Switch*). The last of these three movements, the Cracow Avantgarde, not only formulated the most thorough and innovative poetic program but at the same time offered a synthesis of the other two extreme programs represented by formism and futurism. The formist concept of form was incorporated by the Avantgarde into the broader concept of construction, and the futurist dream of equating art with life found its way—though in a modified fashion—into the concept of "the present," of poetry organically united with its own time. Unlike the other two, the poetic program of the Avantgarde was complete—it comprised the broadest artistic issues as well as the minutest and most professional details of poetic craft. Throughout the 1920s the prestige and range of influence of the Cracow Avantgarde kept growing, and its apogee was the period of *Linia's* publication. By that time its position as the most important and only truly innovative poetic movement was established. The Avantgarde became a fact, almost a tradition toward which every young poet in the thirties felt obliged to assume an attitude.

In distinction to the twenties, which could be seen as "the big laboratory of new ideas," using Brzękowski's phrase, the thirties were the period of discussion either to assimilate and accept these ideas or to criticize and reject them. Aside from the group *Żagary,* no poetic movement or program emerged that could compete with the Avantgarde. Despite some of the best Avantgarde poetry being written in the thirties by poets such as Przyboś or Brzękowski, these should be seen as the post-Avantgarde years. The poetic concepts and prescriptions of the Avantgarde were put on trial, and as there were many judges who differed greatly in their attitudes, the verdicts were both favorable and unfavorable. At the same time, the area in which theoretical discussion about poetry took place widened. Unlike the 1920s when the baton of the avant-garde was passed from hand to hand only among the participants of the relay (formism to futurism to the Cracow Avantgarde) and when theoretical discussion was channeled in a few of its own publications (the *Formists,* futurist manifestoes and leaflets, the *New Art,* the *Switch),* discussion in the thirties covered a much broader spectrum and was carried on in many periodicals, both literary and nonliterary. This decentralization of avant-garde poetic thought coincided with its regionalization. As has been noticed by several critics, the most vital, innovative, and creative voices in the discussion came from outside of Warsaw, from Chełm Lubelski, Lublin, Wilno, and Ostrzeszów Wielkopolski, just as the Avantgarde itself as well as formism and the larger part of futurism had come from Cracow. This curious fact has been explained by the superficial and businesslike nature of literary life in Warsaw characterized by coteries, café-style discussions, and the careerist spirit. It was also a result of the absolute hegemony in the capital, both in the publishing market and among the reading public, of the Skamander group. Its magazine *Literary News* drowned all other voices, and the only choice that remained for those who wanted to be heard was to move beyond its radius.

If the thirties brought a great re-evaluation of the Cracow Avantgarde with a large amount of polemics and the presentation of a variety of new proposals, there was one point upon which the poets of the thirties agreed with the Avantgarde—this was their negative evaluation of the poetry of Skamander. Peiper's original criticism of Skamander attitudes as old-fashioned, *passéist* and catering to the public was shared by the overwhelming majority of young poets; they also agreed with his characterization of their poetics as lacking any aesthetic or ideological program, and of their poetry as sentimental and facile. This total rejection of the Skamander group by the young poets explains why the only school with which they entered a dialogue—and polemics—was the Cracow Avantgarde. Its well-defined and even rigid aesthetic program provided the best foil against which the young poets could define their own attitudes.

The critics of the Avantgarde might be divided into two categories: those who kept their arguments within the sphere of aesthetics, and those who spoke from an extra-aesthetic position criticizing the Cracow group for its lack of involvement in the social and political realities of the time. The most forceful representative of the first group was Karol Irzykowski, who attacked Avantgarde poetics for its exclusive preoccupation with form and its narrow identification of poetry with metaphor. He criticized Avantgarde poetry for being obscure, and considered many of their innovations as trifling and insufficient. He also saw in the Avantgarde influence on young poets a deplorable tendency to narrow poetic horizons. Irzykowski's critical evaluations of the Avantgarde achievements appeared in numerous articles in the mid-thirties[1] and were restatements of his earlier polemics with Peiper. They constituted a large part of his book *An Elephant among Porcelain (Słoń wśród porcelany)* published in 1934. Irzykowski's arguments were picked up by other critics in the thirties, but they did not add any new insights to Irzykowski's original criticisms. They are interesting only because they testify to a certain persistence of arguments, and because they represent the younger generation of critics and poets.

The Authentists and the Return to Experience

It was exactly in this dispute with the Cracow Avantgarde that the new tendencies of the young poets were most clearly revealed. Disagreement with the Avantgarde led the young poets to formulate their own positions; some of the poetic programs of the thirties were formed in reaction to Avantgarde poetics. Such was the case of the group of poets who called themselves "authentists" *(autentyści)* and were associated with the magazine, *The Poets' Region (Okolica Poetów)* published between 1935 and 1939 in the small town of Ostrzeszów. Stanisław Czernik, the editor of the magazine, was also the main theoretician of authentism *(autentyzm)*. His main thesis was that the most essential element in poetry and criterion of its value is the authenticity of the poet's emotions and experiences. The form of a poem was entirely determined by its content, and content in turn was determined by the depth and truth of the poet's experience: "The poet who has not experienced the suffering of hunger is not capable of writing a poem on the subject."[2] The poet's experience can be of an emotional, intellectual, or sensory nature, but it must be "lived through" and not imagined or assimilated. The program of authentism was hazy and its weakness was to have based aesthetic values on purely psychological elements, moving the aesthetic emphasis from the product of the creative process to its genesis. The postulate that truth and faithfulness to experience were the only basis for an aesthetic system of evaluation was difficult to sustain, because it relied on the assumption that a prepoetic reality exists and could be the determining factor in the evaluation of poetry.[3] There is a great gap between an experience—whether truly "authentic" or not—and the verbal rendering of that experience.

The theoretical program and the poetry of authentism are probably less interesting than the very close reflection it gives of its own historical moment. The young poets caught between the conventional poetry of Skamander and the formal experiments of the Cracow Avantgarde looked for new possibilities—authentism was one of their answers. Czernik spoke of the need for a revision of poetic attitudes, for a redefinition of the concepts of form and content and a re-evaluation of their relationship. In the battle between Skamander and the Cracow Avantgarde, the authentists were on the side of the latter; although they considered the period of the Avantgarde as closed, they recognized its revolutionary role and its poetic authority. In defining their own program the poetics of the Avantgarde were a decisive factor, and the theories of authentism acquire significance primarily when seen as reactions against the postulates of the Cracow poets. Seen from this perspective, they translated the desire held by the great majority of the new generation of poets to return to real experience as the source of poetry, to renew the tie of poetry with reality on the one hand and with the poet's own emotions on the other.

The Social Critics of the Avantgarde

The polemics carried on by Irzykowski and the authentists with the Cracow Avantgarde presupposed a common platform: disagreement with some of the Avantgarde theories, and especially with the lack of balance between form and content in its poetics. The critics who followed in the steps of Irzykowski remained within the sphere of aesthetic concerns. They did not question the fundamental premise of the Avantgarde poetic system, its belief in the autonomy of art. However the majority of the criticisms directed against the Avantgarde came from an entirely different vantage point: they questioned the very concept of artistic autonomy. They criticized Avantgarde poetics for its aestheticism, and Avantgarde poetry for its indifference to social and political problems. The social critics repeated the objection to formalism and to a lack of content in Avantgarde poetry, but their interpretation of content differed essentially from Irzykowski's. Compared to his, their concept of content was narrow and specific—they reduced content to subject, and subject to social and political themes. The question of the social commitment of literature had already been raised in the twenties and we have seen Peiper's position on the subject. The discussion continued in the thirties, and one of its most interesting episodes was the polemic between two poets who were both associated with the Avantgarde, Marian Czuchnowski and Józef Czechowicz.

The most persistent criticism of the indifference of the Avantgarde to social matters came from Marian Czuchnowski, a poet close to the Cracow group—his poems appeared regularly in *Linia*—who in his poetry combined Avantgarde poetics with strong social interests. In his article "Socialized Experiments," Czuchnowski criticized Avantgarde poetry for its purposeless experimentation—he saw a need to channel poetic experiments into an organized social force: "All the Avantgarde poets are oriented toward fictitious goals of poetry since they are purely poetic, and because of their social silence they declare themselves on the side of the bourgeoisie."[4] Czuchnowski was inspired by Marxism, and argued that to fulfill its historical role the Avantgarde must become socially involved. In his article "Socialized Absurdities" Józef Czechowicz defended the Avantgarde position.

The voice of Czechowicz is particularly interesting because it broadened the discussion of the social role of poetry by introducing a new element. In appearance, Czechowicz opposed the concept of social poetry from the same position as the Avantgarde (with which he identified), in the name of the autonomy of art and of aesthetic values. But his interpretation of aesthetic values differed essentially from that of the Avantgarde:

> If I and a number of other poets in whose name I speak insist on aesthetic values and criteria in poetry, we do it not because we fail to recognize its social significance, but because we do not want to overestimate it, because we cannot recognize the elements of the social system as something hierarchically above the essence of life. Creativity, its psychology and its products, are

organically united with what is highest in man, highest in peoples and nations, highest on our planet and perhaps everywhere else—with the metaphysical element.[5]

To recognize the metaphysical as the most important element in art, and—even further—to identify it with aesthetic values was an obvious heresy from the Avantgarde point of view. Czechowicz's approach directed the discussion of the social role of poetry onto new tracks: social values were opposed not only to aesthetic values but to metaphysical values as well.

The position taken by Czechowicz was symptomatic because it underlined the evolution of attitudes toward poetry since the time of the Cracow Avantgarde—if the emphasis on aesthetic experience and values connects Czechowicz with the Avantgarde, the consideration of art within a metaphysical category indicates a new stage in the evolution of poetic consciousness. Czechowicz's position provides a bridge between the poetics of the Avantgarde and the generation that would reach maturity in the thirties. If the first of these two generations was devoted to the search for new poetics and new means of expression, the interest of the second shifted away from the poem itself to the broader problem of the role of poetry in general.

The shift of poetic interest in the 1930s had several causes. First, the formal experiments of the Cracow Avantgarde seemed for the time being to have exhausted all possibilities and Polish poetry needed time to assimilate those propositions before proceeding further. If the demand for poetic reform had been fully satisfied, the spiritual and metaphysical claims of poetry had been thwarted by the positivistic nature of the Avantgarde's poetics. Czechowicz's position as well as his poetry were a portent of the oncoming change in attitudes and poetic values; the generation of the thirties revindicated the right of poetry to be more than mere craft. At the same time the social and political situation in Poland changed drastically. Unemployment and inflation together with the continual movement of the government toward a more conservative, right-wing and militaristic position seemed to be leading to an inevitable catastrophe. With the spectacular rise to power of fascism in Germany, the political situation in Europe was more than alarming, and the civilization-oriented optimism of the Cracow Avantgarde appeared anachronistic. The situation inspired a darker outlook on reality and also awoke a sense of moral responsibility in most poets, with the ensuing demand that the poet be involved in social and political life. The literary press of the thirties was flooded with articles on the social responsibility of literature. A few titles taken at random best illustrate the sense of the urgency of the problem: "Polish Contemporary Literature and Life," "The Individual, the Collectivity and the Writer," "The Social Role of Literature," "The Social Functions of Literature," "The Artist, Ordinary Life, and Prometheus."

From Formism to Moralism: Żagary

But the demand for moral responsiblity was also given a deeper and broader interpretation than that implied by the concepts of social and political poetry. Of all the voices taking part in the discussion, the most original and at the same time most representative of the entire young generation came from Wilno, from a group of students known by the name of their periodical, *Żagary*. The name *Żagary* came from a Lithuanian term for "dry twigs, half charred in fire but still glowing."[6] The *Żagary* group is particularly important because it is both the last chapter of the Polish avant-garde and the opening of a new era in Polish poetry.

The vitality and originality of *Żagary* were strong enough to attract immediately the attention of the critics: "Within the context of the oncoming generation, Wilno's *Żagary* is undoubtedly the most lively magazine—because of its spirit, its selection of individualities, thanks to its fundamental approach to truly serious problems, and due, finally, to its provocative temperament which elasticizes and at the same time inclines toward extreme intransigence."[7] In the controversy between the adherents to "pure art" and those who saw art as a social tool, the poets of *Żagary* sided unquestionably with the latter, but they gave their position a much deeper ethical meaning as well as a broader philosophical framework. They believed that the social significance of poetry was found not in the proclamation of certain social and political slogans, but rather in the poet's awareness of social and political reality, in the clear formulation of his *Weltanschauung,* which was the prerogative and basis of any great poetry. The discussion of particular artistic issues was only secondary to the discussion of social and ethical problems.

In his characterization of *Żagary,* Czesław Miłosz described the philosophical position of its members as antiaesthetic and hesitating between "sympathies for Marxism and their metaphysical frame of mind."[8] It stemmed from the historical moment: the *Żagary* poets were extremely aware of the economic, social, and political situation, and in their articles they mentioned time and again unemployment, hunger, strikes, inflation, Stalin, and Hitler. The liberal myth of the supremacy of "people" was crumbling under their eyes, both in Fascist Germany and in Communist Russia. The philosophy of historical materialism, which justified everything in the name of collective welfare, proved to be common both to nationalism and to communism. Whether it was due to political perspicaciousness or perhaps their geographical proximity to the Soviet Union, the Wilno students were much less inclined to believe and accept communist slogans than their contemporaries in Warsaw or Cracow. Their disenchantment with the capitalist world was accompanied by deep skepticism about the benefits of the communist future.

> The myth of the world revolution is flowing, the communized masses dream of trampling the generation of capitalist bedbugs. And what then? What will be founded on the ruins of the capitalist world? What kind of motive powers will act? Perhaps historical materialism and the hopeless struggle with religion. Perhaps the ideal of the barracklike collectivism of consumption. Or perhaps the interest of the trained proletariat living in affluence? And there is no positive answer.[9]

Although the future was uncertain, the sense of an approaching crisis was overpowering for these young men: "The times of the great conflagration of accumulated hatred are approaching, the times of new conquests of Genghis Khan, or else of the great epic, of great transformations. . . . "[10]

In their approach to poetry, the *Żagary* group both continued and drastically diverged from Avantgarde aesthetics. To the extent that they adopted some of the most important poetic propositions of the *Switch* such as rationalism, intellectualism, and constructivism, they might even be seen as continuators of the Cracow Avantgarde. The label of the "Second Avantgarde" applied to them by critics has been based on these premises. The *Żagary* poets themselves considered their endeavor as part of the broad avant-garde movement, and they recognized the Cracow Avantgarde as the strongest and "the most important position in contemporary Polish literature." [11] And yet the most summary reading of the essays in *Żagary* and *Piony* makes it clear that the differences between the two groups were more fundamental than their agreements. There was a deep cleavage between the belief in progress and what might be called the optimistic civilizationalism of the *Switch*, and the catastrophism of *Żagary;* between the fascination with "the present" of the Cracow poets and the dark vision of contemporary reality of the poets from Wilno; between the aestheticism of the "First Avantgarde" and the antiaestheticism of the "Second Avantgarde." The poets of *Żagary* disagreed with the Cracow Avantgarde's fundamental belief in the autonomy of art, and considered as naïve a philosophy that treated reality and art as parallel yet independent phenomena. There was also a cleavage between two different generations. Explaining the negativism and skepticism of their own generation, the poets of *Żagary* complained of the lack of understanding from their elders, and even from those who were only a few years older than themselves. "Between the graduate of a Polish university a few years ago and a student finishing the university now, there is an abyss of mutual misunderstanding, an almost hysterical intolerance." [12] The philosophical attitudes of the poets of *Żagary* and those of the Cracow Avantgarde were not only different, they were irreconcilable and exclusive of each other. This is why discussion became more and more difficult and the wall of misunderstanding, of mutual nonacceptance, grew thicker and thicker until logical argument changed into a passionate outcry.

In 1938 Czesław Miłosz published an article that caused a considerable stir in the literary world and brought not only all the frustrations of the young poet into the open but at the same time marked a new stage in the development of the aesthetic attitudes of the entire younger generation.[13] The article, written with passion, was entitled "The Lie of Today's Poetry"; it attacked all contemporary Polish poetry for its philosophical minimalism and lack of moral responsibility. If the shallow sentimentalism of the older poetry had been a thin disguise over philosophical emptiness, the aestheticism and formalism of the new schools reduced poetry to a sterile game equally shallow and empty. The edge of Miłosz's criticism turned against the recent poetic movements: "I would like to be allowed to proclaim my disgust at all those sterile games called pure poetry.... Enough, enough— let's finish at last with all the 'avantgardes,' the 'imagination,' 'authentism,' with all this babble of the specialists of the new poetics." Outraged by poetry whose main preoccupation was the search for a new metaphor and a "fashionable" combination of words, Miłosz cried out a question whose answer was included in its formulation, as well as a new definition of poetry: "So is this supposed to be poetry, these poems of yours written not to share with people a faith, not to praise or condemn, but only to create a combination of images and sounds? These poems about which it is impossible to say what concept of the world they serve, or what wisdom they express? Poems that do not come under any definition except that they are badly or cleverly made?" Opposed to the formalistic approach to poetry that does not go beyond the poem itself, Miłosz shifted the stress from the poem to the artist. He opposed aesthetic categories with the ethical categories of responsibility, inner discipline, and truth to oneself. It was not the poem but the poet and his *Weltanschauung* that were most important in poetry, and striving for one's own truth meant infinitely more than one's own "expression"—"In my opinion the word should be weighed before it is written, not only for its relation to the words that surround it but also for its relation to what it is at the moment when I write it, what it is as extra-aesthetic consciousness, and how I judge myself, the phenomena of the world and other people." Since for Miłosz the poetic work was an "infinitely personal" creation and a faithful reflection of the poet's intellectual and aesthetic abilities as well as of his moral strength, the flaws in the formal structure of a poem were not a matter of lack of talent or skill, but evidence of the author's "unsolved conflicts with the world and with himself." Greatness in poetry depended on the greatness of the author's individuality, on his internal force and spiritual depth.

For Miłosz the poetic act included a moral responsibility, a responsibility oriented both outward—toward others—and inward—toward himself. If poetry was justified by the poet's certitude that his work "can be helpful to at least one man in his struggle with himself and with the world," it was also a means by which the poet defined himself and his destiny. Poetry was important not as an aesthetic but as an ethical category, as a means for solving the philosophical and moral dilemmas of either the poet or the reader; its ultimate task was to bring the realizations of one's own individuality.

Although Miłosz began his essay with a declaration of independence from any group or movement, insisting that he spoke "in his own name" and did not represent "anyone except himself," he gave expression to the most important inclinations of the new generation: the desire to return to ethical values in art, and the stress on strong individuality. The signs of this total change in poetic attitudes that were so dramatically expressed by Miłosz could be detected earlier. Despite Miłosz's open attack on authentism, which he unjustly identified with the Avantgarde, the authentists' call for the poet's truth to experience and, even more, Czechowicz's insistence on the metaphysical essence of poetry were signals that the formalist poetics of the Cracow Avantgarde were felt even by its own poets to be insufficient. A poll undertaken by *The Poets' Region* in 1935[14] about the situation of contemporary Polish poetry showed the same awareness that it was on the point of entering a new stage. Among the participants of the poll, Stefan Napierski most accurately formulated the strivings of the new generation. Three years before Miłosz's essay, Napierski spoke of the need for heroism and the necessity of impregnating poetry with an ethical attitude. He stressed the importance of the artist's individuality and inner discipline. In the same year Konstanty Troczyński published a book *From Formism to Moralism (Od Formizmu do Moralizmu)* whose title captures the nature of the poetic evolution that took place in the 1930s. Troczyński's theory of art emphasized the decisive role of the moral act or gesture in the artistic process, and following Stanisław Ignacy Witkiewicz he recognized metaphysical feeling as the essence of art. Troczyński's book both reflected the poetic attitudes of the youngest generation and provided their poetry with a theoretical justification.

Catastrophism

In their articles the poets of *Żagary* always explained their philosophical and aesthetic attitudes in terms of the concrete social and political situation, but in their poetry these political concerns were translated into a vision of cosmic apocalypse, a vision that earned them the name of "catastrophists." Czesław Miłosz's poem "On the Book" ("O książce"), considered by the critic Kazimierz Wyka to be the most representative work of catastrophism, is a good example of this poetry; the poem expresses profound pessimism, disenchantment with contemporary reality, and a sense that the destructive force of history has been ominously thickening.

On the Book

We lived in strange, hostile, marvelous times,
bullets sang above our heads
and years no less threatening than tearing shrapnel
taught greatness to those who did not see
war. In the fire of the dryly flaming weeks
we worked hard and were hungry
for bread, for unearthly miracles appearing on earth
and often, unable to sleep, suddenly saddened
we looked through the windows if over the blue night
flocks of zeppelins were not flowing in again,
if a new signal did not explode to the continents
and we looked in the mirror if a stigma did not grow
on the forehead as a sign we were already condemned.
In those times it was not enough to lament
with pure words the eternal pathos of the world,
it was an epoch of storm, the day of the apocalypse,
old nations were destroyed, capitals turning
like a spindle, drunk, under the foaming sky.
Where is the place for you in this tumult,
wise, quiet book, alloy of the elements
reconciled for eternity by the sight of the artist?
Never again from your pages will a foggy evening
glisten for us on the quiet waters as in Conrad's prose,
or the sky break into speech with a Faustian choir,
and the long forgotten song of Hafiz will not touch
our forehead with its coolness, will not rock our heads,
nor will Norwid reveal to us the harsh laws
of history hidden by a red whirlwind of dust.
Anxious, blind, and faithful to our epoch
we are going somewhere far away, above us October
murmurs with a leaf as the other one flapped with a flag.
The laurel is not for us, aware of the punishment
which time allots to those who loved
temporality, deafened by the din of metals.
Thus we were marked to create a fame—nameless,
like a farewell shout of those departing—into darkness.

O książce

W czasach dziwnych i wrogich żyliśmy, wspaniałych,
nad głowami naszymi pociski śpiewały
i lata niemniej groźne od rwących szrapneli
nauczały wielkości tych, co nie widzieli
wojny. W pożarze sucho płonących tygodni
pracowaliśmy ciężko i byliśmy głodni
chleba, cudów nieziemskich zjawionych na ziemi
i często, spać nie mogąc, nagle zasmuceni
patrzyliśmy przez okna, czy nad noce sine
nie przypływają znowu stada zeppelinów,
czy nie wybucha sygnał nowy kontynentom
i sprawdzaliśmy w lustrze, czy na czole piętno
nie wyrosło, na znak, żeśmy już skazani.
W tych czasach nie dość było zawodzić słowami
czystymi, nad patosem świata wiekuistym,
była epoka burzy, dzień apokalipsy,
państwa dawne zburzono, stolice wrzecionem
kręciły się pijane pod niebem spienionym.
Gdzież jest miejsce dla ciebie w tym wieku zamętu
książko mądra, spokojna, stopie elementów
pogodzonych na wieki spojrzeniem artysty?
Już nam z twoich kart nigdy nie zaświeci mglisty
wieczór na cichych wodach jak w prozie Conrada,
ani chórem faustowskim niebo nie zagada
i czoła zapomniany dawno śpiew Hafisa
chłodem swoim nie dotknie, głów nie ukołysze,
ani Norwid surowe nam odkryje prawa
dziejów, które czerwona przesłania kurzawa.
My niespokojni, ślepi i epoce wierni,
gdzieś daleko idziemy, nad nami październik
szumi liściem, jak tamten łopotał sztandarem.
Wawrzyn jest niedostępny nam, świadomym kary
jaką czas tym wyznacza, którzy pokochali
doczesność, ogłuszoną hałasem metali.
Więc sławę nam znaczono stworzyć—bezimienną,
jak okrzyk pożegnalny odchodzących—w ciemność.

The poem was written in 1933, but the vision of war it evokes is so immediate and convincing that it surpasses many descriptions written as a result of experience. If in 1933 the catastrophism of this poem might have seemed groundless, in retrospect it appears genuinely and astonishingly prophetic. Although the poem reveals an extraordinary prescience of the war to come, its catastrophism had its roots in a concrete political situation and in recent political events. In a conversation with Miłosz, Aleksander Wat compared the catastrophism of his own generation to that of the generation of *Żagary,* capturing their differences and pointing out the ominous character of the political situation of the 1930s:

The catastrophism of your generation already took place in the context of Stalinism on the one hand and of Hitler on the other. You were squeezed, especially in Poland, between those scissors. You also had a feeling, perhaps even more profound, that it was the end of an epoch, the end of the world, that civilization was impossible and yet you were at the same time squeezed between monsters of enormous power and dynamics. The situation of Poland in your time was indeed such that the Communist adage seemed absolutely probable: either Fascism or Communism.[15]

The feeling of living in exceptional times, of being both witness and victim of an apocalypse, was the source of the poet's sense of belonging to a condemned, stigmatized generation. The same awareness would become overwhelming among the poets of the post-World War II generation. With them, also, Miłosz shared the tragic conviction that in the time of war, death, and hunger, there was no room for poetry, at least as it had been known before then. History that has grown to the dimensions of an apocalypse left no place for art, just as confusion destroyed harmony and anxiety excluded peace. Miłosz's realization of the obsoleteness of poetry in the face of death and destruction was totally alien to Avantgarde attitudes, but it would become the major dilemma of Polish poetry after 1945. In the evolution of Polish poetry, the importance of Miłosz is that he pushed the critical point—what might be called the watershed, or division between post-World War II and prewar poetry—as far back as 1933, when his first catastrophist poems were written.

FROM A POSTWAR PERSPECTIVE: CONCLUSION

The title "From Formism to Moralism" describes the dialectical nature of the evolution of Polish poetry during the period between the wars, and it also puts into relief the two phases—represented by the avant-garde movements and by post-avant-garde poetry—that proved to be decisive in the development of Polish poetry after 1945. The shattering experience of the Second World War put these two phases into a special perspective in which the avant-garde's revolution in poetic form seemed to the poets starting to write after 1945 to be of lesser importance than the revolution in literary ethics of *Żagary* and a poet like Miłosz. But the perspective was misleading: without the avant-garde experiment there would have been neither the poetry of *Żagary* nor the poetry that came after the end of World War II. Curiously the true importance of the avant-garde came to be felt not in 1945 but in 1956, when the discovery of avant-garde poetry by both poets and critics became not only a poetic but a political event. For those who had been raised on the dogma of socialist realism, the avant-garde experiments in form acquired a revolutionary character. They were attractive for two reasons. On the one hand they had the force of a political gesture; on the other hand—and this is more important—they revealed to young poets the unexplored possibilities of the Polish language, and new exciting poetic models corresponding to a deeply felt need. A young poet wrote in 1972: "I read *Nowe usta* in 1956. I was shaken by it."[16] When he added enthusiastically, "We are all the heirs of Peiper," he spoke not only in the name of his generation but of all postwar Polish poetry. The formal innovations of avant-garde poetry became the common heritage of a wide range of poets from Różewicz, Herbert, and Białoszewski to Grochowiak, Karpowicz, Waśkiewicz, and Krynicki. The formal sophistication of Polish poetry today derives directly from the avant-garde's discoveries—discoveries that it had never superseded. In fact, Polish poetry assimilated the avant-garde experiment so thoroughly that the avant-garde has fused with tradition and become indistinguishable from it.

NOTES

INTRODUCTION

1. To assign exact limits to any literary period is a risky enterprise, and many critics have avoided giving specific dates to the avant-garde movement. For some the beginning of the avant-garde coincides conveniently with that of our own century (R. Delevoy, T. Shapiro, F. Cabanne, V. Boarini and P. Bonfigli, J. Kvapil). Others have designated as the year of origin 1905 (M. Szabolsci), 1909 (P. Restany, J. Holthusen), 1910 (S. Schlenstedt, A. Flaker), 1912 (T. Straus), and also 1918 (G. Torre). The problem of selecting the closing date of the avant-garde period is even more complicated, and the different dates that have been proposed—including our own—are approximate. While 1945 has been accepted by a majority of critics as the termination of the historical avant-garde, some prefer 1938 (M. Szabolsci) or 1939 (G. Torre). In addition, several authors do not consider the avant-garde period to be closed at all (V. Boarini and P. Bonfigli, P. Restany, P. Cabanne), and believe it extends to our own days. Indeed it is safest to speak of different phases of the avant-garde, and the inclusion or exclusion of a particular phase becomes a matter of the individual perspective and interpretation adopted by the critic. Although P. Restany sees 1924 as a turning point in the evolution of the avant-garde, most critics push this point to 1930, when the rebellious, nonconforming spirit of the movement began to falter and the avant-garde pre-empted a position of authority that contradicted its very premises.

2. Most critics have emphasized that one essential characteristic of avant-garde movements is the existence of groups, or collectivities, having well-defined artistic and philosophical programs. E. Bojtar has spoken of "groupements à programme," M. Bakoš of collective movements with "a common program-theory," V. Effenberger of groups and collective ideas. For M. Szabolsci, programs and communities serve as the very terms of his definition of the avant-garde. Prior to Marinetti's

1909 manifesto no group or program existed that could qualify as avant-garde. To be sure the manifesto was preceded by years of artisitic and poetic activities, not only among the futurists but the cubists and expressionists as well. However, they were private rather than public, individual and not collective. These activities mark the period of gestation that must be distinguished from the moment at which gestation comes to a point of conscious formulation. And it is only from this moment of self-realization—translated by theories and manifestoes—that we can speak of the avant-garde as a historical phenomenon.

3. Many critics have pointed out the importance of the revolt against tradition in the avant-garde. Guillermo Torre considers antitraditionalism together with its corollary, internationalism, as the two most prominent characteristics of the avant-garde. For Matei Calinescu the struggle with the past, with tradition and older artistic forms, is a prerequisite for the existence of an avant-garde; E. Bojtar states that the aspiration for artistic and social change is the single fundamental factor underlying all avant-garde tendencies. A. Marino defines the avant-garde by its continual opposition to artistic tradition—he calls the confrontation between the tradition of "order" and that of "adventure" one of the constants of all avant-garde movements, echoing E. H. Holthusen's assertion that the avant-garde reopened the eternal discussion between the "old" and the "new." Marino perceives the antitraditional, insurrectional spirit of the avant-garde in broad terms, the break with artistic tradition being only part of a more global rebellion against the old moral, social, political order. In a similar manner M. Grygar sees the "iconoclastic antitraditionalism" of the avant-garde directed against artistic forms as part of a more general criticism of the role art plays in a bourgeois society.

However the antitraditionalism of the avant-garde did not preclude the eventual establishment of its own values, norms, and canons, its own "poncifs." Destruction and construction, disintegration followed by reintegration, destitution, and restitution, are some of the most important phenomena of the avant-garde resulting in what A. Marino has called its "internal cycle." Similarly Alexander Flaker distinguishes between negative determinants of the avant-garde—the de-hierarchization of genres, antiaestheticism, the dehumanization of art, destruction of syntax and established poetic structures—and positive contributions such as the acceptance of open structures, the combination and interrelation of different genres, the enlargement of the semantic field, and the principles of associationism, montage, and simultaneity. Flaker also speaks of internal oppositions and polarities within the avant-garde such as the coexistence of both technicism and primitivism, of individualism and collectivism, of experimentation and hermeticism together with the desire to create a new language for the masses, of rationalism and constructivism together with irrationalism and the denial of structures. The critic Jan Mukarovski believes that the desire of the avant-garde to integrate itself into the cultural tradition of a country and—at the same time—its effort to distinguish itself from this tradition is one of its fundamental dialectical contradictions.

4. M. Bakoš, for whom the avant-garde period continues to and includes the present, has called the period between the wars one of pioneering research, the phase of analysis and experimentation leading to the period of synthesis we are witnessing in our own time. The orientation toward the future of the avant-garde has

been repeatedly pointed out; A. Marino has written that "the future" is a major avant-garde *topos,* and E. Bojtar considers this to be one of its most important poetic categories.

5. Recent evaluations of the movement have stressed its lack of direction and the inability of *Zdrój* to form an artistic program of its own. Józef Ratajczak has pointed out that its preference for metaphysical and ontological themes was dangerous from the artistic point of view, often inducing the poets of the movement to treat art as an extension of religion or philosophy. After defining the characteristics of expressionist aesthetics, Jan Józef Lipski has admitted that not a single work in Polish literature of the period after World War I contains all of them. Both critics concluded with a negative evaluation of the movement's contribution to Polish poetry.

CHAPTER ONE

1. Bruno Jasieński, "Futuryzm polski (Bilans)" (1923), *Utwory poetyckie, manifesty, szkice,* p. 231.

2. Ibid., p. 223.

3. Aleksander Wat, "Wspomnienia o futuryźmie," *Miesięcznik Literacki,* no. 2 (1930), p. 71.

4. B. Jasieński, "Futuryzm polski (Bilans)," p. 229.

5. Adam Ważyk, *Dziwna historia awangardy,* p. 45.

6. Anatol Stern and Aleksander Wat, "Prymitywiści do narodów świata i do Polski" *(Gga,* 1920), in *Antologia polskiego futuryzmu i Nowej Sztuki,* p. 3. All subsequent quotes from this manifesto are taken from the same anthology.

7. F. T. Marinetti, "The Founding and Manifesto of Futurism, 1909" *(Le Figaro,* Paris, 20 Feb. 1909), in *Futurist Manifestoes,* ed. Umbro Apollonio. Statements in this manifesto such as "We will glorify war—the world's only hygiene" (p. 22), or "Art, in fact, can be nothing but violence, cruelty, and injustice" (p. 23), provoked the counterstatements of Wat and Stern.

8. A. Wat, *Mój wiek. Pamiętnik mówiony,* p. 24.

9. Tytus Czyżewski, "O 'Zielonym Oku' i o swoim malarstwie," *(Jednodniówka futurystów,* 1921), in *Polska awangarda poetycka,* ed. Andrzej Lam, 2:227.

10. A. Wat, "Wspomnienia o futuryźmie," p. 71.

11. A. Wat, *Mój wiek,* p. 25.

12. See F. T. Marinetti, "Destruction of Syntax—Imagination without Strings—Words-in-Freedom" (1913), *Futurist Manifestoes,* p. 104: "We Futurists initiate the constant, audacious use of onomatopoeia." In the same manifesto, Marinetti maintained that onomatopoeia "vivifies lyricism with crude and brutal elements of reality." See Guillaume Apollinaire, "The New Spirit and the Poets" (1918), in *Selected Writings of Guillaume Apollinaire,* trans. Roger Shattuck, especially pp. 230-31.

13. "Do narodu polskiego. Manifest w sprawie natychmiastowej futuryzacji życia" [A manifesto to the Polish nation concerning the immediate futurization of life], "Manifest w sprawie poezji futurystycznej" [A manifesto concerning futurist poetry], "Manifest w sprawie krytyki artystycznej" [Manifesto concerning

artistic criticism], and "Manifest w sprawie ortografii fonetycznej" [A manifesto concerning phonetic orthography], in *Jednodniówka futurystów*. *Manifesty polskiego futuryzmu* (1921), reprinted in *Antologia polskiego futuryzmu i Nowej Sztuki.*

14. B. Jasieński, "Futuryzm polski (Bilans)," p. 234.
15. A. Wat, *Mój wiek*, p. 42.
16. "Wstęp od Redakcji," *Nowa Sztuka*, no. 1 (November 1929), p. 4.
17. Jan Józef Lipski, "O poezji Tytusa Czyżewskiego," *Twórczość*, no. 6 (1960), p. 67.
18. B. Jasieński, "Futuryzm polski (Bilans)," p. 232.
19. Leon Chwistek, "Twórcza siła formizmu," *(Głos Plastyków,* nos. 8-12 [1938]), in *O Nową Sztukę,* ed. Helena Zaworska, pp. 128-29.
20. A. Wat, *Mój wiek*, p. 39.
21. B. Jasieński, A. Stern, "Wstęp do *Ziemi na lewo"* (1924), in Jasieński's *Utwory poetyckie...* , p. 240.
22. A. Wat, "Wspomnienia o futuryźmie," p. 71.
23. A. Wat, *Mój wiek*, p. 162.
24. Ibid., p. 59.
25. A. Stern, *Głód jednoznaczności i inne szkice*, p. 255.
26. A. Wat, *Mój wiek*, p. 23. The following two quotations come from the same passage.
27. Although Jasieński's early poems as well as his pose of a dandy were far from revolutionary, Wat seems to overlook that Jasieński's change of attitude from dada to social commitment occurred in a shorter period than similar change in other Polish futurists.
28. They were both older than the other futurists; Czyżewski was born in 1880 and Młodożeniec in 1895. From the beginning, Czyżewski and Młodożeniec kept aloof from futurist activities, and characteristically they never became politically involved, although in the thirties, Młodożeniec was active in peasant political parties.
29. A. Wat, *Mój wiek*, p. 79.
30. This choice has been suggested, it seems to me incorrectly, by Helena Jaworska in *O Nową Sztukę.*
31. A. Stern gives an account of Mayakovski's visit to Poland in his essay "Majakowski po 40 latach," *Głód jednoznaczności*, pp. 237-51.
32. B. Jasieński, "Futuryzm polski (Bilans)," p. 235.
33. Wat maintains in *Mój wiek* that Polish futurism "remained without influence" (p. 26), and agrees with the criticism of Karol Irzykowski that Polish futurism was a "miscarriage" (p. 43). Traces of futurist influence can be found in postwar Polish poetry, for example the poetry of Miron Białoszewski, but they are rare and their similarity might be coincidental rather than deliberate. As both Wat and Ważyk noted, of all writers only Witold Gombrowicz certainly read the futurists and was inspired by them in his plays and novels. But what he appreciated and took from them was their use of nonsense, probably the least "futurist" ingredient in their poetry.
34. B. Jasieński, "Futuryzm polski (Bilans)," p. 239.

35. T. Czyżewski, "Mój futuryzm," (Zwrotnica, no. 6 [1923]), in Polska awangarda poetycka, ed. Lam, 2:397.

36. Yet Czyżewski's poetic solutions were entirely different from those of Peiper. While Peiper based his poetics on the value of the sentence as the primary compositional element, Czyżewski rejected syntax and, following futurist poetics, took the word as his point of departure.

37. T. Czyżewski, Noc-dzień. Mechaniczny instynkt elektryczny, p. 39.

38. Ibid., p. 41.

39. T. Czyżewski, Lajkonik w chmurach. Poezje, p. 63.

40. Ibid.

41. Ibid., p. 65.

42. L. Chwistek, Tytus Czyżewski a kryzys Formizmu, pages not numbered.

43. Kazimierz Wyka, Rzecz wyobraźni, p. 18.

44. T. Czyżewski, Wąż, Orfeusz i Eurydyka, wizje antyczne, pages not numbered.

45. K. Wyka, Rzecz wyobraźni, p. 15.

46. An excellent analysis of the Pastorals has been made in ibid.

47. Jan Józef Lipski, "O poezji Tytusa Czyżewskiego," Twórczość, no. 6 (1960), p. 77.

48. Renato Poggioli, The Poets of Russia, 1890-1930, p. 266.

49. Edward Balcerzan uses the term contractors in his excellent introduction to Jasieński's Utwory poetyckie . . . , p. lvi.

50. Ibid., p. lviii.

51. B. Jasieński, Nogi Izoldy Morgan (1923), ibid., p. 222.

52. E. Balcerzan, in Jasieński's Utwory poetyckie . . . , p. lv.

53. Ibid., p. liv.

54. Nina S. Kolesnikoff, "Polish Futurism: The Quest to Renovate Poetic Language," Slavic and East European Journal 21, no. 1 (Spring 1977):66.

55. Balcerzan made an attempt to "translate" the first stanza, in Jasieński's Utwory poetyckie . . . , p. lxvi.

56. B. Jasieński, "Manifest w sprawie poezji futurystycznej" (1921), Utwory poetyckie . . . , p. 213.

57. See the poem, "Song of the Engineers" ("Pieśń maszynistów").

58. B. Jasieński, "Coś w rodzaju autobiografii" (in Russian) (1931), Utwory poetyckie . . . , p. 248.

59. St. Młodożeniec, "Krakowskie spotkania," Orka (December 1958), nos. 51-52, p. 15.

60. St. Młodożeniec, preface to Futuro-gamy i futuro-pejzaże (1934), in his Utwory poetyckie, p. 505.

61. Janusz Sławiński, "Poezje Młodożeńca," Twórczość, no. 5 (1959), p. 121.

62. St. Młodożeniec, "O poezji" (1936), Utwory poetyckie, p. 43.

63. Ibid., p. 44.

64. Ibid., p. 45.

65. J. Sławiński, "Poezje Młodożeńca," p. 124.

66. Tomasz Burek, "Sztandar futuryzmu na chłopskim wąkopie albo o poezji Stanisława Młodożeńca," in Młodożeniec's Utwory poetyckie, p. 22.

67. K. Wyka, *Rzecz wyobraźni*, p. 246.

68. Stefan Gacki, "List do Anatola Sterna," *Almanach Nowej Sztuki*, no. 1 (1924), p. 26.

69. A. Stern, *Poezja zbuntowana*, p. 339.

70. N. Kolesnikoff, "Polish Futurism: The Quest to Renovate Poetic Language," p. 73.

71. A. Stern, *Głód jednoznaczności*, pp. 65-66.

72. A. Wat, *Ciemne świecidło*, p. 233.

73. "Linguo choas ranis, cra corvis vanaque vanis ad logicam pergo quae mortis non timet ergo" [I abandon the croaking of frogs, the cawing of crows, and I turn from empty nothingness to logic which is not afraid of death's "therefore"]. Wat took the quote from Jacopo da Voragine's *Legenda aurea*.

"Tu verras dans ce tableau un promeneur sombre et solitaire plonger dans le flot mouvant de multitudes et envoyant son coeur et sa pensée à une Electre lointaine qui essuyait naguère son front baigné de sueur et rafraîchissait ses lèvres parcheminées par la fièvre." (Charles Baudelaire)

74. A. Wat, *Ciemne świecidło*, p. 230.

75. A. Wat, *Mój wiek*, pp. 54, 55-56.

76. A. Wat, *Ciemne świecidło*, p. 233.

77. Ibid., p. 230.

78. André Breton, "Manifeste du surréalisme" (1924) in *Manifestes du surréalisme* (Paris: Jean-Jacques Pauvert, 1962).

79. Adam Ważyk, *Dziwna historia awangardy*, p. 41.

80. A. Wat, *Mój wiek*, pp. 154-55.

81. Czesław Miłosz, preface to *Mój wiek*, p. 8.

82. A. Wat, *Mój wiek*, p. 155.

CHAPTER TWO

1. Leon Chwistek, "Zagadnienia współczesnej architektury," *Nowa Sztuka*, no. 1 (1921), p. 10.

2. Tadeusz Peiper, "O jedności," *Zwrotnica*, no. 4 (1923), p. 90.

3. T. Peiper, *Nowe usta* (1925), reprinted in his collected works, *Tędy. Nowe usta*. All quotations come from the 1972 edition of *Nowe usta;* the quotations from Peiper's other writings are indicated in the notes.

4. T. Peiper, *Tędy. Nowe usta*, pp. 155-56.

5. T. Peiper mentions his poems, "Odezwa" [Appeal], and "Zwycięzca" [The victor], ibid., p. 349.

6. *Blok*, no. 1 (1924), p. 1.

7. Andrzej K. Waśkiewicz, *Rygor i marzenie*, p. 44.

8. Karol Irzykowski, "Metaphoritis i złota plomba," *Walka o treść. Beniaminek*, p. 71.

9. Ibid., p. 259.

10. Stanisław Jaworski, *U podstaw awangardy. Tadeusz Peiper. Pisarz i teoretyk*, p. 168.

11. Ibid., p. 168.

12. T. Peiper, *Tędy. Nowe usta*, pp. 302-3.
13. S. Jaworski, *U podstaw awangardy*, p. 197.
14. K. Irzykowski, quoted by T. Peiper, "Oskarżenie obrońcy" (1928), in *O wszystkim i jeszcze o czymś*, p. 176.
15. Julian Przyboś, *Linia i gwar*, 1:5.
16. Ibid.
17. Ibid.
18. J. Przyboś, "Człowiek w rzeczach" (1926), *Linia i gwar*, 1:16.
19. Janusz Sławiński, *Koncepcja języka poetyckiego awangardy krakowskiej*, p. 57.
20. Ibid., p. 65.
21. J. Przyboś, "Ku poezji powszechnej," *Linia i gwar*, 2:182.
22. Ibid., p. 183.
23. J. Przyboś, "O rymie," *Najmniej słów*, p. 168.
24. J. Sławiński, *Koncepcja języka poetyckiego awangardy krakowskiej*, p. 59. Sławiński quotes Jan Prokop, "Budowa obrazu u Przybosia," *Ruch Literacki*, no. 1-2 (1960), p. 77.
25. J. Przyboś, "Pytanie o miejsce na Ziemi," *Sens poetycki*, 2:245.
26. Karol Irzykowski, "Od metafory do metonimii," *Wybór pism krytyczno-literackich*, p. 650.
27. Kazimierz Wyka, "Wola wymiernego kształtu," *Rzecz wyobraźni*, p. 228.
28. Artur Sandauer, "Esceta czy Scyta? albo robotnik wyobraźni," *Poeci czterech pokoleń*, p. 158.
29. K. Wyka, *Wędrując po tematach*, 2 *(Puścizna)*:374-75.
30. Ibid., p. 378.
31. J. Przyboś, "Nowatorstwo Władysława Strzemińskiego," in *Linia i gwar*, p. 131.
32. See Salvador Dali, "L'Ane pourri," *Surréalisme au service de la révolution*, vol. 1 (1930).
33. See Sigmund Freud, *The Interpretation of Dreams*, the chapter "The Dream-Work."
34. J. Przyboś, "Realizm 'rytmu fizjologicznego,'" *Linia i gwar*, 1:145.
35. J. Przyboś, "Przygody awangardy," *Linia i gwar*, 1:75.
36. J. Przyboś, "Sens poetycki," *Sens poetycki*, p. 50.
37. J. Przyboś, "Przygody awangardy," p. 61.
38. Ibid., p. 60.
39. J. Przyboś, "O poezji integralnej," *Linia i gwar*, p. 32.
40. J. Przyboś, "Dwa głosy," *Linia i gwar*, p. 53.
41. J. Przyboś, "Przyjaciel poetycki," *Sens poetycki*, p. 195.
42. Jan Brzękowski, "O klasycznym i romantycznym widzeniu poezji," *Wyobraźnia wyzwolona*, p. 74.
43. Ibid., p. 78.
44. Ibid., p. 75.
45. Janusz Sławiński, "O poezji Jana Brzękowskiego," *Twórczość*, no. 9 (1961), p. 92.
46. J. Brzękowski, "Wyobraźnia wyzwolona," *Wyobraźnia wyzwolona*, p. 63.

47. J. Brzękowski, "Poezja integralna," *Wyobraźnia wyzwolona,* p. 13.
48. J. Brzękowski, "Wyobraźnia wyzwolona," p. 62.
49. J. Brzękowski, "Integralizm w czasie," *Wyobraźnia wyzwolona,* p. 56.
50. Ibid., p. 60.
51. J. Brzękowski, "Czas poetycki," *Wyobraźnia wyzwolona,* p. 69.
52. J. Sławiński, "O poezji Jana Brzękowskiego," p. 91.
53. Ibid., p. 90.
54. J. Brzękowski, "Integralizm w czasie," p. 58.
55. Ibid., p. 59.
56. J. Brzękowski, "Poezja integralna," p. 21.
57. Ibid., p. 39.
58. J. Sławiński, "O poezji Jana Brzękowskiego," p. 88.
59. J. Brzękowski, "Poezja integralna," p. 37.
60. Ibid., pp. 38-39.
61. J. Brzękowski, "Integralizm w czasie," p. 53.
62. J. Brzękowski, "Wyobraźnia wyzwolona," p. 65.
63. S. Jaworski, introduction to *Wiersze awangardowe,* by Jalu Kurek, p. 12.
64. Quoted by Jaworski, ibid., p. 11.
65. Jalu Kurek, *Zmierzch natchnienia,* p. 23.
66. Ibid., p. 6.
67. Ibid., p. 183.
68. Ibid., p. 41.
69. Ibid., p. 53.
70. Ibid., p. 24.
71. Ibid., p. 42.
72. Ibid.
73. Ibid., p. 98.

CHAPTER THREE

1. Adam Ważyk, *Dziwna historia awangardy,* p. 78.
2. Ibid., p. 81.
3. Edward Fry, *Cubism* (New York: McGraw-Hill, 1966), p. 14.
4. A. Ważyk, *Dziwna historia awangardy,* p. 80.
5. Because Ważyk's book is trenchant and to the point, and because it is also written from a broad perspective, it is the best book on the avant-garde that has appeared in Poland. It is often biased and impressionistic in its appraisals, however—for example, Ważyk's description of the *Almanac of New Art* as representing "the critical years" in the history of the Polish avant-garde is unjustified by the facts and cannot be accepted unreservedly. Some of Ważyk's generalizations about avant-garde poetry stem from reflections on his own poetry, and apply to other poets only to a limited degree.
6. Józef Czechowicz, "Treść i forma w poezji," *Wyobraźnia stwarzająca. Szkice literackie,* p. 29.
7. J. Czechowicz, "Przemówienie wygłoszone na inauguracyjnym zebraniu Związku Literatów w Lublinie w dniu 21 maja 1932," *Wyobraźnia stwarzająca,* p. 26.

8. Kazimierz Wyka, "O Józefie Czechowiczu," *Rzecz wyobraźni*, p. 40.

9. Czesław Miłosz, *The History of Polish Literature*, p. 412.

10. J. Czechowicz, "Z mojego warsztatu literackiego," *Wyobraźnia stwarzająca*, p. 120.

11. J. Czechowicz, "Wschodzi poemat," *Wyobraźnia stwarzająca*, p. 36.

12. J. Czechowicz, "Tezy do manifestu," *Wyobraźnia stwarzająca*, p. 90.

13. J. Czechowicz, "Uspołecznione absurdy," *Kamena*, no. 8 (1934), p. 148.

14. J. Czechowicz, "Odpowiedź na ankietę," *Wyobraźnia stwarzająca*, p. 57.

CHAPTER FOUR

1. A series of articles by Irzykowski about the Avantgarde appeared in several issues of *Pion* in 1934 and 1935, which carried the common subtitle "Wycieczki w lirykę" [Excursions into poetry]. They included "Zgiełk a ścisk tzw. walorów" (no. 39, 1934), "Awangardą a pogardą" (no. 40, 1934), "Niczego nie zrozumieć–wszystko przebaczyć" (no. 41, 1934), "Noli iurare, domine Przyboś, in verba Peiperi" (no. 5, 1935), "Jeszcze raz ucieczka w kontekst" (no. 19, 1935), and "Niezrozumialstwo, metafory i kto nie będzie rozstrzelany" (no. 52, 1935).

2. Stanisław Czernik, "Styl w liryce," *Okolica Poetów*, no. 1 (1935), p. 4.

3. An excellent critique of the position of the authentists appeared in the article by Ignacy Fik, "W sprawie autentyzmu," *Okolica Poetów*, no. 12 (1936).

4. Marian Czuchnowski, "Uspołecznione eksperymenty," *Kamena*, no. 6 (1934), p. 99.

5. Józef Czechowicz, "Uspołecznione absurdy," *Kamena*, no. 8 (1934), pp. 147-48.

6. Czesław Miłosz, *The History of Polish Literature*, p. 412. *Żagary* had a complicated history and was published in two phases. The first comprised eight numbers that appeared between April 1931 and May 1932; the four numbers of the second series appeared between November 1933 and March 1934. During the break between the two series, the group of *Żagary* continued to publish in the magazines *Piony* (five issues, 1932) and *Smuga* (eight issues, 1933). To stress the continuity of their initiative, the second series of *Żagary* started with "number 22." An editorial note declared that the three magazines represent "a common uniform front of young literary Wilno," and that together "they covered nearly all the avantgarde endeavors of the last few years" *(Żagary*, no. 1 [no. 22] [1933], p. 1).

7. Stefan Napierski, "Prowincjonalne pisma literackie," *Droga*, no. 9 (1934), pp. 829-30.

8. Cz. Miłosz, *History of Polish Literature*, p. 412.

9. Henryk Dembiński, "Defilada umarłych bogów," *Żagary*, no. 3 (1931), p. 2.

10. Ibid., p. 12.

11. Teodor Bujnicki, in his review of the magazine *Linia*, in *Piony*, no. 3 (1932), p. 4.

12. A note from the editors, *Żagary*, no. 3 (1931), p. 2.

13. Cz. Miłosz, "Kłamstwo dzisiejszej poezji," *Orka na Ugorze*, no. 5 (1938).

14. *Okolica Poetów,* nos. 4/5 (1953).

15. A. Wat, *Mój wiek,* pp. 24-25.

16. Jerzy Leszin-Koperski, Preface to Tadeusz Peiper, *Wybór wierszy,* Warsaw, 1972.

BIOGRAPHICAL NOTES

BRZĘKOWSKI, JAN. Born in 1903 in Wiśnicz near Tarnów, he received a doctorate in philosophy from the Jagellonian University in Cracow. After studying at the Sorbonne and École du Journalisme in Paris, in 1928 Brzękowski settled permanently in France. During 1929-30 he edited the bilingual French-Polish magazine *l'Art contemporain–Sztuka Współczesna*. Following the war he served as director of the spa Amélie-les-Bains, and currently he lives in Paris, writing poetry and criticism both in Polish and in French.

CZECHOWICZ, JÓZEF. A native of Lublin, born in 1903, he studied pedagogy for elementary school teachers and later worked as a teacher in several towns and villages. While in Lublin, he edited a short-lived literary magazine *Searchlight (Reflektor)*. Besides poetry he wrote essays, reviews, and children's poetry, and he made numerous translations from Russian, Czech, French, and English poetry. In Warsaw his apartment was a meeting place for the younger generation of poets. Czechowicz collaborated with several leading literary magazines, and from 1938 to 1939 he edited *Pen (Pióro)*. While at a barber shop in Lublin in September 1939, he was killed by a German bomb.

CZYŻEWSKI, TYTUS. Born in 1880 into a family of gentry in Berdychów, he later studied at the Academy of Fine Arts in Cracow. After working intermittently as an art teacher in high schools, in 1908 he traveled to Paris, where he attended the École du Louvre from 1910 to 1912. Czyżewski's first individual painting exhibition was held in 1910, and in 1917 he founded the group "Polish expressionists" with the brothers Zbigniew and Andrzej Pronaszko; soon they changed their name to "formists." The group included the philosopher Leon Chwistek, the writer and painter Stanisław Ignacy Witkiewicz, and the sculptor August Zamoyski. It organized several exhibits and the artistic club The Nutmeg (Gałka Muszkatołowa). In 1917 Czyżewski joined the futurists, and from 1919 to 1921 was editor of the magazine the *Formists (Formiści)*. Between 1922 and 1925 he worked in the Polish Embassy in Paris and corresponded with the *Switch*. Czyżewski continued to paint and write poetry and criticism until his death in 1945.

JASIEŃSKI, BRUNO. The son of a country doctor (Jakub Zysman) known for his philanthropy, Jasieński was born in 1901 in Klimontów near Sandomierz. He attended the Polish gymnasium in Moscow during the years 1914-18, and later studied philosophy at the Jagellonian University in Cracow. From 1919 to 1923 he was actively involved in futuristic activities and in 1923 he began to collaborate with the communist newspaper the *Workers' Tribune (Trybuna Robotnicza)*. In 1925 he left for France, where he organized a theater among Polish mine workers and collaborated with *l'Humanité*. Having been deported from France in 1929 for his novel *I Burn Paris (Palę Paryż)*, Jasieński went first to Leningrad, and later settled in Moscow, taking an active part in Soviet literary life. In 1930 he became a member of the board of directors of the Moscow Association of Proletarian Writers (MAPP) and the editor of two magazines: *Culture of the Masses (Kultura Mas)*, published in Polish, and *International Literature*, published in four languages. Jasieński wrote poetry, short stories, and novels in Russian, and he was a friend of the eminent Russian poet Vladimir Mayakovski, whom he defended against official criticism. Arrested in 1937, Jasieński died in 1939 in a labor camp near Vladivostok. His books disappeared from libraries until his "rehabilitation" in 1955. In 1956-57, after an interval of almost thirty years, his writings began to be published in Poland.

KUREK, JALU. Born in 1904 in Cracow, he studied Polish literature and Romance languages at the Jagellonian University, where his father was a janitor. During his travels to Italy in 1924, he met Marinetti and later became his spokesman in Poland. Kurek worked as a journalist before World War II, but after the war he supported himself by writing. A prolific author of more than forty books, fifteen volumes of which are poetry, he currently lives in Cracow.

MIŁOSZ, CZESŁAW. A native of Lithuania, born in 1911, he received a master's degree in law from Stefan Batory University in Wilno. In 1937 he moved to Warsaw, and during the German occupation he edited a clandestine anthology of poetry. From 1946-50 he worked in the diplomatic service of People's Poland, but he broke with the Polish government in 1951 and settled in France. In 1960 he moved to Berkeley, California, where he held the position of Professor of Polish Literature at the University of California until 1981. Extremely active as a poet and writer, between 1945 and 1975 Miłosz published nine volumes of poetry, two novels, and a number of critical essays and other books, among them the widely known *The Captive Mind (Zniewolony umysł*, 1953). In 1969 he authored *The History of Polish Literature* in English. Miłosz received numerous awards and prizes, including the Prix littéraire européen (1953), the Marian Kister Literary Award (New York, 1967), the Jurzykowski Foundation Award, the award of the Polish P. E. N. Club in Warsaw for translations of poetry, a Guggenheim Fellowship (1976), an honorary Doctor of Letters from the University of Michigan, and the Neustadt International Prize for Literature (1978). In 1980 he was awarded the Nobel Prize for Literature.

MŁODOŻENIEC, STANISŁAW. He was born to a well-to-do peasant family in 1895 in the village of Dobrocice, near Sandomierz. Captured in 1915 by the retreating Russian army, Młodożeniec was taken to Moscow where he attended the Polish gymnasium in order to avoid military service. After returning to Poland in 1918, he studied Polish literature at the Jagellonian University. Along with Czyżewski and Jasieński he founded the futurist club Katarynka and participated in futurist activities. Between 1922 and 1939 he worked as a high school teacher, and during the 1930s he became politically active in the peasants' party. After the war he lived in London, before returning in 1958 to Poland, where he died in 1959 in Warsaw.

PEIPER, TADEUSZ. Born in 1891 in Cracow, he studied in Cracow, Berlin, and Paris, before spending five years (1914-20) in Spain, where he became acquainted with Spanish "ultraists." After returning to Poland he collaborated with the *New Art (Nowa Sztuka)* and in 1922 founded the *Switch (Zwrotnica)*. After the closure of the *Switch* in the thirties, a large number of his polemical articles were published in various periodicals. Peiper spent the war years in the Soviet Union, returning to Poland in 1944 and settling in Warsaw, where he wrote theater and film reviews. Suffering from acute hypochondria, he lived his last years in total isolation and died in 1969.

PRZYBOŚ, JULIAN. Born into a peasant family in the southern Polish town of Gwoźnica he studied Polish literature at the Jagellonian University. For many years Przyboś worked as a high school teacher, and after World War II he served for two years as the first chairman of the Writers' Union. From 1947 to 1951 he was a delegate of the Polish government in Switzerland. Besides poetry he wrote essays on painting and Polish literature, among them a well-known study of Mickiewicz. Przyboś died in Warsaw in 1970.

STERN, ANATOL. The son of a journalist, Stern was born in 1899 in Warsaw. After studying Polish literature at Wilno University, he served as editor of the magazine the *New Art (Nowa Sztuka)*. Since he held a keen interest in film and theater in addition to poetry, in 1924 he became editor-in-chief of *Film News (Wiadomości Filmowe)*. Stern was a translator of Mayakovski, as well as an author of novels, short stories, film scenarios, and critical essays. He died in Warsaw in 1968.

WAT, ALEKSANDER. Born in 1900 in Warsaw, he studied philosophy at Warsaw University, and after a short period of futurist activities, Wat became the editor-in-chief of the communist *The Literary Monthly (Miesięcznik Literacki)* from 1929 to

1930. He severed his relations with communism after 1930 and worked as an editor for a publishing house. During World War II he fled from the Germans and was imprisoned by the Soviets in Lwów. Wat spent the war in prisons and labor camps in the Soviet Union and returned to Poland in 1946. He was attacked as a political deviationist during the Stalinist period. In 1956, after a thirty-year interval, he started to write poetry again. His *Poems (Wiersze, 1957)* received a prize from the liberal weekly *New Culture (Nowa Kultura)*. In 1958 Wat emigrated to France, where he died in 1967. His "spoken diary" *My Century (Mój wiek)*, published posthumously in London in 1977, is a powerful account of his tragic association with communism.

WAŻYK, ADAM. A native of Warsaw, Ważyk was born in 1905 and later studied mathematics at the University of Warsaw. He co-edited *Almanac of the New Art (Almanach Nowej Sztuki)*, and after the war he became a spokesman of the new regime, the feared "terroretician" of Socialist Realism. In 1955 he wrote *Poem for Adults (Poemat dla dorosłych)*, a bitter denunciation of Stalinism. Until his death in Warsaw in 1982, Ważyk wrote poetry, criticism, and translations. He is the author of a very personal account of the Polish avant-garde entitled *The Strange Story of the Avant-garde (Dziwna historia awangardy, 1976)*.

BIBLIOGRAPHY

The bibliography is arranged according to chapters. Within each section, the group publications and critical literature about a movement precedes the bibliography of individual authors. The secondary literature about literary movements is divided into two parts: first, contemporary judgments and polemics, and then critical literature that includes surveys and evaluations written mostly after the second world war. The primary sources as well as sections on contemporary judgments and polemics are chronological, while the secondary sources are arranged alphabetically.

The bibliography opens with a list of all the avant-garde periodicals and ends with general reference works. It is selective, and only those volumes of poetry that belong to the avant-garde period of the individual poets are listed. With the exception of theoretical writings and essays, prose works are not included (for example novels, short stories, and plays). I have attempted to avoid duplications, but some were inevitable.

GENERAL AVANT-GARDE PERIODICALS

Formiści, Cracow, 6 numbers, 1919-22.

Nowa Sztuka, Warsaw-Cracow, 1919-21.

Zwrotnica, Cracow, 2 series: first series (6 numbers) 1922-23; second series (6 numbers) 1926-27.

Almanach Nowej Sztuki, Warsaw, 4 numbers, 1924-25.

Reflektor, Lublin, 3 numbers, 1924-25.
Blok, Warsaw, 11 numbers, 1924-26.
Praesens, Warsaw, 2 numbers, 1926-30.
Art Contemporain - Sztuka Współczesna, Paris, 3 numbers, 1929-30.
a.r., Łódź, 2 "communications," 1930 and 1932.
Linia, Cracow, 5 numbers, 1931-33.
Żagary, Wilno, 2 series: first series (8 numbers) 1931-32; second series (4 numbers) 1933-34.
Piony, Wilno, 5 numbers, 1932.
Smuga, Wilno, 8 numbers, 1933.
Okolica Poetów, Ostrzeszów Wielkopolski, 42 numbers, 1935-39.
Pióro, Warsaw, 2 numbers, 1938-39.

FUTURISM

Group Publications

Gga. Pierwszy almanach poezji futurystycznej. Dwumiesięcznik prymitywistów. Warsaw, 1920.
To są niebieskie pięty, które trzeba pomalować. Warsaw, 1920.
Nieśmiertelny tom futuryz. Warsaw, 1921.
Jednodniówka futurystów. Manifesty polskiego futuryzmu. Wydanie nadzwyczajne na całą Rzeczpospolitą Polską. Cracow, 1921.
Nuż w bżuhu. Druga jednodniówka futurystów. Cracow-Warsaw, 1921.

Contemporary Judgments on Futurism and Polemics

Krajewski, Radosław. "Futuryzm polski." *Zdrój*, vol. 9, no. 3 (1919).
Hulewicz, Jerzy. "O 'futuryźmie polskim'," *Zdrój*, vol. 9, no. 6 (1919).
——. A note on the Warsaw futurists without a title. *Zdrój*, vol 10, nos. 1-2 (1920).
Irzykowski, Karol. "Futuryzm a szachy." *Ponowa*, no. 1 (1921). Reprinted in his *Słoń wśród porcelany. Lżejszy kaliber.* Cracow: Wydawnictwo Literackie, 1976.
Nowaczyński, Adolf. "Fetoryści." In his *Pogrom. Ramoty i gawędy (1915-1919).* Warsaw: Bogusławski, 1921.
Witkiewicz, Stanisław Ignacy. "Parę zarzutów przeciw futuryzmowi." *Czartak*, no. 1 (1922).
Chwistek, Leon. "Nowa poezja polska. (Cztery wykłady o poezji futurystycznej wygłoszone na kursach literackich w Krakowie)." *Nowa Sztuka*, no. 2 (1922).
Irzykowski, Karol. "Plagiatowy charakter przełomów literackich w Polsce." *Robotnik*, nos. 29 and 31 (1922). Replied to by Bruno Jasieński in *Ilustrowany Kurier Codzienny*, nos. 37 and 43 (1922), and Anatol Stern in "Emeryt merytoryzmu. Z powodu ostatniego artykułu Irzykowskiego pt. 'Plagiatowy charakter przełomów literackich w Polsce' czyli jeszcze o wiatrologii," *Skamander*, no. 17 (1922). Answered by Irzykowski in "Futurystyczny tapir. (Przyczynek do sprawy zwyczajów literackich i do sprawy plagiatu)," *Ponowa*, no. 5 (1922).

Irzykowski's articles were reprinted in *Słoń wśród porcelany. Lżejszy kaliber.* Cracow: Wydawnictwo Literackie, 1976.

Peiper, Tadeusz. "Futuryzm. (Analiza i krytyka)." *Zwrotnica,* no. 6 (1923). Reprinted in his *Tędy. Nowe Usta.* Cracow: Wydawnictwo Literackie, 1972.

Witkiewicz, Stanisław Ignacy. "O naszym futuryźmie." In *Teatr.* Cracow, 1923.

Irzykowski, Karol. "Likwidacja futuryzmu." *Wiadomości Literackie,* no. 5 (1924). Reprinted in *Słoń wśród porcelany. Lżejszy kaliber.* Cracow: Wydawnictwo Literackie, 1976.

Gacki, Kordian. "Sztuka ludzka." *Almanach Nowej Sztuki,* no. 1 (1924).

Brucz, Stanisław. "Zarys nowej poetyki." *Almanach Nowej Sztuki,* no. 2 (1924).

Kurek, Jalu. "Poezja futuryzmu polskiego." *Głos Narodu,* no. 170 (1924).

Wielowieyska, Helena. "We wszystich kolorach." *Nasz Wyraz,* no. 6 (1938).

Literature about Futurism

Balcerzan, Edward. "Futuryzm." In *Literatura polska w okresie międzywojennym,* edited by J. Kądziela, J. Kwiatkowski, and I. Wyczańska. Vol. 1. Cracow: Wydawnictwo Literackie, 1979.

Folejewski, Zbigniew. "The Place of Futurism in West and South Slavic Poetry." In *Canadian Contributions to the 8th International Congress of Slavists,* edited by Zbigniew Folejewski. Ottawa: Canadian Association of Slavists, 1978.

Folejewski, Zbigniew. *Futurism and its Place in the Development of Modern Poetry: A Comparative Study and Anthology.* Ottawa: University of Ottawa Press, 1980.

Jarosiński, Zbigniew. Introduction to *Antologia polskiego futuryzmu i Nowej Sztuki.* Wrocław: Ossolineum, 1978.

Jasieński, Bruno. "Futuryzm polski. (Bilans)." (1923). In his *Utwory poetyckie, manifesty, szkice.* Wrocław: Ossolineum, 1972.

Kolesnikoff, Nina. "Polish Futurism: Its Origin and the Aesthetic Programme." *Canadian Slavonic Papers,* no. 17 (1976), pp. 301-11.

——. "Polish Futurism: The Quest to Renovate Poetic Language." *Slavic and East European Journal,* vol. 21, no. 1 (Spring 1977), pp. 64-77.

Kowalczykowa, Alina. "O pewnych paradoksach futurystycznego programu." *Poezja,* no. 6 (1969).

Lam, Andrzej. *Polska awangarda poetycka. Programy lat 1917-1923.* Cracow: Wydawnictwo Literackie, 1969.

Młodożeniec, Stanisław. "U narodzin krakowskiej awangardy." *Orka,* no. 34 (August 1958).

——. "Krakowskie spotkania." *Orka,* nos. 51-52 (December 1958).

Stern, Anatol. "Futuryści polscy i inni." In his *Poezja zbuntowana. Szkice i wspomnienia.* Warsaw: PIW, 1964.

——."Niezwykła historia polskiego futuryzmu (1918-1968)." In his *Głód jednoznaczności i inne szkice.* Warsaw: Czytelnik, 1972.

Wat, Aleksander. "Wspomnienia o futuryźmie." *Miesięcznik Literacki,* no. 3 (February 1930).

——. "Metamorfozy futuryzmu." *Miesięcznik Literacki,* no. 3 (February 1930).
——. *Mój wiek. Pamiętnik mówiony.* Vol. 1. London: Polonia Book Fund Ltd., 1977.
Ważyk, Adam. *Dziwna historia awangardy.* Warsaw: Czytelnik, 1976.
Zaworska, Helena. *O Nową Sztukę. Polskie programy artystyczne lat 1917-1922.* Warsaw: PIW, 1963.

Jerzy Jankowski

Tram wpopszek ulicy. Skruty prozy i poemy. Warsaw: Wydawnictwo Futuryzm Polski, 1920.

Horzyca, Wilam. Review of *Tram wpopszek ulicy* in *Skamander,* no. 1 (1920).

Tytus Czyżewski

Zielone oko. Poezje formistyczne. Elektryczne wizje. Cracow: Gebethner, 1920.
Noc-dzień. Mechaniczny instynkt elektryczny. Cracow: Gebethner, 1922.
Wąż, Orfeusz i Eurydyka. Wizja antyczna. Cracow: Instytut Wydawniczy "Niezależnych," 1922.
Pastorałki. Paris: Polskie Towarzystwo Przyjaciół Książki, 1925.
Robespierre. Rapsod. Cinema. Od romantyzmu do cynizmu. Paris-Warsaw: Leon Nowak, 1927.
Lajkonik w chmurach. Poezje. Warsaw: Gebethner i Wolff, 1936.

Chwistek, Leon. *Tytus Czyżewski a kryzys Formizmu.* Cracow: Gebethner, 1922.
Lipski, Jan Józef. "O poezji Tytusa Czyżewskiego." *Twórczość,* no. 6 (1960).
Młodożeniec, Stanisław. "Tytus Czyżewski pierwszy w awangardzie." *Orka,* no. 6 (February 1959).
Wyka, Kazimierz. *Rzecz wyobraźni.* Warsaw: PIW, 1977.

Bruno Jasieński

But w butonierce. Warsaw: Klub Futurystów "Katarynka," 1921.
Pieśń o głodzie. Cracow: Instytut Wydawniczy "Niezależnych," 1922.
Ziemia na lewo. Warsaw: Spółdzielnia "Książka," 1924.
Słowo o Jakubie Szeli. Paris, 1926.
Utwory poetyckie. Warsaw: Czytelnik, 1960.
Utwory poetyckie, manifesty, szkice. Wrocław: Ossolineum, 1972.

Balcerzan, Edward. *Styl i poetyka twórczości dwujęzycznej Brunona Jasieńskiego.* Wrocław: Ossolineum, 1968.
——. Introduction to *Utwory poetyckie, manifesty, szkice* by B. Jasieński. Wrocław: Ossolineum, 1972.
Gacki, Stefan. Review of the volume *Ziemia na lewo* in *Almanach Nowej Sztuki,* no. 2 (1924).

Lasota, Grzegorz. "Początek drogi B. Jasieńskiego." *Przegląd Kulturalny*, no. 7 (1956).
Rawiński, Marian. "U genezy wczesnej twórczości poetyckiej Brunona Jasieńskiego." In *O wzajemnych powiązaniach literackich polsko-rosyjskich*. Volume dedicated to the 6th International Congress of Slavists in Prague, edited by S. Fiszman and K. Sierocka. Wrocław: Ossolineum, 1969.
——. "'Archaistów' i 'Nowatorów' racje rewolucji" (Nad *Słowem o Jakubie Szeli* Brunona Jasieńskiego). In his *Po obu stronach granicy*. Wrocław: Ossolineum, 1972.
Stern, Anatol. *Bruno Jasieński*. Warsaw: Wiedza Powszechna, 1969.

Stanisław Młodożeniec

Kreski i futureski. Cracow: Klub Futurystów "Katarynka," 1921.
Kwadraty. Zamość: Zamojskie Koło Miłośników Książki, 1925.
Niedziela. Warsaw: Europa, 1930.
Futuro-gamy i futuro-pejzaże. Warsaw: Wąkopy, 1934.
Utwory poetyckie. Warsaw: Ludowa Spółdzielnia Wydawnicza, 1973.

Burek, Tomasz. "Sztandar futuryzmu na chłopskim wąkopie albo o poezji Stanisława Młodożeńca." In *Utwory poetyckie* by Młodożeniec. Warsaw: Ludowa Spółdzielnia Wydawnicza, 1973.
Sławiński, Janusz. "Poezje Młodożeńca." In *Twórczość*, no. 5 (1959), pp. 121-25.

Anatol Stern

Futuryzje. Warsaw: Wszechczas, 1919.
Nagi człowiek w śródmieściu. Poemat. Warsaw: Wszechczas, 1919.
Anielski cham. Warsaw: F. Hoesick, 1924.
Ziemia na lewo. Warsaw: Spółdzielnia "Książka," 1924.
Bieg do bieguna. Warsaw: F. Hoesick, 1927.
Europa. Warsaw, 1929.
Piłsudski. Poemat. Warsaw: F. Hoesick, 1934.
Rozmowa z Apollinem. Warsaw: F. Hoesick, 1938.
Wiersze dawne i nowe. Warsaw: Czytelnik, 1957.
Wspomnienia z Atlantydy. Warsaw, 1959.
Poezja zbuntowana. Szkice i wspomnienia. Warsaw: PIW, 1964.
Poezje. Warsaw: PIW, 1969.
Alarm nocny. Warsaw: Czytelnik, 1970.
Głód jednoznaczności i inne szkice. Warsaw: Czytelnik, 1972.

Gacki, Stefan. "List do Anatola Sterna." *Almanach Nowej Sztuki*, no. 1 (1924).
——. Review of the volume *Ziemia na lewo* in *Almanach Nowej Sztuki*, no. 2 (1924).
Matuszewski, Ryszard. Introduction to *Alarm nocny* by A. Stern. Warsaw: Czytelnik, 1970.
Prokop, Jan. "Uwagi o poezji Anatola Sterna." *Poezja*, no. 10 (1969).
Wyka, Kazimierz. *Rzecz wyobraźni*. Warsaw: PIW, 1977.

Aleksander Wat

Ja z jednej strony i Ja z drugiej strony mego mopsożelaznego piecyka. Warsaw: Wszechczas, 1920.

Wiersze. Cracow: Wydawnictwo Literackie, 1957.

Ciemne świecidło. Paris: Libella, 1968.

Mój wiek. Pamiętnik mówiony. 2 vols. London: Polonia Book Fund Ltd., 1977.

Miłosz, Czesław. "O wierszach Aleksandra Wata." In *Prywatne obowiązki.* Paris: Instytut Literacki, 1972.

THE CRACOW AVANTGARDE

Group publications

Zwrotnica. Cracow, 2 series. First series (6 numbers), 1922-23; second series (6 numbers), 1926-27.

Linia. Cracow, 5 numbers, 1931-33.

Contemporary Judgments on the Avantgarde and Polemics

Iwaszkiewicz, Jarosław. "*Zwrotnica.* Garść luźnych uwag o nowym piśmie." *Kurier Polski,* no. 353 (1922).

Borowy, Wacław. "Ruch literacki w czasopismach." *Przegląd Warszawski,* no. 17 (1923).

Winkler, Kazimierz. "Zwrotnica." *Naprzód,* nos. 114-115 (1923).

Irzykowski, Karol. "Likwidacja futuryzmu." *Wiadomości Literackie,* no. 5 (1924). Reprinted in his *Słoń wśród porcelany. Lżejszy kaliber.* Cracow: Wydawnictwo Literackie, 1976.

——. "Awangardzistom utarcie nosa," *Wiadomości Literackie,* no. 10 (1924).

——. "Metaforitis i złota plomba," *Wiadomości Literackie,* nos. 52-53 (1928). Reprinted in his *Walka o treść. Beniaminek.* Cracow: Wydawnictwo Literackie, 1976.

Czachowski, Kazimierz. "Młody Kraków literacki." *Tygodnik Ilustrowany,* no. 31 (1929).

Bronner, Juliusz. "W mieście awangardy." *Tygodnik Artystów,* no. 2 (1934).

Czernik, Stanisław. "Treść i forma." *Kamena,* no. 7 (1934). Answered by Julian Przyboś in "Na marginesie artykułu Czernika," *Kamena,* no. 9 (1934); and by Jan Brzękowski in "Rewizja w imię treści," *Kamena,* no. 9 (1934).

Czuchnowski, Marian. "Uspołecznione eksperymenty." *Kamena,* no. 6 (1934). Answered by Józef Czechowicz in "Uspołecznione absurdy," *Kamena,* no. 8 (1934).

Irzykowski, Karol. "Wycieczki w lirykę. I-VI." *Pion,* nos. 39-41 (1934), and nos. 5, 19, 52 (1935). Answered by Julian Przyboś in "Uwagi o nowej liryce," *Pion,* no. 2 (1935).

Mainskij, Aleksander. "Wśród zdobyczy i nieporozumień." *Dźwigary*, no. 1 (1934).

Marienholz, Szymon. "Antynomie poezji współczesnej." *Dźwigary*, no. 1 (1934).

Piwowar, Lech. "Kieszonkowy podręcznik nowej poezji." *Gazeta Artystów*, no. 6 (1934).

——. "Awangardziści przeciw awangardzie." *Tygodnik Artystów*, no. 3 (1934). Continued by Juliusz Bronner in "Konfrontacja," *Tygodnik Artystów*, no. 4 (1934). Answered by Julian Przyboś in "Uzupełnienie do 'Konfrontacji'," *Tygodnik Artystów*, no. 8 (1935).

——. "Idąc z Marianem Czuchnowskim." *Tygodnik Artystów*, nos. 6-7 (1934).

Czachowski, Kazimierz. "Polska poezja awangardowa." *Polska Zachodnia*, no. 267 (1935).

Czuchnowski, Marian. *"Linia* bez linii." *Tygodnik Artystów*, nos. 12 and 13 (1935).

Kott, Jan. "Drogi awangardy poetyckiej w Polsce." *Przegląd Współczesny*, no. 54 (1935).

Okolica Poetów, nos. 4-5 (1935). A poll under the title "Wymiana poglądów" about contemporary poetry and the Avantgarde.

Zawodziński, Karol W. "Pegaz to nie samochód bezkołowy." *Skamander*, no. 57 (1935). Reprinted in his *Wśród poetów*. Cracow: Wydawnictwo Literackie, 1964.

Piechal, Marian. "Krytyka od podstaw. (Rzecz o awangardzie poetyckiej)." *Pion*, no. 33 (1936).

Chmielowiec, Michał. "Rozważania o poezji." *Sygnały*, no. 35 (1937).

Bujnicki, Teodor. "Podzwonne awangardzie." *Słowo*, no. 247 (1938).

Fik, Ignacy. "Awangarda i awangardziści." *Sygnały*, no. 39 (1938).

Frasik, Józef Andrzej. "Hurtownie, detaliści a my." *Nasz Wyraz*, no. 2 (1938).

Fryde, Ludwik. "Dwa pokolenia." *Pióro*, no. 1 (1938).

——. "Trzy pokolenia literackie." *Pion*, no. 45 (1938).

Kott, Jan. "Pyrrusowe zwycięstwo awangardy." *Sygnały*, no. 37 (1938).

Miłosz, Czesław. "Kłamstwo dzisiejszej poezji." *Orka na Ugorze*, no. 5 (1938). Answered by Gustaw Herling-Grudziński in "Obrona metafory," *Orka na Ugorze*, no. 6 (1938); Jan Król in "Przeciw wyrażaniu siebie," *Orka na Ugorze*, no. 7 (1938); Jerzy Putrament in "O 'finis operantis'," *Orka na Ugorze*, no. 8 (1938); Józef Maśliński in "Środki nie tylko cele," and G. Herling-Grudziński in "Bilans i wnioski," *Orka na Ugorze*, no. 9 (1938).

Nasz Wyraz, nos. 7-8 and 10 (1938). A poll about avant-garde poetry.

Wymiary, no. 3 (1938). A discussion under the title "Dokąd zmierza młoda literatura?"

Zawodziński, Karol W. "Awangarda, jej apogeum i likwidacja." *Przegląd Współczesny*, vol. 68 (1938). Reprinted in his *Wśród poetów*. Cracow: Wydawnictwo Literackie, 1964.

Bieńkowski, Zbigniew. "Język poetycki." *Nasz Wyraz*, no. 4 (1939).

Śpiewak, Jan. "Rozmowa z Adamem Ważykiem." *Sygnały*, no. 65 (1939).

Irzykowski, Karol. "Od metafory do metonimii." *Kurier Literacko-Naukowy*, no. 15, 1939. Reprinted in his *Wybór pism krytyczno-literackich*. Wrocław: Ossolineum, 1975.

224	BIBLIOGRAPHY

Literature about the Cracow Avantgarde

Brzękowski, Jan. "Awangarda. (Rys historyczny)." *Kultura* (Paris), nos. 7-8 (1955).

——. "Awangarda. (Szkic historyczno-teoretyczny)." *Przegląd Humanistyczny,* no. 1 (1958). Reprinted in his *Wyobraźnia wyzwolona.* Cracow: Wydawnictwo Literackie, 1976.

——. *W Krakowie i w Paryżu. Wspomnienia i szkice.* Cracow: Wydawnictwo Literackie, 1968.

Jaworski, Stanisław. *Między awangardą a nadrealizmem.* Cracow: Wydawnictwo Literackie, 1976.

——. "Awangarda ('Zwrotnica' 1922-1923, 1926-1927; 'Linia' 1931-1933)." In his *Literatura polska w okresie międzywojennym.* Cracow: Wydawnictwo Literackie, 1979.

Kłak, Tadeusz. *Czasopisma awangardy. Cześć I: 1919-1931.* Wrocław: Ossolineum, 1978.

Kurek, Jalu. *Mój Kraków.* Cracow: Wydawnictwo Literackie, 1963.

——. *Zmierzch natchnienia? Szkice o poezji.* Cracow: Wydawnictwo Literackie, 1976.

Lam, Andrzej. *Polska awangarda poetycka. Programy lat 1917-1923.* 2 vols. Cracow: Wydawnictwo Literackie, 1969.

——. *Z teorii i praktyki awangardyzmu.* Warsaw: Uniwersytet, 1976.

Matuszewski, Ryszard. "Rzecz o narodzinach polskiej awangardy poetyckiej." *Miesięcznik Literacki,* no. 9 (1970).

Okopień-Sławińska, Aleksandra. "Wiersz awangardowy dwudziestolecia międzywojennego. (Podstawy, granice, możliwości)." *Pamiętnik Literacki,* vol. 56, no. 2 (1965).

Peiper, Tadeusz. *O wszystkim i jeszcze o czymś. Artykuły, eseje, wywiady (1918-1939).* Cracow: Wydawnictwo Literackie, 1974.

Piechal, Marian. "Zaklęte kręgi." *Poezja,* no. 1 (1967).

Sławiński, Janusz. *Koncepcja języka poetyckiego awangardy krakowskiej.* Wrocław: Ossolineum, 1965.

Stanisławski, Ryszard, ed. *Constructivism in Poland 1923-1936. BLOK. Praesens. a.r.* A catalogue prepared for the exhibition in the Museum Folkwang, Essen, May 5-June 24 1973. Stuttgart, 1973.

Szymański, Wiesław Paweł. *Z dziejów czasopism literackich w dwudziestoleciu międzywojennym.* Cracow: Wydawnictwo Literackie, 1970.

Ważyk, Adam. *Dziwna historia awangardy.* Warsaw: Czytelnik, 1976.

Wyka, Kazimierz. "Z lawy metafor." In his *Rzecz wyobraźni.* Warsaw: PIW, 1977.

Zaworska, Helena. *O Nową Sztukę. Polskie programy artystyczne lat 1917-1922.* Warsaw: PIW, 1963.

Tadeusz Peiper

A. Cracow: Zwrotnica, 1924.
Żywe linie. Cracow: Zwrotnica, 1924.
Nowe usta. Lwów: Ateneum, 1925.
Raz. Warsaw: F. Hoesick, 1929.

Tędy. Warsaw: F. Hoesick, 1930.
Na przykład. Poemat aktualny. Cracow: Zwrotnica, 1931.
Poematy (Zbiór). Cracow: Koło Wydawnicze "Teraz," 1935.
Wybór wierszy. Warsaw, 1972.
Tędy. Nowe usta. Cracow: Wydawnictwo Literackie, 1972.
O wszystkim i jeszcze o czymś. Artykuły, eseje, wywiady (1918-1939). Cracow: Wydawnictwo Literackie, 1974.

Chmielowiec, Michał. "Obrona poety Peipera." *Sygnały,* no. 33 (1937).
Czernik, Stanisław. "Kroki ku epice." *Okolica Poetów,* no. 3 (1935).
Irzykowski, Karol. "Burmistrz marzeń niezamieszkanych." In his *Słoń wśród porcelany. Studia nad nowszą myślą literacką w Polsce.* Warsaw: Rój, 1934. Reprinted in his *Słoń wśród porcelany. Lżejszy kaliber.* Cracow: Wydawnictwo Literackie, 1976.
Jaworski, Stanisław. *U podstaw awangardy. Tadeusz Peiper. Pisarz i teoretyk.* Cracow: Wydawnictwo Literackie, 1968.
Sebyła, Władysław. Review of the volume *Poematy* in *Pion,* no. 3 (1936).
Sławiński, Janusz. "Poetyka i poezja Tadeusza Peipera." *Twórczość,* no. 6 (1958).
Stern, Anatol. "Twórca zdań rozkwitających (O poezji Tadeusza Peipera)" (1924). In his *Głód jednoznaczności i inne szkice.* Warsaw: Czytelnik, 1972.
Walińska, Hanna. "Systemy Tadeusza Peipera." *Nowy Wyraz,* no. 4 (1972).
Waśkiewicz, Andrzej K. "Woń rzeźni i róż." In his *Rygor i marzenie.* Łódź: Wydawnictwo Łódzkie, 1973.

Julian Przyboś

Śruby. Cracow: Zwrotnica, 1925.
Oburącz. Cracow: Zwrotnica, 1926.
Sponad. Łódź: biblioteka "a.r.," 1930.
W głąb las. Łódź: biblioteka "a.r.," 1932.
Równanie serca. Warsaw: F. Hoesick, 1938.
Miejsce na ziemi. Warsaw: Czytelnik, 1945.
Wybór poezji. Warsaw: Książka i Wiedza, 1949.
Najmniej słów. Cracow: Wydawnictwo Literackie, 1955.
Linia i gwar. Szkice. 2 vols. Cracow: Wydawnictwo Literackie, 1959.
Sens poetycki. 2 vols. Cracow: Wydawnictwo Literackie, 1967.
Zapiski bez daty. Warsaw: PIW, 1970.
Utwory poetyckie. Zbiór. Warsaw: Ludowa Spółdzielnia Wydawnicza, 1975.

Kwiatkowski, Jerzy. *Świat poetycki Juliana Przybosia.* Warsaw: PIW, 1972.
Łaszowski, Alfred. "Liryzm przestrzenny." *Pion,* no. 11 (1937).
Okopień-Sławińska, Aleksandra. "Pomysły de teorii wiersza współczesnego. (Na przykładzie poezji Przybosia.)" In *Styl. Kompozycja. Konferencje teoretycznoliterackie w Toruniu i Ustroniu,* ed. by Jan Trzynadlowski. Wrocław: Ossolineum, 1965.
Prokop, Jan. "Wokół Przybosia. (Marginalia interpretacyjne.)" *Twórczość,* no. 9 (1958), pp. 95-106.

——. "Budowa obrazu u Przybosia." *Ruch Literacki,* nos. 1-2 (1960), pp. 72-78.
Sandauer, Artur. *Przyboś.* Warsaw: Agencja Autorska i Dom Książki, 1970.
——. *Poeci czterech pokoleń.* Cracow: Wydawnictwo Literackie, 1977.
Sebyła, Władysław. Review of the volume *W głąb las* in *Pion,* no. 11 (1933).
Sławiński, Janusz, ed. *Wspomnienia o Julianie Przybosiu.* Warsaw: Ludowa Spół-
dzielnia Wydawnicza, 1976.
Waśkiewicz, Andrzej K. "Wobec Przybosia." In his *Rygor i marzenie.* Łódź: Wy-
dawnictwo Łódzkie, 1973.
Wyka, Kazimierz. "Przyboś." In his *Wędrując po tematach.* Vol. 2 *(Puścizna).*
Cracow: Wydawnictwo Literackie, 1971.
——. "Wola wymiernego kształtu." In his *Rzecz wyobraźni.* Warsaw: PIW, 1977.

Jan Brzękowski

Tętno. Cracow: Zwrotnica, 1925.
na katodzie. Paris: collection des d. i. de l'esprit nouveau, 1929.
W drugiej osobie. Łódź: biblioteka "a. r.," 1933.
Zaciśnięte dookoła ust. Warsaw: biblioteka "a. r.," 1936.
Poezje wybrane. London: Oficyna Poetów i Malarzy, 1960.
Życie w czasie. Studia i szkice. London: Oficyna Poetów i Malarzy, 1963.
Wybór poezji. Warsaw: Czytelnik, 1966.
Poezje. Warsaw: PIW, 1973.
W Krakowie i w Paryżu. Cracow: Wydawnictwo Literackie, 1975.
Wyobraźnia wyzwolona. Szkice i wspomnienia. Cracow: Wydawnictwo Literackie,
1976.

Łaszowski, Alfred. "'Kwiaty grzechu' Awangardy." *Pion,* no. 8 (1937).
Michalski, Hieronim. Review of the volume *Zaciśnięte dookoła ust* in *Kamena,*
no. 2 (1937).
Przyboś, Julian. "Przyjaciel poetycki." In his *Sens poetycki.* Cracow: Wydawnictwo
Literackie, 1967.
Sławiński, Janusz. "O poezji Jana Brzękowskiego." *Twórczość,* no. 9 (1961).
Szymański, Wiesław Paweł. "Tropiciel snów niewyśnionych. (O poezji Jana Brzę-
kowskiego)." *Twórczość,* no. 8 (1967).
Waśkiewicz, Andrzej K. "Wyobraźnia wyzwolona (O poetyce Jana Brzękowskiego)."
Wiatraki, no. 2 (1967).
——. "Między snem a nieśnieniem." In his *Rygor i marzenie.* Łódź: Wydawnictwo
Łódzkie, 1973.

Jalu Kurek

Upały. Warsaw: Almanach Nowej Sztuki, 1925.
Śpiewy o Rzeczypospolitej. Warsaw: Dom Książki Polskiej, 1930.
II śpiewy o Rzeczypospolitej. Cracow, 1932.
Usta na pomoc. Warsaw: F. Hoesick, 1933.
Mohigangas. Warsaw: F. Hoesick, 1934.

Mój Kraków. Cracow: Wydawnictwo Literackie, 1970.
Zmierzch natchnienia? Szkice o poezji. Cracow: Wydawnictwo Literackie, 1976.
wiersze awangardowe (retrospektywa). Cracow: Wydawnictwo Literackie, 1977.

Kucharski, Zbigniew. Review of the volume *Usta na pomoc* in *Pion,* no. 13 (1933).
Waśkiewicz, Andrzej K. "Kurek czyli ewolucje poetyki." In his *Rygor i marzenie.*
  Łódź: Wydawnictwo Łódzkie, 1973.

POETS ASSOCIATED WITH THE AVANT-GARDE BUT OUTSIDE ANY GROUP

Adam Ważyk

Semafory. Warsaw: Almanach Nowej Sztuki, 1924.
Oczy i usta. Cracow: Zwrotnica, 1926.
Wiersze zebrane. Warsaw: F. Hoesick, 1934.
Wybór poezji. Warsaw: PIW, 1967.
Gra i doświadczenie. Eseje. Warsaw: PIW, 1974.
dziwna historia awangardy. Warsaw: Czytelnik, 1976.

Bobrowski, Czesław. Review of the volume *Semafory* in *Reflektor,* no. 2 (1925).
Napierski, Stefan. "Poezja Ważyka." *Droga,* no. 11 (1935).
Sebyła, Władysław. Review of the volume *Wiersze zebrane* in *Pion,* no. 3 (1935).
Trznadel, Jacek. Introduction to *Wybór poezji* by A. Ważyk. Warsaw: PIW, 1967.

Józef Czechowicz

Kamień. Lublin: Biblioteka Reflektora, 1927.
dzień jak codzień. Warsaw: F. Hoesick, 1930.
ballada z tamtej strony. Warsaw: F. Hoesick, 1932.
Stare kamienie. Warsaw: F. Hoesick, 1934.
z błyskawicy. Warsaw: F. Hoesick, 1934.
nic więcej. Warsaw: F. Hoesick, 1936.
Arkusz poetycki. Warsaw: F. Hoesick, 1937.
nuta człowiecza. Warsaw: F. Hoesick, 1939.
Wiersze. Lublin: Wydawnictwo Lubelskie, 1963.
Wiersze wybrane. Warsaw: Czytelnik, 1955.
Wyobraźnia stwarzająca. Szkice literackie. Lublin: Wydawnictwo Lubelskie, 1972.

Herbert, Zbigniew. "Uwagi o poezji Józefa Czechowicza." *Twórczość,* no. 9 (1955).
Kłak, Tadeusz. *Czechowicz—mity i magia.* Cracow: Wydawnictwo Literackie, 1973.
——. *Reporter róż.* Katowice: Wydawnictwo "Śląsk," 1978.
Napierski, Stefan. "Dwie książki Czechowicza." *Droga,* no. 6 (1935). About the
  two volumes *ballada z tamtej strony* and *z błyskawicy.*
Pollak, Seweryn, ed. *Spotkania z Czechowiczem. Wspomnienia i szkice.* Lublin:
  Wydawnictwo Lubelskie, 1971.

Różewicz, Tadeusz. "Z umarłych rąk Czechowicza." Introduction to *Wiersze wybrane.* Warsaw: Czytelnik, 1955.

Sandauer, Artur. "Upiory, półsen, muzyka (Rzecz o Józefie Czechowiczu)." In his *Poeci czterech pokoleń.* Cracow: Wydawnictwo Literackie, 1977.

Sebyła, Władysław. Review of the volume *z błyskawicy* in *Pion,* no. 16 (1934).

Stern, Anatol. "Poeta wielkiej ciszy. (O Józefie Czechowiczu)." In his *Głód jednoznaczności i inne szkice.* Warsaw: Czytelnik, 1972.

Wyka, Kazimierz. "O Józefie Czechowiczu." In his *Rzecz wyobraźni.* Warsaw: PIW, 1977.

REFERENCE WORKS

Antologia polskiego futuryzmu i Nowej Sztuki. Introduction and commentary by Zbigniew Jarosiński. Wrocław: Ossolineum, 1978.

Bakoš, Miluláš. *Avantgarda 38.* Bratislava: Slovenský spisovatel, 1969.

Baranowicz, Zofia. *Polska awangarda artystyczna 1918-1939.* Warsaw: Wydawnictwa Artystyczne i Filmowe, 1975.

Bieńkowski, Zbigniew. *Poezja i niepoezja.* Warsaw: PIW, 1972.

Boarini, Vittorio, and Pietro Bonfigli. *Avanguardia e Restaurazione. La cultura del novocento: testi e interpretazioni.* Bologna: Zanichelli, 1976.

Bojtar, E. "Le problème des tendances dans la poésie est-européenne entre les deux guerres." *Studia Slavica Academiae Scientarum Hungaricae,* vol. 14, nos. 1-4 (1968).

Bürger, Peter. *Theorie der Avantgarde.* Frankfurt am Main: Suhrkamp Verlag, 1974.

Cabanne, Pierre, and Pierre Restany. *L'avant-garde au XXe siècle.* Paris: André Balland, 1969.

Calinescu, Matei. "Avant-Garde, Neo-Avant-Garde, Post Modernism: the Culture of Crisis." *Clio: An Interdisciplinary Journal of Literature, History, and the Philosophy of History,* no. 4 (1975), University of Wisconsin, pp. 317-40.

——. *Faces of Modernity: avant-garde, decadence, kitsch.* Bloomington: Indiana University Press, 1977.

Czernik, Stanisław. "Wstęp do dziejów polskiej poezji powojennej." *Okolica Poetów,* no. 4 (1937).

Delevoy, Robert L. *Dimensions of the 20th Century 1900-1945.* Translated from the French by Stuart Gilbert. Geneva: Skira, 1965.

Fik, Ignacy. *20 lat litaratury polskiej. (1918-1938).* Cracow: "Placówka," 1939. Reprinted in his *Wybór pism krytycznych.* Warsaw: PIW, 1961.

Flaker, Aleksandar. "Je potrebný termin avantgarda?" *Slovenska Literatura,* Bratislava, no. 19 (1972), pp. 264-70. Translated by Z. K.

Fryde, Ludwik. "Trzy pokolenia literackie." *Pion,* no. 45 (1938).

Holthusen, H. E. *Avantgardismus und die Zukunft der modernen Kunst.* Munich: Piper, 1964.

Holthusen, Johannes. *Twentieth-Century Russian Literature. A Critical Study.* Translated from the German by Theodore Huebener. New York: Frederick Ungar Publishing Co., 1972.

Hutnikiewicz, Artur. *Od czystej formy do literatury faktu. Główne teorie i programy literackie XX stulecia.* Toruń: Towarzystwo Naukowe w Toruniu, 1965.

Illes, Laszlo. "Die Avantgarde, als kunstlerische Haltung." *Proceedings of the 5th Congress of the International Comparative Literature Association. Belgrade, 1967,* edited by Nikola Banasevic. Belgrade: University of Belgrade, 1969.

Kłak, Tadeusz. *Czasopisma awangardy. Część I: 1919-1931.* Wrocław: Ossolineum, 1978.

Kądziela, Jerzy, Jerzy Kwiatkowski, and Irena Wyczańska, eds. *Literatura polska w okresie międzywojennym.* 2 vols. Cracow: Wydawnictwo Literackie, 1979.

Lam, Andrzej. *Polska awangarda poetycka. Programy lat 1917-1923.* Cracow: Wydawnictwo Literackie, 1969.

Lipski, Jan Józef. "Expressionism in Poland." In *Expressionism as an International Literary Phenomenon,* edited by Ulrich Weisstein. Paris: Didier; Budapest: Akadémiai Kiadó, 1973.

Marill René (Alberes). *L'aventure intellectuelle du XXᵉ siècle, 1900-1950.* Paris: Nouvelle Edition, 1950.

———. *Bilan littéraire du XXᵉ siècle.* Paris: A.-G. Nizet, 1970.

Marino, Adrian. "L'avant-garde et la 'révolution' du langage poètique." *Cahiers roumains d'études littéraires,* no. 2 (1975), pp. 92-107.

———. "Le comparatisme des invariants: le cas des avant-gardes." *Cahiers roumains d'études littéraires,* no. 1 (1976), pp. 81-95.

———. "L'avant-garde historique et la question du réalisme." *Cahiers roumains d'études littéraires,* no. 1 (1978), pp. 72-78.

———. "Analyse comparatiste du cycle de l'avant-garde." *Cahiers roumains d'études littéraires,* no. 1 (1979), pp. 84-93.

Mathauser, Zdenek. "L'histoire des avant-gardes européennes du point de vue de deux problèmes du Congrès de l'A.I.L.C." *Proceedings of the 6th Congress of the International Comparative Literature Association. Bordeaux 1970,* edited by Michel Cadot, David Malone, and Miklós Szabolcsi. Stuttgart: Bieber, 1975.

Matuszewski, Ryszard. *Doświadczenia i mity.* Warsaw: PIW, 1964.

Micheli, Mario de. *Le avanguardie artistiche del Novecento.* Milan: Schwarz, 1959.

Miłosz, Czesław. *The History of Polish Literature.* London: Macmillan, 1969.

Napierski, Stefan. "Prowincjonalne pisma literackie." *Droga,* no. 9 (1934).

Poggioli, Renato. *The Theory of the Avant-garde.* Translated from the Italian by Gerald Fitzgerald. Cambridge, Mass.: Harvard University Press, 1968.

Pollakówna, Joanna. *Formiści.* Wrocław: Ossolineum, 1972.

Problemy literarnej avantgardy. Conference of the Slovak Academy of Sciences in Smolenice, October 25-27 1965. Bratislava: SAV, 1968.

Restany, Pierre. *L'autre face de l'Art.* Paris: Editions galilée, 1979.

Schlenstedt, Silvia. "Problem Avantgarde: Ein Diskussionsvorschlag." *Weimarer Beitrage: Zeitschrift für Literaturwissenschaft, Ästhetik und Kulturtheorie,* vol. 23, no. 1 (1977), pp. 126-44.

Shapiro, Theda. *Painters and Politics. The European Avant-Garde and Society, 1900-1925.* New York: Elsevier, 1976.

Szabolcsi, Miklós. "L'avant-garde littéraire et artistique comme phénomène international." *Proceedings of the 5th Congress of the International Comparative Literature Association, Belgrade, 1967,* edited by Nikola Banasevic. Belgrade: University of Belgrade, 1969.

——. "L'avant-garde littéraire et artistique comme phénomène international." *Pensée,* no. 142 (1968), pp. 94-112.

——. "Avant-garde, Neo-avant-garde, Modernism: Questions and Suggestions." *New Literary History* (University of Virginia), no. 3 (1971), pp. 49-70.

——. *Jel es kialtas.* Budapest: Gondolat, 1971.

Szymański, Wiesław Paweł. *Z dziejów czasopism literackich w dwudziestoleciu międzywojennym.* Cracow: Wydawnictwo Literackie, 1970.

Torre, Guillermo. *Historia de las Literaturas de Vanguardia.* Madrid: Ediciones Guadarrama, 1965.

Troczyński, Konstanty. *Od Formizmu do Moralizmu.* Poznań: Księgarnia Uniwersytecka Jan Jachowski, 1935.

Weisberger, Jean. "Les Avant-Gardes littéraires au XXe siècle. Problèmes théoriques et pratiques." *Neohelicon,* vol 3-4, no. 2 (1974).

Zawodziński, Karol. *Wśród poetów.* Cracow: Wydawnictwo Literackie, 1964.

Zaworska, Helena. *O Nową Sztukę. Polskie programy artystyczne lat 1917-1922.* Warsaw: PIW, 1963.

INDEX

PUBLICATIONS ON RUSSIA AND EASTERN EUROPE OF
THE SCHOOL OF INTERNATIONAL STUDIES

Nationalism in Eastern Europe
PETER F. SUGAR & IVO J. LEDERER

*Agrarian Policies and Problems
in Communist and Non-Communist Countries*
W. A. DOUGLAS JACKSON

The Spiritual Regulation *of
Peter the Great*
ALEXANDER V. MULLER

The Octobrists in the Third Duma, 1907-1912
BEN-CION PINCHUCK

*Legitimacy through Liberalism:
Vladimir Jovanović and the Transformation of Serbian Politics*
GALE STOKES

*Vladivostok under Red and White Rule:
Revolution and Counterrevolution in the Russian Far East,
1920-1922*
CANFIELD F. SMITH

*The Anarchism of Nestor Makhno, 1918-1921:
An Aspect of the Ukrainian Revolution*
MICHAEL PALIJ

Petr Tkachev, the Critic as Jacobin
DEBORAH HARDY

The February Revolution: Petrograd 1917
TSUYOSHI HASEGAWA

Witnesses to the Origins of the Cold War
THOMAS T. HAMMOND

The Poetic Avant-garde in Poland, 1918—1939
BOGDANA CARPENTER

The Balkan City, 1400-1900
NIKOLAI TODOROV